1996-102
Cleargreen—113, etc.

FILMING CASTANEDA

THE HUNT FOR MAGIC AND REASON

Mary Joan Barker—118

By

GABY GEUTER

Unopened letter—140

Caught—172

Nuri Alexander—188

~~Marriages~~ Marriages—198

Two years!—217

Rachel?—221

ISBN: 1-4140-4614-6 (e-book)
ISBN: 1-4140-4612-X (Paperback)
ISBN: 1-4140-4613-8 (Dust Jacket)

Library of Congress Control Number: 2003099405

This book is printed on acid free paper.

Printed in the United States of America
Bloomington, IN

Cover design: Jeff Lin hybrid studios

1stBooks - rev. 02/10/04

Acknowledgements

My thanks go to Nicky and Jeff Lin, for not abandoning me during these years,

To Greg, for his generosity and understanding,

To Martin Prechtel, for putting me on the right writer's path with his astounding workshops,

To Melissa, for her patience and support with editing.

I will never be able to thank all the countless souls that in some form or another inspired me to go on and finish this book, but for a few:

Dave Worrell, Rich Jennings, Valerie Kadium, Susan Salonisen, Petra Ziebarth, Isabella Groeschel, Dorothea Birngruber, Steve and Eve Rockow, Jane Downes, Franz Benton, Alex, Tanya and Greg Senofsky, Margaret and C.J. Castaneda, Grete Lang, Roswitha Geuther, Durga, Rasa and Paul Thies, Lucy from the Golden China Restaurant, Rachel Wolpern, Joseph Dostal, Matt Guest, Frank Kenton, Paulette Kerr, Ron Goldstein, Don Fleishman, James Barger, Chris Rogers, Steve Levinson, Pamela Weir-Quiton, Larry Hoisterman, Amy Wallace, Amalia Marquez, Jim Cleveland, Regina Thal, Leigh Goldstein, Mike Sager, Barry Klein and Patty, Amanda Foulger, Gloria Garvin, Jim and Veralyn Tawyesva, Mili Sangama and Jeff, John Shroeder, Manuela and Roberto Ammendola, Marianne Powell, James Seligman, Trudy and Saber Stehelin, Nancy Shanderae, Deena Metzger and Michael Ortiz, Marija Gimbutas, Vicky Komie and the Beyond Baroque nonfiction writer's group.

To all of us who remember

I am going to give you a fartby fart account
Yes, yes. That's wonderful, a five part
account

-Carlos Castaneda

Table of Contents

Acknowledgements.. iii

Author's Foreword...ix

Chapter One: How Did I Get Here?...1

Chapter Two: Suspending Judgment..11

Chapter Three: Charlie's Spider Web 25

Chapter Four: The Puzzle Of Reason.......................................47

Chapter Five: Pandora's Box...73

Chapter Six: In The Bowels Of The Twin World.....................95

Chapter Seven: Digging For Bones...109

Chapter Eight: Back From Hell With Trophies.......................123

Chapter Nine: Caught In Westwood..165

Chapter Ten: Back To The Beginning.....................................187

Chapter Eleven: Countdown To Infinity 209

Epilogue...227

Appendix A: Time Line...231

Appendix B: Have You Seen These Women?..........................235

Appendix C: Miscellaneous Photo Gallery 239

Appendix D: Paper Trail From Trash Archives 243

Author's Foreword

The story you are about to read, more than anything else, aspires to be a gift, as well as a marker for myself, to never forget the ripple caused by the pebble of word memory that dropped into my pond and that lies now shimmering like a jewel on the bottom of the water.

But before I begin, I'd like to caution the esteemed reader. According to Plato, "a written discourse on any subject is bound to contain much that is fanciful".

And even though, I did my best not to stray from the path, in no way do I claim to present an objective view of past events, of which, by my contention, we are in general incapable of, by our very nature of perceiving.

Immersed in seeing, hearing, and sensing with my own selective mechanisms, compounded by the added variable of a fallible memory, retraced from a certain hindsight position, in a strict sense my tale might not be close to the original experience at all, and could very well be considered fiction, with the people in it products of my imagination.

And taking you, the reader, into account the act of your deciphering will keep the story alive and change it again. By the distinction of your interpretative preferences it will become your design.

Nevertheless, one must consider that the events are told with good intentions, and the people in this narration represent fleeting facets of a whole, often unseen reality, hidden behind the surface of the mundane, rooted in the experience of a particular time space.

Thus my gift, this story is to be taken at your own risk. Let it rumble around in you, reverberate in your ribcage, knock on your heart, and trace its echo in your bones.

Gaby Geuter

Chapter One

How Did I Get Here?

You are here because you know something.
What you know you can't explain.
But you feel it. You felt it your entire life.
                              -Morpheus in *The Matrix,* 1999

The question of the man standing in front slowly seeped into my barricaded mind. Was he talking to me? Or the other twenty in the room? Evenly spaced on the honey colored floor we stood like sentinels motionless, waiting for someone to answer. His black eyes rested loosely on me.

In his gaze I felt exposed. "I am nobody, I am nothing," I said without words. He saw me and I saw him with the pores of my skin, with the feelers of my neck.

What does he mean? How did I get here? In general or in particular? What brought me here? To this room in this city, to this country, into his elusive presence? The walls stopped to exhale. The light above crackled in blaring neon, growing nuances stronger.

His probing question tore into the void of silence and grew a myriad of tentacles rooting through the muck of possibilities like dark matter in space. In the bright glare of this spotlight my mind raced, bouncing the question like a ping-pong ball off the many walls of the elaborate mansion that houses my memory.

In a sense, it was not a miracle to suddenly stand in front of him. Hadn't I prepared all my life for this moment? It was the wishing, longing, hating, mocking and sneering that dropped me into this dream of illusions turned reality. But then it came as a complete shock.

For thirteen years I've lived in this never-ending sea of houses that stretches two driving hours from East to West and is harnessed only inconsequentially by the Pacific Ocean. A mythical movie-town with her everyday street corners and crossings eternalized on celluloid, a magic carpet of invented miracles, heroic deeds and heart-wrenching dramas packaged for fast consumption. As if this city, The City of the Angels, that feeds its self-generated illusions to the rest of the world could also give birth and form to my fantasies!

Conceivably, I had walked the same sidewalks and touched the same door handles he had, possibly even rubbed elbows without ever seeing him. So close, and yet unreachable.

Why did it happen now after so many years? Utter coincidence, a whimsy of the universe. There has to be a reason for it. I did not look for him, not here or in Yuma and Nogales, like so many others. I knew that to find someone hiding purposefully in the anonymity of a city of millions was more difficult than searching for the proverbial needle in a haystack.

It was not my scheming that brought me here. Maybe it was my soul mourning for its loss in nightmares of hunger? Or was it the hole she left behind staring out of my eye sockets, gnawing and scratching in my throat, gliding in dreams over Spain like a witch in a red silk robe? For millennia she held me by the hand, ridiculing love, religion, authority and power, but never letting me grow blind. And if I only stumbled wearily behind her once in a while, I caught the seam of her dress.

Whatever it was that prompted me to leave the narrow-minded village of my youth and to throw myself into the unknown expanse, this mysterious force pushed me over the western ocean like a nutshell and suddenly reeled me into this man's presence.

This is how I happened to meet the sorcerer.

He slipped into my life like a sock long lost in the wash that suddenly reappeared, unexpectedly anticipated. My insides shook uncontrollably. My mind ripped from the indolent daily routine, drew slow circles of disbelief. Cognitive dissonance.

I was still far away searching for a plausible, honest and comprehensive reply to the unanswerable question when the pregnant silence became unbearable. What by now seemed like an eon later, I gushed: "From Germany, I came from Germany", as if that would explain my whole story!

With one glance he had reduced my razor-sharp tongue to stammering. This bothered me afterwards immensely. I felt like an idiot - the worst insult to my self-image.

The simplest answer would have been that it was Kylie who had invited me to the private instructions of the magical movements. Kylie, the Nordic looking bodyguard, who follows the witches to all public appearances. She is the guardian of the outer door. She accompanied Florinda to the Sisterhood bookstore anniversary celebration in Westwood. Was it not a wondrous coincidence that I heard Florinda's name mentioned during the ten minutes of my daily radio time? A decade of listening went by before I caught this precise moment.

A handful of people, mostly my friends, crammed into the small room of the women's bookshop. Florinda, the author of "A Witch's Dream", sat only inches away from us. Her short spiked hair glowed in golden blond. Piercing blue shot from her eyes.

Wondering about her age, I scanned her face for telltale signs of cosmetic surgery. With the female habit of critical comparison, my gaze scrutinized her carefully combed eyebrow arches, her perfectly smooth, peachy complexion and an almond-shaped face featuring a delicate small nose and a strong chin, used to getting her way. She wore no offensive perfume but an immaculately pressed blouse and well fitting tailored pants on her evenly proportioned slender frame.

With her freshness and understated elegance she seemed to have stepped down from a reclining pose on an Armani billboard from which she languidly watched over the neon palm tree sunsets of Los Angeles with the indifference of nobility.

Did I expect a turquoise laden Lynn Andrew's sister draped with amulets, or maybe a robust, colorful woman with braids and ruffled skirts wearing no panties? Perhaps an exotic creature reeking with mystery?

Instead, there was a female Johnny Carson impersonator with the same smirk on her face balanced on a daintily thin neck.

She rode on a wave of gushing confidence with unscarred pixie-like youthfulness. She smiled readily and spoke loudly in exuberant bursts without a moment hesitation. Was she playing a game with us, feeding our hungry eyes from her addictive lips? Did she bask in our attention? The allotted fifteen minutes were too short to answer our questions. I needed more time to probe the enigma of her sudden appearance into my world.

Outside, on the sidewalk in front of the bookstore on Westwood Boulevard, I summoned all my courage and addressed her in German. "Kann ich Sie wiedersehen?"

Through her book I knew about her German upbringing in Venezuela and with this clever maneuver I was hoping to place a foot into the suddenly opened doorway of the sorcerers' world before it would close again. Her eye flickered for a second.

Was she flattered? Maybe it was our German connection, maybe she enjoyed my obvious ardor, or possibly it was just a fleeting whim that made her promise me another opportunity for a longer talk. Kylie, the androgynous guardian, gave me her telephone number.

Months passed. Bill Clinton became president; Audrey Hepburn died from colon cancer; Erich Honecker was free to fly to Chile since it violated his human rights to stand trial in front of a judge with an illness; the World Trade Center in New York was damaged in a bomb attack; the Christian sect in Waco incinerated by the government; and yes, Prince Charles and his wife Diana decided on a separation. A report that must have brought tears to my mother's eyes.

My sporadic telephone conversations with Kylie resulted in shrunken expectations and always the same polite excuse of an out-of-the-country-traveling Florinda. Was she testing my persistence? Did she want to soften me up, turn me into easy prey, and marinate me like a piece of meat? Or was this crack in the door to the unknown nothing but a glimpse, a fleeting facet on the random tapestry of chaos?

My hopes had all but disappeared, when, unexpectedly, and without explanation, Florinda was ready to talk. So I saw her again, the female embodiment of confidence and the emissary of an unknown world.

She agreed to appear at the apartment of a friend, in front of an assembled group of people who met there for weekly discussions on shamanism. I would have liked to tell her how long I had waited for this opportunity to encounter a bona fide sorceress; what an honor it was to welcome her, and how curious I was to hear her story, but she cut me off. She didn't need someone else's introduction. She would present herself.

Florinda Donner-Grau, the name given to her by her master, becomes real through dreaming. She did not want to be the explanation of another, but rather the image of her own fabrication.

In the ensuing conversation she enjoyed answering questions. She was so full of life, so full of energy. She did not seem to be worn out by the daily grind, or scarred by the role of wife, mother, grandmother and consumed by the common struggle for survival? No, she was childless and unmarried, devoted to a life of sorcery.

My mind circulated a thousand questions that grew insignificant in her presence, but I felt compelled to tell the strange dream I had had a few nights before. Although I sensed her momentary apprehension, I abandoned my usual restraints and sputtered away.

In my ordinary unconscious dream world I heard the name Florinda Donner. It was followed by a violent punch into my stomach region that catapulted me into an awareness of crystalline proportions. Suddenly, I found myself crawling cautiously through a narrowing mint-green wooden chute.

My friend Greg, whom I had met a few months earlier through a personal ad, was holding on to my right ankle. I continued forward in a slow crawl, pulling him like a log behind me.

Finally, I arrived at an opening that widened into a small room. It was full of tiny things: toys, dollhouses and figurines placed neatly in the middle. I looked them over carefully. They reminded me of nothing. Soon the dream images weakened and my concentration waned. Or was I found out? Nobody seemed to be in the room.

Florinda had listened to my account in amusement. She exchanged knowing glances with her attendant and said that it was Taisha's room.

How could it have been Taisha's room?

Nobody mentioned who was leading the sorcery passes the first time I stood in the dance studio on Stewart Street. In my ignorance I assumed it would be Kylie and Aricele, the chacmools who dragged a hundred participants from physical stagnation at the seminar in Arizona with their animalistic flexibility and the strength of Amazons. Since that day, together with a friend, I pestered Kylie to start a practice group in Los Angeles.

When the small gray-haired man took his place between the two guardians, he seemed to me a generously tolerated Mexican who told funny stories with a mellow Latin singsong lilt. Friendly and unassuming in his dark blue shirt, designer jeans and beige windbreaker, he looked nothing like the sorcerer of my subconscious mind. Missing was the colorful headdress, the extravagantly bold clothing, the ominous beard and a brooding countenance. The deep lines crisscrossing his smiling great-uncle face gave him the shrunken-head-appearance of a dried apple with unruly hair.

Surrounded by the laughter of the invited group, he talked about his search for gurus in which he encountered the last real guru, who fell down a long staircase, breaking his neck right in front of him. All of the twenty or more attending students and the three witches standing behind us were under the spell of this inconspicuous man, who pulled our puppet strings with effortless ingenuity. His existence had suddenly penetrated through a small hole in the wall separating the world of fantastic literature from my ordinary reality. But where had this leak begun?

I was searching one slow seething Sunday afternoon, driven by memories of empty choking village Sundays when after church service and lunch not even the leaves of the linden trees ventured to stir, and the houses turned into faces with sleepy vacuous eyes. On these summer afternoons of thunderstorms, when the first drops whipped down on the musty earth, and I threw myself in giant leaps against the wind that squalled around the sandstone barn I was hunting for a way out, out of the village, out of the habitual labyrinth of my world of thoughts. I longed to be the wind, the house, the wash table, the child, the jump, the sensation of flying. I thirsted for inspiration, for hope and answers, for a small step forward.

On this nameless shabby Sunday afternoon I had gone to the Phoenix Bookstore. The eager clerk recommended the book of a fellow sorceress in lieu of the dried up river from the master's typewriter. He sensed my resistance in the skeptical composure that expected warmed up, watered down and pilfered ideas, prompting him to point out that I could paint my own picture of the validity of this self-proclaimed witch at the author's upcoming book signing.

Trained in a fabulist-father course and enough hard-won practice to see through my mother's thick curtain of self-absorption, I believed myself to be fully prepared to smell out prevarication of any sort.

But the woman's clarity, sincerity and simplicity surprised me the more. Taisha Abelar, as she called herself, sat next to a small card table dressed in the businesslike attire of an accountant with a subdued patterned silk blouse, while her manicured, fine-boned hands without nail polish brushed calmly over her matching fashionable pants.

She wore her hair in a short mouse-brown bob, possibly a wig, with substantial gold hoop earrings. Her clean alabastrine complexion showed no trace of make-up during her talk about her apprenticeship as a sorceress. Without the obligatory feather adornments, quartz crystals, beaded necklaces and Celtic jewelry she was no contender for the contemporary new-age witch. Plain and unobtrusive, she reminded me of a Buddhist nun.

Her steel-gray eyes wandered openly in a steady gaze over the crowded room. The execution of her thought processes appeared logical, of continuous rational clarity bordering on beauty. Only a superior actress could hide her true feelings and thoughts so thoroughly, preventing the seepage of even the tiniest fleck of a lie in her body language and tone during this marvelous performance.

Or did I cloud my rational mind with sugar plums? Did I hunger for the fantastic and wondrous imaginative opposite of my world and therefore read clarity in empty vacant eyes, perceive beauty in parroted rote ideas? Was my believing her not just a desperate act of grasping for straw? Or could this really be a new pathway providing physical answers to the mysteries of existence?

I bought her book off hand and she signed it on the first page, wishing me the best. My stammered question was as unimportant as her polite answer, since I wanted her undivided attention for one solipsistic moment. And the moment betrayed no lies. She was as solid as a rock, convinced of the authenticity of her experiences.

Just like he was. Steeped in a blank stare I oscillated in front of him. The sudden realization of vast possibilities overpowered me. His words poured over me in the overwhelming force of a landslide, that crushed and shook me in my boots, unlocking endless vistas of grandeur, a sublime landscape, that had been only raw fantasy until the moment I stood in the proximity of the electrifying energy running through his wiry body and his ubiquitously penetrating eyes.

His words pierced me like darts on a bulls-eye.

The sorcerer is no ordinary man. He has adventitious opportunities in life as well as in death. At the hour of his departure he turns his total self into a single ball of energy passing by death with grit and bravado whizzing into infinity.

Ordinary humans have no other way than the total annihilation and destruction of their awareness by the eagle of death that waits like a bird of prey for the moment the awareness separates from the body. The sorcerer buys his freedom through the constant and willing release of all identifications, memories and feelings.

In the velvet indigo of the night he saw between tears the streaming lights of his master sorcerer and cohorts jump over the wall of the compound, disappearing on a spiraling course with a last gesture of farewell like silent firework rockets into the purple vastness of the universe.

The Disneyfication of a lost story from the collected works of the Grimm Brothers? No, he maintained this to be the truth, as concrete and real as the wooden floor on which our feet squealed back and forth in horse stance. He does not want money. He only wants to show us the way. We do not have to believe him. We should test the veracity of his teachings ourselves. His words were urgent. The time is short. Soon he would leave.

There was no speckle of a doubt, no furrow of deceit, not one gesture that betrayed him. Or is he himself a phantom? Is he like the incestuous mind-coloring of his books a mere product of my imagination? This man, who calls himself Carlos Castaneda.

GABY GEUTER

Chapter Two

Suspending Judgment

*The stars that once confused me seem now to light a path that
is clear, that in truth I have been traveling for all these days,
when in what came I left behind my sorrows, and I'm traveling
still.*

-Robert Merivel in *Restoration,* 1995

Coastal sagebrush washes against my thighs in muted smoke-green as I wind my way past the simmering bushes of the buckwheat that have been toasted to a rusty brown. Ever the artist's daughter, my eyes arrange palettes of colors, compositions of light and dark, pictures that soothe. The empty deer-weed bushes narrow the yellow-ochre sandstone path with wine-red broom stalks. The days of green exuberance are only memory. A gray stiff heat holds the landscape in a vice. Indian summer. The season of fire.

I walk to feel the ground under my feet.

Turkey vultures that usually hunt inland cut silent circles over the glimmering hills. Meager shadows lick across my face under the mountain mahogany and the thorny wild lilac bushes, an arched tunnel gracefully bowing over the footpath.

The hot breath of the desert engulfs me with dust and exhaust on its way to the Pacific Ocean, where it accumulates in a yellow-brown layer of smog on the curve of the horizon. In a few days, when the wind switches, the saturated coolness of the ocean will bring the biting stench back and lap it over the city like a cloth.

The aroma of singed black sage wafts in shivers. Cicadas pierce the silence. Pearls of sweat creep down my forehead.

He tells us, we know nothing. We catalogue, and name, and our society calls it knowledge. I have learned the names of the plants in these hills, as if the words could grow new roots for me in this adopted land. An effort of marking home with sounds of recognition.

The tiny and twisted prickly leaves of the evergreen brush oaks, the delicate fronds of the Chamiso, the Toyon, and the smooth waxy shoots of the Sumac with its oily seeds, the Sugar bush and Lemonade berry give the Santa Monica Mountains even in the deadest time of the year a tenacious tinge of faded moss.

The hawks have gone somewhere else. Only troops of quail cluck unencumbered like a herd of schoolchildren with supervision between the leaves in the underbrush.

He says, there is more out there than what we are willing to see. Where? Have I not searched for it all my life, hopelessly plumbing the flat surface of appearances for some depth of meaning?

A melancholic rattle startles me into the present. The steel colored spears of the yucca ache in the wind surrendering to the heat like the cracking skin on my arms. Shriveled up mummies of the Hummingbird Sage and the wild Gooseberry bush stand as ghostly remnants of a plentiful past.

Hidden within all waits for revival.

The steep path turning away from the sun leads down into the rupture of the ravine. Here sycamores, California laurels, white alders, ancient crippled oaks and scrubby elderberry bushes jostle for space and light. My hands caress the reeds on the decent. They rustle reassuringly against my hips.

Meeting him still seems unreal, just as the sudden possibility that all those cloud castles in my mind could actually be true.

I avoid the touch of the red-colored leaves of Poison Oak. Just in case. Even though I have not gotten the nerve itching rashes for several years after trying the native cure of eating a tiny bud of the young leaves in the early spring. The Chumash and Tongva that lived here in the canyon built their roundhouses from the reeds.

Everything they needed was available in abundance. Acorns, roots, seeds in the fall, berries, fresh greens and plate-sized Chanterelle in the spring, plenty of game in the mountains and fish in the near ocean. In my childhood hills I knew when and where to find the edible plants to supplement our post-war diet in the tradition of prehistoric gatherers like the first Californians.

In the dense shade under the big trees the smell of tired ferns, dried moss, decayed mushrooms, frogs and moist sand oozes around the polished ironstone rocks that testify the ravenous power of the water during the rainy season.

On top of the cliff, balancing her black twisted branches over the abyss, the oak ballerina claws her feet into the rock arrested in a timeless dance. The air rushes like a cool river following the trickle of water in the bottom of the ravine. A small corner of cerulean blue flickers in a puddle. Los Angeles is light years away.

I'm leaning against the rough wood railing of the bridge, gazing at the light reflections in the water. The Sycamore leaves crunch under my feet like dried five-fingered hands.

The outer silence betrays the weltering tumult of thoughts possessing my mind. I deem myself on the threshold of a new adventurous land. At last I'm in motion, after the eddy of an all too familiar reality. The reference points of memories and relationships, that once were my net of identification, are fading. A new landscape is about to open up in front of me.

The last picture I painted during my wordless hunt for the unknown ended with a dark prussic blue blotch that filled the whole canvas. I sat on the edge staring into the blue and I saw nothing. Now in the landscape of my mind, unfamiliar colorful dark glittering lines unveil, as shimmering surfaces and fantastic holograms whisper mysteriously. They unlock an endless universe full of strange corners into which I peer with astonishment.

I don't know who I am anymore and for the first time in my life, I don't care. A Sinbad sailing into unknown expanses, a Winnetou in a dangerous land.

He says that people waste too much energy on the daily defense of self-representation.

Ninety percent of our energy serves to maintain our self-reflection. What we experience as the self is only our system of interpretation.

There is nothing else, but the interpretation of energy in flux.

To see energy as it flows in the universe is the goal of the sorcerer.

All he wants is to help us get out of the cage. We are like chicken in a coop, unaware of our demise, waiting for death. There is more. The farmer that feeds us is not our friend. We are his crop, his food.

The universe is predatory. He says, there are no gods, only interpretation.

Our reality is an accumulation and organized sorting of endless information. Anything that does not fit we ignore.

When my father came home he would hide behind the cow barn and sneak like a thief along the hedge of horse chestnut trees. We chased over these gnarled elephant trunks screaming like a flock of noisy parrots, competing with each other in sure-footed childhood mastery.

I clung to the supple top of the oak that stood its ground between the chestnuts, whipping back and forth with gusts of the approaching storm. The oak was the ocean; I was the storm, rootless and free.

On the corner of the upper garden where the giant pear tree fell and buried me despite evasive maneuvers under the tips of its soft branches like a scratchy crochet blanket, parked the drab green tanks so massive they barely fit through the narrow streets of our village. The young men in uniform brought my mother to a state of flutter I seldom saw in her. I could not understand what was so exiting about the inside of a tank. And the chewing gum did not impress me much either.

On the long narrow stone staircase that led to the lower garden my mother photographed my younger sister with a crown of dandelions. She seemed to forget my birthdays.

Apple trees, expansive enough to build tree houses in them, stretched their arms in long established generosity. We children were forbidden to pick apples or anything else, as if we were a plague of locusts decimating everything in sight. Through openings in the wooden fence the young men of the village peered at my mother, posing invitingly in her bathing suit. How could they smell when she would be in the garden?

Zacher's fruit orchard next door tempted with plums, apples and pears. From there we ran past the hedge of wild roses across the meadow of sorrel down to the brook. Around its dark waters anchored battered tall willows and black alder trees surrounded by a thicket of blackberry and filberts that one could separate only with imaginary machetes.

On this mill brook he hid brightly colored sugar eggs in the hollowed trunk of a silver willow. He exclaimed that the Easter bunny had just been here. Between the yellow and white anemones danced a soft spring breeze and the water of the brook sprayed in white silver veins.

I wondered how the Easter bunny could know when we would come to the streamlet, and how he could have carried the immaculately clean sugar eggs without wrappings. But this bewilderment melted away with the rarely enjoyed sweetness and I could almost see him.

With the egg basket on his back, he was a figure as genuine as my father, whose unexplainable absences and sudden reappearances alternately triggered fear and joy in me. The secrecy made it unreal.

The underbrush rustles, stronger than the rummaging of the brown Towhees. Suddenly it is quiet. I become a bridge posts. A knowing inside of me, a visceral feeler, stretches out and searches through the thicket.

Between the oak leaves appear the cautiously twitching ears of a coyote, a proud strong specimen with a gray rusty stripe along his back. He glides down the slope in a smooth feathery motion, looking at me nonchalantly as he crosses the path. A good omen. Coyote is my friend.

He dribbles down the path to the small waterfall and throws me another one of his mischievous glances asking if I am coming or not.

Amused I follow him. At the edge of the riffled ironstone I sit down and listen to the gurgling of the thin streamlet that tumbles twenty feet into a small bowl. The sound resembles distant human voices in a language I cannot decipher. Can you hear the whispering?

The coyote is long gone. The dry stalks of the Humboldt Lily tower between the rocks. Green algae cones in the dripping stream of water.

The drone of a hummingbird buzzes nervously between branches and comes closer. Some call him lightning bird. Allen's hummingbird is even smaller than others, with rufous sides and a metallic pink bib. He hurtles around me. Because of his speed and agility he can afford to be bold and daring. He has no equal. It doesn't let him rest.

He comes back to test my human impatience. Then he whizzes over the water, extending his miniature claws and unbelievably alights on the crest of the waterfall where the stream flows fastest. He attaches his claws to the mossy algae, ducks his head and upper body under the brown, amber streaked whirling cord of water, splashing with spread out wings and keeping his tongue stuck in the wet sucking.

He is close enough to touch. In the helter-skelter of my mind, my body instinctively seeks the calming effect of the natural world. Slowly I'm groping my way back to the beginning, on the rope that leads into the haze of oblivion.

In the dance studio we silently wait for him. Everyday words are too ordinary to transmit the flood of energy that rattles us chosen ones on the inside. The atmosphere of the room changes as soon as he enters. A fresh wind drives away the paralyzing silence of expectation. His squinting eyes wink imperceptibly. He rubs his hands with a smirk.

He tells us to suspend judgment. Death and Dying are not linear concepts. Out there is nothing but pure energy. He moves his lower arm with a jerking motion to the side and clenches his fist at the last moment. Relaxing and tensing. He walks between the participants back and forth listening to the snapping sound of our fists.

Next to me willows a long legged model from New York that is unable to make a fist with her oversized red fingernails. My arms

16

move automatically. My mind watches, bundled to a single point that pushes along the wall of perception like a laser tip of glowing nerves.

Who is he?

The net of my senses vibrates in high gear as if awakened from a long sleep. Even at work, while following the explanations of my boss, I simultaneously register every nuance, every muscle spasm, flutter of eyelashes, the acrid smell of her mouth when she gets nervous or angry, our sweat that accumulates microscopically, the rattle of the printer, the clicking of the computer, the movement of the big hand on the clock, the ringing of the phone, all as one big grid of awareness.

On a wordless level, all my sensory devices convene to touch this wiry man in front of me. Is he the person in his books? Is there something else behind the man? The witches behind me don't seem very familiar with the movements. In front of me is a woman with the face of a cow. She and her boyfriend smell like sweat.

Death dissolves us slowly. The sorcerer changes his destiny. He gives death a facsimile of his life with the hope to be spared. The repeated contemplation of all past interactions establishes a platform of distance from which the sorcerer can observe himself and his behavior more clearly.

All relationships, every encounter I've ever had with people, I'm supposed to regurgitate? To free the energy that is trapped there? As if I was not already wading enough through my memories. Taisha thought I should recapitulate despite my Primal Therapy years, in which I screamed out all my painful childhood memories until I came to the collective ocean of tears too big to be drained by my eyes.

That aside, death does not scare me. The total disintegration of self, the worm-invested composting of my borrowed cellblocks, and the dispersing of memories into the blackness of the universe has always been my ultimate comfort. After all, my brother went there. Is the threat of our end the only way to motivate and control people?

Death sits riding on the left shoulder to whisper into the ear of the sorcerer.

At the end of the classes a cluster of eager proffering fans surround him lusting for personal attention. I stand apart. Doesn't he

17

tell us everything during the class, and all I need to do is use it? I refrain from acting like a groupie or a dumb puppet that nods and prattles in blinded conviction. Or maybe it is only my engrained shyness that keeps me from approaching him.

Nevertheless, I catch a private moment with him. I touch the sleeve of his jacket, addressing him with "Carlos...," and nearly jump out of my skin. The cloth feels almost empty, like a ghost. Barely recovering I ask him to grace the Castaneda discussion group of my friends with a visit, who have no knowledge of my participation in this secretly held private class. He refuses without explanation.

A few weeks later I ask him again, suddenly overcome by an image of my ignorant friends fabricating convoluted ideas about Castaneda, as he sits among them incognito and their surprised faces when he discloses his identity. This time, without explanation, he consents.

He arrives in a small white car, escorted by Kylie. In the hallway he touches my hair. "You have nice long hair". For a moment I am irritated.

Obviously he prefers short hair on women. Even though the big sorceresses of his books sported long thick black braids, all his current companions have a boyish Peter Pan cut. Why is he complementing my long hair? Does he see his hands with barber tools?

He is disappointed about the small size of the apartment living room, and that he has to stand with his back against a window. The thirty-five people crowded into the space listen breathlessly to the foundation of the pre-historic Mexican sorcery tradition.

The sorcerer lives without expecting reward.

The social order cares nothing about the individual. It leads us to our destruction, shapes us into repeating idiots, and teaches us self-pity.

Discipline is the only deterrent. The fantasy of self-importance in normal life pushes infinity out of sight.

The sorcerer prepares himself with discipline to face infinity. Our birthright is to be free, not a wheel in the machine.

We are wanderers; we have to fulfill our destiny.

We are all bored fucks, conceived in total boredom. That's why our energy level is low. We have to struggle harder to get out of the cage.

He answers questions. They are harmless little questions, no irreverent ones. The room is in awe, captured by the omnipresence of this legendary writer, this icon of the sixties. He appears to be used to it.

As usual, I have not one good question, one that he could use, one that would lure the next step out of him. Years ago, at the Phoenix Bookstore, he was waiting for the right question. Only such a question would be worthwhile to pose. After three hours of generous talk he disappears as quickly as he arrived.

From the audience at the apartment three women as well as Greg have been invited to join the private movement classes. Sexual relations are not condoned, so we act in the class as neutral as possible.

Frequently, during the day at work, I receive telephone calls from Kylie asking me for the phone number of one or the other of the new women. It is beginning to annoy me. She uses me as a telephone directory. Can't she take her own telephone book with her when Carlos wants to call women from the restaurant?

Not knowing what importance and meaning his conversations have, I feel a slight touch of being used and passed over. Does he have to rub it in my face that I am less important than others?

Or is this only another test of my ego? Do Kylie's calls offer me an opportunity I don't recognize, to voice my enthusiasm about the teachings? Does she want to be friends? Within earshot of my colleagues at work I can hardly talk about sorcery in the open.

Sarcastic citizens assign Los Angeles four seasons, respectively earthquakes, fires, mudslides and riots. All of which happen in a seemingly independent cycle and in undetermined order. We have entered the season of fire.

Over the distant blue hills swell ominous orange tinted clouds of smoke. With a wind force of sixty miles per hour the arson flames race to the ocean. There they change direction with the flipping of the wind that hurtles the wall of fire back into the canyons.

The road home on PCH, full of other wide-eyed worried drivers, slows down to a crawl with the tail of cars growing aproportionally to the head of the snake. On one side is the ocean, on the other, the cliffs. There is no way out. Everybody fears the loss of precious possessions.

At the Topanga turnoff they don't let me go any further. No one is allowed to enter the burning area. The smoke column billows threateningly over the mountain rim. From the restaurant on the beach I call my daughter to tell her to pack our cat and all photographs she can find into her car and then get out of the canyon as quickly as possible.

For two days we watch on the news as firefighting helicopters scoop water from the ocean with large buckets dropping it on the west side of our canyon.

Is everything gone, turned to ash? The robe I wore giving birth, the self-made baby jeans, the mother's day presents of wobbly ceramic bowls, refrigerator drawings, the recipe of the pine nut cake from Jimena de la Frontera, diaries full of complaints, seeds of memories? I let them go.

But this time the fire spared our side of Topanga. Tuna Canyon, though, resembles the surface of the moon. Through an ankle deep blanket of white and gray powder loom the black charred fingers of the once succulent greenery into the empty sky. They grab after my clothing and paint Ash Wednesday salvation markings on my cheeks.

He is unhappy. Maybe because of the unpleasant smell of sweat generated by the participants in the first row, or he might be annoyed by the lacking attention of some that disregard his demand to come to class wearing closed shoes, and not flimsy sandals. Greg must believe, as long as Carlos does not take him aside personally and speak to him in confidentiality - lemee tell you somezin - that it does not apply to him. What ignorance!

Or maybe Carlos is weakened by the constant dental work he is undergoing. He says we are not taking his efforts seriously. He is pumped full of Novocain and we are limp.

I don't understand what he expects from me. I'm trained at paying strict attention. My body is in good physical shape to readily absorb the movements he is teaching. I take everything he says seriously. On the other hand, the sarcastic criticizing that he thinly disguises as jokes does not bother me. That I'm wound up dancing around with Greg in insolence is a direct result of the dammed up tremendous energy raging inside of me, the energy of hope for something new, precious and lasting.

Am I too modest, too unassuming, and too good again? Should I force myself into the foreground? Should I call Kylie with a pretext, trying to become friends? She has never been very open or communicative towards me. She seems to be turned inward, totally wrapped up in her task of being a sorcerer's apprentice, wound tight like a spring, ready, focused and changeable at any moment.

Carlos' dissatisfaction disturbs me, and I approach him before the class starts. "Carlos, do you think I have a chance? Am I going to make it? I am German".

Carol, the nagual woman, waves from the studio door pointing towards the time.

"Oh, she is such a dog", he exclaims and with a gesture of his hand shoos her away, like a mongrel. He listens intently to my question, unperturbed by Greg's presence, which is spurred by a curiosity that has no decorum or subtlety.

Germans possess good qualities, especially discipline, sobriety and sincerity. His answer is not conclusive, but appeasing. I am relieved that he did not dismiss me harshly.

The gray grass lies on the hills like shaggy fur, flattened by the early rains. Beneath the skeletons of bleached mustard rods and silver hairs, blink the first delicate tips of green. The orange flaming hands of the Sycamore leaves dance stiffly, deformed to origami figures on the white-flecked bone branches.

The silence now breathes quieter, more hopeful. Sailboats of leaves crash noisily down into the brook that tattles in several voices again. The mealy berries of the Toyon, the Christmas berry bush, blush like children's cheeks in winter snow.

At night the coyotes howl. They chase through the canyon in a wild horde. I encountered them once in the moonless mountains on the same path. Glowing eyes, pointed ears, a panting busy din. They barely moved out of my way. For them I was not human. Humans gasp loudly yelling in shorts, in broad daylight, limited to the wide paths, protected from the tick infested poisonous world of the bushes. In the blackness we passed like shadows of breath recognizing each other on a level beyond the five senses.

Christmas is approaching. The classes of the magical movements are temporarily suspended because a number of the participants are leaving town to be with family. I'm not leaving. Kylie will notify us as soon as the classes start up again.

Greg, who tends to read only the last sentence of any book in his own brand of Zen minimalism, is finally breaking down to read Carlos' books, sufficiently impressed by the master's presence.

Orion the Hunter migrates over the southwesterly sky in the crystal clear and frosty nights. I have placed my bed out on the deck to watch the blanket of stars over me. Maybe they will convey their secrets to me at night during my unguarded sleep state like the books that Carlos puts under his pillow.

When the feet don't warm up the whole night I take an electrical heating pad to bed with me. Mother heated bricks on top of the stove and wrapped them in old towels so we wouldn't burn our feet on them. With the hot stones we went into the ice flower bedroom, where on moist walls grew green-black ice crystal designs and we cuddled under the feather beds.

Carlos visits me in a dream. I rarely have dreams with people that I actually know from waking life. He comes into my dream without great fanfare, asking me how I am doing. A polite flourish I answer without thinking with the same superficial politeness.

The next instant my consciousness rails, "That was a unique opportunity to talk with him. How stupid of you! A meeting on your level, without interference, without obstructions or masquerade and pretense. In your dream!" I could have asked him any question I wanted. What secrets he teaches his selected students, if I am good enough to become one of them, what future our planet has, if we can dream together.

In this moment of scorn that is driving me from my dream, an owl suddenly lifts from the swaying branch it has been sitting on over the deck. It flutters, briefly illuminates and then glides over me into the blackness of night, awakening me completely.

That Carlos visited me in this dream is without a doubt. The owl in exactly the same moment was too strange. What are the odds of having an unusual dream and the close encounter with a night bird at the same time? Carlos the owl touched me with his wings and disappeared with a gentle whoosh fanning over me.

Kylie regrets during my repeated telephone inquiries that Carlos has not resumed teaching the movement classes. Maybe I should tell her my strange dream?

One evening, on a drive with Greg through town, passing Stewart Street, the stray thought appears between us, if Carlos might possibly be teaching again. This prompts Greg to turn spontaneously onto the parking lot in front of the studio.

Through the big windows we clearly see familiar faces lined up in the neon light of the foyer waiting for Carlos. In a purple haze they seem suspended in non-animation, staring into the space in front of them. The classes are still going!

Shock stifles my body. Unable to move, I sit in the cab of Greg's truck while he jumps out like stung by a wasp and runs into the hallway. To me the presence of the others in the dance studio is confirmation enough. It is obvious! The meaning of our discovery is that we are not wanted anymore, uninvited!

But why did Kylie lie to me for weeks on the phone? Why couldn't she tell me to my face that I am not invited anymore? I can understand if the group of sorcerers protect themselves with secrecy and deception from the general world as a precaution. What reason do they have to lie to me? The lies hurt more then the exclusion.

Death rides on the left shoulder and whispers into the ear of the sorcerer.

Chapter Three

Charlie's Spider Web

There can be only one.

-Connor McCloud in *The Highlander,* 1986

What went wrong? Why did he silently remove me from his presence without telling me the truth? Did I neglect to prostrate myself deep enough to satisfy his attention? Was I too proud to flatter and show my enthusiasm?

I don't understand why they have to lie to me! Could he not see the grateful excitement in my eyes and the spellbound rapture that kept me upright like a rod?

Or did I fail to recognize the chance he offered during those months, garbled in nuances of cultural misunderstandings? When he expressed his disappointment in the class I should have approached him and affirmed my sincerity.

This is the result of my self-centered pride, my cynical antipodal attitude and secret fear of rejection. A missed opportunity! They have, as he threatened, passed me by, gone to a different place!

Has the door to the sorcerer's world shut again? Is everything over? Has the drive for self-preservation, that helped me to survive and catapulted me into this scenario, finally become my stumbling block?

Oh, such self-flagellation.

As always, I was too modest, too shy to tell him the dreams with my strange energetic connection. My report card read every year: She is very quiet and unpretentious. Silent listening was rewarded. I've never learned the art of asking. The bread on the table winked invitingly at me, but despite my stomach-growling longing I could not manage to ask for a second slice. To be inconspicuous was my survival tactic. In order to slip by the sleeping beast of erratic flickering anger I learned to sacrifice my needs, to modify them. Through voluntary relinquishment I had at least some control over the extent of my cession. So I was not at the mercy of the adults. They appeared to me like a plateau of posteriors absorbed in their self-destructive world, throwing only rare hasty sideways glances.

Hidden behind their orders and explanations I sensed their self-serving motives. "What are the neighbors going to say?" was not an acceptable reason for me. "You don't do that," was not enough.

I lived behind my eyes withdrawn in obstinate seclusion. I was too proud to beg, too modest to ask, too sober to demand. Only the drive for truth and authenticity pushed me forward.

My carefully chosen and painstakingly mined questions are outwitted again by Greg's quick reaction. Instinctively, he shocks Kylie with a rash phone call and throws her into unprepared stuttering. The scared deer caught in the headlights of the dance studio foyer must not have said anything about our nightly surprise visit. Or, Kylie did not expect the audacity of a foolhardy call to ask for an explanation. Maybe she thought we would recoil in shame.

When she receives my call she reacts in a cool and collected manner. Her voice vibrates with meditated animosity and frosty defense.

Why did they lie to me?

They owe me no explanation. They can invite whomever they like.

Of course, I understand the class was free, but why did they have to lie to me? Couldn't she tell me to my face?

26

My co-workers are getting curious, always interested in personal drama and gossip. I lower my voice and obscure the mouthpiece.

I'm not mad, only disappointed and surprised. I was under the impression that I had an alliance forged through the secret meetings, a commonality in contrast to the rest of the world.

She does not give me any room, presents only a smooth hard wall.

They don't want my energy.

What is that supposed to mean?

Sorcerers owe nothing to anybody.

That ends my reservoir of replies. Even in my native language I lack a range of pleading words. If they don't want my energy, whatever that means, so be it. But the lies continue to be a caustic sore. Lies are a weakness, a gutless avoidance. Winnetou, the noble savage, would not have lied. I'm still looking for the ideal, the perfect uebermensch.

A sorcerer has to be patient, cunning, ruthless and sweet, so he said.

Somehow I did not grasp the workings of the sorcerer's group, what motivates their wheels into spinning, what counts in their circle. I would have expected a rational explanation from the reservoir of the sorcerer's universe, even if it had crushed my self-importance.

For example, the standard concept: The normal behaviors of our society have no validity in the world of the sorcerers. Or more creative: At the request of the Nagual, who constantly scans the horizon of the dark sea of awareness they had to lie to me. In fact, it is not a lie at all, but merely a temporary pausing, a catching of breath, before the next pomegranate ink message appears on the writing wall.

Maybe the reason for my exclusion is the peripheral relationship with Greg. We are sitting high up in the eye of a toad-like rock that guards the top of the mountain ridge. From the backside of this boulder one can easily climb onto the sandstone head. Five feet below, on the "brow" runs a ledge that leads to a small cave, just big enough for two people.

The first time we met, I noticed his pinpoint stare, then his oversized nose that makes him appear as if he is about to fall over, and then his humor. Looking at him I wonder why he follows me around. Either because he has nothing better to do, or he is lonely, or sometimes I think it is just a random coin toss, for no reason at all.

"Someone said this used to be one of Carlos' power spots".

"Could be. It's breathtaking."

From the eye of the toad one can see the white necklace of the ocean bay, the coastal islands, Catalina, St. Barbara, a smidgen of Anacapa, swimming in the glitter of the oceanic soup like croutons. To the left stretches a flat carpet of houses and buildings, interrupted only by the occasional pile of vertical blocks, Century City, Down Town L.A. On the other side roll the curly-haired mountain mother giants with furrowed rock faces over the canyon to the San Fernando Valley, and the snowy peaks of the Frazier Mountain range.

"Maybe our dismissal had something to do with our relationship".

"Do you think they know?"

Shredded fog chases past our faces like ghostly fingers of moist cotton candy. A flock of crows practice their aerial stunts in front of our noses with their wings smacking, whistling, hissing and spitting in the wind like a concert for feather instruments.

Greg does not seem to be deeply affected by his silent expulsion from the private classes. He took Kylie's excuse with compliant understanding.

"Maybe Carlos wants to be the only comedian in the room".

The sound of a taught shiny black crow's wing stroking the warm air pockets sweeping upward and folding space reverberates in distant corners of ancient memories talking in an almost forgotten, primeval language.

Greg believes to have been expelled from the magical classes because of his clowning around. Jokingly he warned the other students to watch out for Carlos driving the van. Florinda said with a laugh that they were going to kick him out of the group. Without me, he would not have given Carlos and the sorcerers a second look. He did not dream for twenty years to meet a wise master. He has no doubts, and he never questioned the meaning of life. For him it may be just another distraction that is quickly and easily replaced with the next one. What does he have to lose?

Silently, I cull through my own reasons. Maybe I'm not cut out to be a sorcerer. I am too critical, too stubborn and I'm never satisfied with easy explanations. I want to see an overview, the whole view. Possibly even explore my own way. I hate to follow the dot-to-dot chalk marks of previous climbers on a rock-climbing wall.

The crows are not distracted by Greg's offerings of flying breadcrumbs. The wind tunnel around the rock face affords perfect conditions for elaborate sailing maneuvers, which are interrupted only through the sudden dive-off into the ravine below us and a circling along the floor to catch the updraft again. The feather coats shine like polished blue-black metal and the crow eyes flicker savagely as they pass us within arms length in tolerant superiority. Their joyful cries bounce from the cliffs and they chase after each other in frivolous abandon, avoiding collisions by the width of a feather. They are riding the wind in total surrender as if weaving a pattern into the cloth of life.

Distant views to the minute blue ridges expand my range of thought as well. Am I not the perfect candidate, fulfilling almost all sorcerer's requirements? I grew up on their basic weltanschauung, I don't live shackled to society, my ego plays a minor role, and I am willing to make sacrifices. I have distanced myself long ago from my family. Having confronted my fears, nothing can scare me away, can it?

Or does it? Maybe deep down there is a defining last vestige of resistance: the fear of having to give up my daughter. Carol, the nagual woman, who supposedly left her children like dona Soledad from Carlos' books, gave me the standard answer to my question if I must denounce the bond to my daughter in order to be with them. First, I should recapitulate.

One of my worst nightmares was the neglect of my future children. My daughter is my only commitment, an almost sacred pledge I've made in my life never to abandon her. She saved me from self-destruction. For her sake, I did not want to take his blows anymore and ran off. It mattered little to me if he hurt me. He carried the pain just as I did. Death catches up with all of us. Time takes place in circles.

29

I never left her behind when she was small, or gave her to my mother. She is my responsibility. My mother and grandmother did not care much for their grandchildren. For them we were nothing more than bothersome accidents created in the youthful fallacy of a euphoric postwar negligence. Indescribably murky circumstances, unforgivable sins, ineffable guilt-ridden secrets surrounded our childhood and colored the attitude of relatives towards us. In their words, the smooth lake turned into a murderer, the green forest became evil and behind the house of my great-grandmother, the two white he-goats battled each other in a menacing public display.

And, not to forget, there was the uncle with a hushed up past in a certain brown uniform.

Would I have been prepared to give up the motor of my life to trade it for the shaky world of the sorcerers? As long as the commitment to my daughter is not dissolved on its own I cannot desert her.

Kylie's last words, still ringing in my ears, puzzle me. They don't want my energy? Is this a subtle way of saying they don't want me? Or is something wrong with my energy? Is it not compatible with theirs, or is it lacking in general? What curious secret lies behind this concept of needing energy? Once again I'm at a loss of understanding despite the decades of culture cramming in front of the TV to understand the web of connotations in this country.

The underlying meaning of words that are not dead ink prints in the dictionary, but more like shifting schools of fish, is contrived by the context, the emphasis and overall intention of the speaker. Everyday Los Angeles is driven by an informal and friendly exchange of common sociological movie and TV metaphors. If language is rooted in a place then the world of the sorcerers is an unfamiliar realm, whose features and very ground of coherence still escapes me.

He taught us that the energy of a person hinges on the magnitude of excitement the mother experienced during the time of conception. My mother certainly did enjoy the process; otherwise she would not have produced a herd of eight.

But it does not explain my admittedly lacking abundance of energy. Did it get lost during pregnancy? At the time it was discovered that my father was not the blue-blood aristocrat with Eastern Pomeranian land holdings, but a bigamist, a no good impostor who took the identification papers of a dead soldier in the war to cover up his self-granted furlough, disappearing acts for which he could expect the death penalty. He was not the decorated hero, draped with the "Ritterkreuz" medal of a paratrooper jumping behind enemy lines, but exposed as the sordid liar and small-time opportunist. At the time of my birth he was behind bars. Maybe that siphoned off the energy in her belly that I shared with my brother. And when I was spit out unexpectedly instead of the placenta, all she had left to give was rejection.

It just can't be over. The sand has not run through my fingers yet, the silica crystals still glitter in the sun.

The earthquake comes early on Monday morning, before the gray dawn, before the soft pink clouds, just as all life is turning over once more with a sigh to cherish another round of sleep. It arrives rattling like a freight train, taking hold of the house, the garden, and the spaces in the air. In its powerful grip the house moans and clatters, rumbles and creaks, becomes an old worm-eaten rollercoaster. The wooden deck I'm sleeping on suddenly jumps alive and writhes into an automatic massage mattress.

Earthquake, no dream, I shake. The realization crashes into my awakening mind. The air vibrates in rippling waves. With a half appeasing, half anticipating glance at the glass doors, I'm expecting them to burst any moment; I leap from the deck, grabbing shoes and flashlight. I call my daughter. In the lurid light of the night the water of the pool sloshes back and forth over the rim in a giant seesaw motion. We hold on to each other in the open air without breathing.

It lasted only thirty seconds. Long enough to panic. Each one of these seconds stretched in slow motion, selecting with painful hesitance the next move, usuriously growing into milestone events, licking towards sweeping possibilities. Was this the beginning or is it over? We are waiting for the aftershock; there is always an aftershock. The quake passed like a wave, jerking us awake to leave us shaken in its wake. It must have been a strong earthquake, or at least close under the surface to bring our heavy basalt ground into motion.

The repertoire of earthquakes acquired since living in Los Angeles includes the short, softly vibrating shiver, friendly like a baby's crib; the sudden concise hard kick from below, a slap in the face of the complacent mind; the mild spongy consistent quivering, causing alarm only at the extended duration; the meandering rattling equivalent to several large trucks on a narrow bridge, and the hefty back and forth jerking of all surface structures that turns refrigerators into projectiles.

Quietly we absorb the night waiting for the color of dawn, as if everything is more harmless in the light of day. Or maybe to put some distance between the scare and us.

Many brick walls in Santa Monica succumbed to the quaking. My work place resembles the inside of a trashcan, a total chaos of files, brochures, computers and broken pictures. No car ventures into the streets. Deep cracks gape like entrances to the underworld, yawning black in the tar. The freeway is empty and quiet, eerily reminiscent of the aftermath in an end-of-the-world movie.

My heart rejoices in the unusual opportunity to bicycle on the deserted highway. One part of me welcomes the sudden suspension of all normal activities and even admires the power of nature. It is not evil; it only is, just like death. In the valley, in the center of the quake, under collapsed houses people lie dead.

In crisis situations I react collected, instinctively sober, logical and goal oriented. The everyday life between the adrenaline driven emergencies wears me out. The curlicues of the quiet life tear me apart. In dangerous situations I am fully alive and awake. The shaking has rattled my obstinate pride long enough like the metal shavings on a magnetized surface to call Kylie. Without circumventing I ask to be taken back into the group.

To my own surprise, my begging is successful.

Eyes wide-open and breathless, on the crested awareness of finitude, I ride back into the class of the magical movements. The journey into the unknown has not come to an end! His secrets lie waiting to be plumbed.

The decision for my reacceptance surely was Carlos'. My humiliation must have appealed to him. Greg has not been invited back. Only one of us is allowed. In consolation, I promise Greg to show him all of the magical movements, even though it is forbidden.

They must have made the connection between us. As sorcerer's apprentices we are advised to avoid sexual relations in order to save energy, collecting it instead to use for dreaming. Taisha was told sex leaves webs of wormlike energy strings attached to the body of the woman through which the man can supplement his own energy needs. The woman stays chained in this symbiotic trap unless she becomes abstinent for more then seven years.

I suspend my rational mind on selected occasions, but this seems slightly fantastical even for my tolerant ears. Having grown up in the carefree sixties, the act of love was not a means of control for the man but rather a commonly accepted process of getting to know each other. The agreement was given by free will. Except the first time. He tore the zipper of my pants and threatened to beat me. His small penis did not accomplish much and I hissed at him not to get me pregnant. Inhale, exhale from left to right. Ahh! Cut the connection, retrieve the energy, and sever the strings. As usual I only take what I can use?

Still in the same studio I take my old spot between the other chosen ones. They move aside only reluctantly, as if they have a greater right to the patch of wooden floor than me. In class Carlos picks on me repeatedly, rubbing in how offended I was over my previous expulsion. My timid objection that it was not the exclusion, but the lies that hurt me, remain unnoticed. He uses me as a lecture example. I am embarrassed over the unwanted attention. Kylie, on the other hand, receives a public commendation for her unscrupulousness, which she obviously had to practice first. His sarcastic goading is not aimed at hurting. He wants to reduce me, squash my pride like cockroaches. Kylie says they spit on the ego. My ego resists like a squirming snake.

But I'm not the only one he criticizes. Reni, who screams in her bathroom incessantly "intent, intent, intent" with the neighbors on the verge of calling the police, is teased for her catholic zeal.

I regard his vitriolic derision as an act of kindness, like the smell of over-ripe pears in the summer on the street to Weiboldshausen, smashed on the gravel road, sweet and putrefied, covered in wasps. The pear tree is no more. And the village as it was exists only in my memory: hacked, robbed, destroyed, tortured in the middle ages, re-settled by Hutterers with centuries old dung heaps, stone age oxen, heavy horses, blacksmith caves, flocks of sheep, geese shepherds, gnarled linden trees, an onion church tower with unblinking eyes and a village forest where you chopped your own Christmas tree.

Once again I have the opportunity to chase the unknown. But I am not received with open arms. I have to earn my place. Keenly aware of his scything intolerance I monitor my gestures and body language. During his lecturing, the minutes of physical inactivity, I copy Kylie's postures, arms hanging straight down on the sides of the body, or loosely hooked behind the back, weight resting on both legs. I don't want to appear arrogant or bored with cross-armed foot tapping impatience.

The cold stares of the others in the group don't bother be. They are huddling with their backs turned to me like a herd of musk oxen praising the energetic advantage of short hair. Am I a leper, the only longhaired left in the group?

Do they know more then I do? That this is only my probation?

I am used to being an outsider, a gypsy in the village of incestuously agglutinated houses that differentiated themselves from the next hamlet a couple of miles away through a variance in pronunciation and animosities. Newcomers were observed with suspicion and every limping chicken was our fault. Not completely unwarranted, what with our parents arrogance and my fathers sojourns in prison.

They are awaiting the Electric Warrior, the sparking energetic fighter, as prophesized by don Juan, who would fulfill their goal by giving the group a final push. Without training, this promised bundle of power, the last link in the circle, will be fully equipped to give them the definitive lift to leave this world in full awareness and travel like astronauts into infinity.

Maybe the long-legged model next to me is the long awaited savior that he fawns over. It can't be me that I'm sure of. He would have recognized the potential in me from the start, I would think. It may be my own resistance, his obvious disbelief in me and my energy, or a combination of both, that prevents me from expecting to join his group in their transformation into pure energy. I have to escape on my own, salvaging bits and pieces leading to my own rescue. I don't know why he took me back, but I will make the most of it.

With innocent curiosity I explore the colors and shapes of this new world like floating on a piece of drift ice in the ocean swaying in uncertainty. They shimmer in constant change and fade into the far nothing. From my modest position in the third row, close to the door, a safe distance from the brunt of his caustic love, I am afforded a perspective with a partial overview to observe his actions and appearance.

He creates an engulfing atmosphere of anticipation, rallying our wishes and hopes for something great, the arrival, birth, and the culmination of something extraordinary, destiny changing. A prowling tiger, his resilient ropy ball of energy plays like a conductor with the strings of our universe.

In his presence I leave the stable ground and its habitual buoys behind, or did I ever really know them at all? You don't get seasick if you keep looking at the horizon. I am listening to the hum, to the meaning between the sounds, to the real voice, like the gurgle of the brook. Be it hunger, humiliation, praise, fear, approval, exclusion and denial, it all runs off my left side like water from oilcloth. I am a survivor. My inner drive is unstoppable. Holding on to the table rim in a tight grip I pick up the breadcrumbs that fall from the master's plate. Through him I am facing the infinite that pulls me irresistibly closer. There is only now.

Jim is half-naked, painted red, yellow and blue. He wears a black wig in the traditional style over his short hair, chest-long with square bangs over his eyebrows, crowned with downy eagle feathers. Over his massive chest drapes a diagonal red sash, around his hips wraps a short skirt from natural cotton with woven black and red scenes. The ends of a white belt dangle around his calves that are ringed with little bells. For two days, without food and sleep in the kiva, he prepared for the dance. I traveled all through the night to the mesas that loom above me in the softly lit morning sky.

Up there in the old town the audience gathers on the rectangular mud square surrounded by ocher stone houses. Young people sit in droves on the flat roofs. Each house is cooking buckets of hominy stew with meat outside on open fires on the edge of the cliffs next to the ancient outhouses where the updraft dumps dust from hundreds of miles away.

Weeks of preparations making the parchment thin piki bread from blue corn or spiced with red chili on hot stones have gone into this day. The clouds drift by in the clear blue of the desert, closer then usual.

And then they dance, men and women in pairs forming a giant colorful snake that stomps, twists and turns, swells, rattles and chants. Between all the short black-haired people I hardly draw any attention. Jim invited me to this butterfly dance, because my friendship helped him to stay sober. In general, the Hopi don't like tourists to watch their ceremonies anymore.

Even though the dance spectacle is repeated four or five times into the smallest detail during the day, the audience assembles every time and watches in total rapture. The memory of a millennia old tradition stands between untouched houses and dusty alleys, forgotten in the 11th century: A tradition of self-sufficiency in barren surroundings, forced into tight social and religious survival patterns, overwhelming in their exuberant intensity, variety and blooming color palette, in stark contrast to the harsh life in the desert.

Jim has little influence in the hierarchy of his village. Most of his adult life he spent seeped in alcohol. His ninety-year-old mother, a leather-skinned skeleton who lives in Polacca, in whose house we women cooked and gossiped the whole night, speaks only Hopi. As much as they try, their way of life seems like a dead butterfly, whose iridescent pigments all but adhere to the skin of the hand of progress, irrevocably lost.

We are meeting now three times a week for the magical movements, which takes a lot of time away from my commitments at home, especially from my daughter. Even though the two-hour classes are not strenuous physically, the undivided attention he demands from us students tears at my reserves. He expects total presence. The slightest umbrage of a wavering attention could result in termination.

He promises to show us the photograph of a flyer. The head of the Tibet house in Mexico City unintentionally photographed the figure of a voladore, a shadow leaping from one hill to the next during a visit of the Dalai Lama.

We are listening with astonishment to the incredulous description of parasitic beings that attach themselves to us in order to lick the sheen of our awareness. One can see them only from the corner of the eyes. They creep across the ground flat like shadows. They control our brain in a back and forth motion.

The sorcerers hesitated to talk about these creatures for many years to avoid drawing their attention unnecessarily. Only discipline can make us unpalatable to them. Only iron discipline keeps them at bay. They are unable to land in trees. That's why sorcerers might spend long periods in trees during their training.

Half of my childhood I lived in trees: oaks, horse chestnuts, pines, beeches, cherry trees, apple trees, willows and linden trees. Maybe this is why I feel so poorly rooted in society.

In the emerald shade of the linden tree my legs dangled over the village road, unnoticed by the busy rattling of tractors below, hidden deep in the world of shaking leaves, gnarled crusty skin and friendly insects. I sat with the boys in the outstretched arms of the linden tree on the Village Square, like oversized plums.

Until the moment when they began to whistle after girls, there was no difference between Winnetou, the noble savage hero of Karl May's American Indian stories, and me. Overnight an abyss opened. Suddenly I belonged to one sex, whereas until then I was none, could do and be what my strength and desire permitted me to.

On the open north side of the village, between meadows and fields, stood a lonely linden tree with wide-stretching branches in all directions. Gamekeepers had built a hunting and observation platform reaching from the bottom into the top nestles of leaves. On the longest day of the year I jumped out of the bedroom window and ran through the lifeless village in the first light of dawn to the linden tree with the stand.

And then I saw her. Blood-red, she rose from the ground, a whirling disk as big as a barn that danced and flickered as if she wanted to hold on to the forest. Slowly like the bubbles in a lava lamp she finally let go, changing to bright gold on her journey towards the zenith. Like pearls on a string these undivided pictures are imprinted forever on my inner eye.

He says that sorcerers collect a treasure chest of memorable events that are retrievable at will. As an example he gives the story of his visit to a hooker that posed naked in front of her mirror like a music box ballerina. This moment touched him in a melancholic way. Sorcerers collect moments like these into an album.

I don't quite understand the peculiarity of his story. But many of my engraved moments, the ones I would rather forget and throw into the black hole of oblivion, don't fit into this personal album of indelible pages. The long, flat days of immeasurable stagnation, the guilt over the death of my brother, the self-imposed punishment of hateful relationships, the robberies of empty consumption, the humiliation of a mother driven by lower instincts, the silencing strangle-hold of crazy misunderstandings, the worthlessness of a nonexistent father, the unbridgeable abyss between adults and myself, the poison-berry hedge with the scary man, the deserted village, the meager feelings of superficial people.

"We are secrets forever looking for resolve," said Oswald Spengler.

Such moments I don't mind giving to the eagle that is waiting, hunched on its talons to tear them into tiny shreds and devour them into nothingness. The picture of the lonely shepherd wanderer in the summer dry hills of Spain is close to me. I preferred the wordless pathless conifer forest to the narrow, steeply gabled cobblestone alleys of the worm-eaten, satiated cities.

My suppressed coughing draws his attention and when I answer "Yes, I do have a cold," in a barely detectable voice, he dismisses me in the middle of the class with a "Come back when you are better". The breaths and evading looks behind my back suggesting no pity carry me out the door. The group of sorcerers must be extremely vulnerable to infections, minimizing their exposure in the secluded environment I imagine they live in.

Spring arrives in Topanga as soon as the rain gushes through the ravines and over the smooth rock faces in white-veined waterfalls, and veils of mist steam from the leafy canopy of the soaked landscape. It peaks out from under the blanket of Ceonopsis that covers the January hills under a full moon like powdered sugar, followed by the cloak of wild lilac blossoms wafting sweetly in the February air.

Its viridious soul jumps from the crevices of the canyon belly and sprays green tones in every conceivable nuance like a painter intoxicated by green ecstasy across his canvas. Thousands of frog voices echo in the wet gullies in a grand rock concert. With every exhale the spring gusts blow, swaying down of grass over the skeletons of winter, then dress the hills in mustard yellow bleeding into a cobalt sky. The blue-green ridges swell with deep breaths, humming in the sound of colors.

He tantalizes us with the promise of an invitation from the witches to a sorcery theater. Something we have never seen before, that will blow us away. In my imagination, I see a party with magic in half dark rooms, laughter, clinking and clatter and unexplainable secrets. Are the unattainable promises even more attractive?

Brown-skinned, sparsely dressed women from the hula class next door hush through our room to the back exit. There is the gleam of a lecherous old man in his eyes. He licks his lips and grins. A cynical mocking of our sex-crazed societal behavior?

Or is there a glimpse of his grandfather lurking in his face? The Brazilian grandfather whose only legacy was his obsession with women. He took lovers into his ripe old age without committing himself to anyone of them, courting, seducing, showering them with gifts, all the while considering them inferior.

With his leering glances at the young hula dancers, Carlos surely appears to be like the grandfather of his stories. The women in our class dress modestly in oversized tee shirts, sweatpants and tennis shoes, asexual, unadorned, shorthaired and without makeup. In their eyes I'm reading admiration, devotion and even something like love.

In the very corner in the back stands a gray-streaked delicate being that oftentimes comes in late, but is never reprimanded by Carlos. This is his "daughter", the Blue Scout, who originates from a place far away, so far from the human circle of imagination, that her ways are completely foreign to us.

She does not like to be the center of attention, nor does she acknowledge her assigned position. She was rescued as a blue energy from the world of the inorganic beings and took the form of a young and boyish woman. Obviously she can't be Carlos' and Carol's physical daughter. These stories I regard as a sweeping symbolic gesture reaching into mythological dimensions. But still it conceals the miraculous, the strange. Sometimes I slink close to her, but she does not like me. She ignores me.

He promises us class participants a special lecture, no magical movements, but eagerly anticipated theoretical teachings, the college course of sorcery. New perceptions, realizations? The fleshing out of the knowledge described in his books? Or maybe a journey into the other reality, the left magical side, and the unveiling of unspeakable secrets?

Kylie and I search for an appropriate place, a studio large enough without mirrors and windows. None of our suggestions appeal to Carlos. Finally he settles on the Dance Home studio despite its view obstructing columns. It seems incredible, how handicapped they appear when making decisions that are contingent on invisible nebulous circumstances and omens.

He uses a small loudspeaker. About a hundred people sit in front of him on mats and pillows as he starts again from the beginning. The explanation of the human energy cocoon, the manipulated apparatus of perception, the world view of the sorcerers.

He points to the "nagual woman", who has a book full of energy tales to tell as soon as she starts piecing together the memory of her ten-year absence from our everyday world.

In one recessed corner of my mind map I have to admit to myself that I am slightly disappointed. No continuing teachings, steps and new realizations that build on the previous ones. Didn't he intend to give us special instructions just for the participants of his private movement classes? Are we too unripe to understand the next level? Is there a plan at all? Repetition does not harm, I presume. Sometimes I block things out too easily, like the recapitulation. Only recently I have begun compiling my list of names.

The round-faced nagual woman, sea-gray eyes, with speckles of silver in her short brown hair, has suddenly become attractive again. During the Rim Institute seminar men glommed to her like moths to light, after she admitted publicly to use her equipment in contrast to the other two witches that proclaimed sexual abstinence.

So far, she has not written anything. Where was she during her 10 years of absence, when she disappeared with don Juan into infinity to act as a bridge for the next group of sorcerers? What was her experience? With unbridled curiosity I ask to be invited to her promised talk about her incredible journey. She smiles painfully and turns away from me even before she finishes her politely evasive reply.

In the class, the exercises seem to be growing more complex, not only loose fragments and simple poses anymore. They remind me somewhat of Asian martial arts practices. Otherwise, the format stays the same, some movements, and then he tells his ironic stories about crazy lackadaisical people.

Silently, I agree with him. We people are dumb, shortsighted, like small unruly children without discipline. Even his sometime obscene choice of words bothers me little. Where he comes from death, sex, injustice and tragedy are the openly shared normality. The bland and prudish Americans have to be shaken from their barricades.

The master moves effortlessly, with smooth suppleness and the flexibility of a panther, a precise machine of powerful knowledge stored in his limbs. Despite his age he surpasses most of us. Only Kylie, the chacmool guardian, embodies the magical movements with focused perfection. Carlos' hand is flat, stretched out, straight as a ruler but still relaxed. My hand has to strain to stretch the fingers, to angle the thumb on the side of the hand.

The sorcerer presents a flat hand, no beggar's cup.

The sorcerer asks, demands, he claims his birth right to freedom.

My tendons burn. Some stretch their fingers so far they bend backwards. I admire Carlos' ease and agility. Gracefully he sweeps his arm through the air. He says, once we begin to bend our elbows on the side of the body in the shower, it is all over, and resignation sets in. His angled arms creep up slowly along his body, then he slaps his hands down drowning in the laughter of the attending group. Down boy!

With the help of the chacmools, he adapts the individual magical movements, taught to him and the witches by don Juan, making them usable for general consumption.

These movements prepare the body for the point from which the sorcerers perceive their world. Their intended effect has been established thousands of years ago and does not need our assurance. Only practice, only the doing, can convince us.

He encourages us, if just for a moment, to forget about our engrained ordinary world. I have not seen the witches behind me teach any of the movements; they seem curiously unfamiliar with many of the passes.

Carlos' energy carries us like a cloud on which we float over the everyday world. He creates a bridge, a net that catches us if we fall. He takes responsibility for us. We can tell him our physical ailments and he will address our problems. In response to the small note about my migraine attacks he answers as quick as a bullet, "Sugar, it comes from sugar". That answer could have come from the health column of a magazine, or the monthly newsletter of your health insurance. Sure, sugar is the convenient culprit for any illness. I hoped for a shamanic explanation and a permanent resolve for my reoccurring headaches.

He says that we should take responsibility for our death and not live in the belief of our immortality. We should look death and infinity into the eye at night in the mirror when we are alone.

No need to tell me about death. Death has been my constant companion. Only centimeters away he stared out of my eyes. That's why I did not hold him back but admired the suicide attempts of my brother, wrapping himself airtight in sheets to suffocate after he painted his body with gold bronze. In a dream I saw him in a mental institution. Alarmed I called, "Brother, what are you doing here? I know why I am here, but you? I love you so much". One day he succeeded. They found him frozen in the German forest. He had been lying there for too long to determine the real cause of his death.

On a pale dreary winter day when we were children, my twin brother and I found two coal black ravens in the crusty-white powder snow near the river behind the village. They laid there, stretched out, just brushed by death, immaculate in their winged perfection as if they had bedded themselves next to each other to die. Two twin ravens in the snow resting metallic black on blue-white as if they were dreaming of flying over red speckled summer roofs in the fenceless expanse of a stark blue sky in the whirlwind aerial dance of white doves.

Our eyes followed their dreams. In tandem they flew over the roofs, orchards, fields, hills and forests, higher to the place where the ocean blue joins the turquoise sky, still higher until the midnight space swallowed us all.

My brother picked them up, the ones that only the wind had touched until then. And with the thought of a raven beak necklace we carried them secretly like thieves into the village just as the approaching evening shadows crawled from the forest wrinkles.

Behind the old pigsty, hidden from the disapproving eyes of our mother, who regularly raided our treasure chest shoeboxes full of snake skins, elderberry cigarettes, hazelnuts and rodent skulls, we used a dull knife to saw off first the raven heads, and then removed their surprisingly soft beaks. Shreds of meat, sinews and tiny hairy feathers stuck to them, a sad sight.

Our follow-up attempt to burn away the gunk in the stove did not help either, but instead turned the once proud beaks, that had seen the world from high above, into an unsightly mess of stinking shriveled prunes. The twin ravens would not continue their flight on our chests.

I wish my brother had waited. He was the only one close to me, as close as my belly.

43

In the course of his training the sorcerer arrives at a point, where he meets the 'mold of man', the blueprint. Men experience this as a male presence; to women it appears as the quintessence of femaleness.

Years ago in a lucid dream I encountered in searing clarity a shining female figure that radiated an overwhelming generosity that brought me to my knees to pledge with sobbing admiration my lasting loyalty. Wondering who she was, what her name was, she raised me from my knees and with exuding kindness told me: Your name is Deirdre. For many years I searched in vain for the meaning of this dream image.

Carlos' account of meeting his own 'mold' is so eerily close to my dream experience, it is as if he had witnessed it or read my thoughts. He laughs about his experience in which he believed to see God and reacted just as emotionally as I did.

On the evening of a summery April day, when the turquoise sky falls all the way into the cracks of the clapboard houses, and the ocean glitters with cobalt-jade reflections in the sand crystals, on this Wednesday evening, standing in the milky yellow light of the dance studio, at my usual spot, next to the fashion model and the artist behind me who drives a Jaguar, wrapped in a quiet agreement and the rare absence of my self-chastising chatter, my right eye catches something strange behind his left shoulder, next to his ear: an elliptical rotating vortex, a vibrating change of air texture.

Amazed, my eyes blink, and immediately it disappears. A phantom? For one moment I freeze. My sarcastic cynicism does not tend to hallucinations; I never touched drugs, not even in the licentious sixties. Am I losing what is left of my objectivity?

What is real? The shimmering spider-web reflections of the ocean kaleidoscope or the labyrinth of my world of thoughts in which I wander alone like a lost slipper? My gullible naiveté desires for the reality of concrete proof in order to believe without a doubt. It wants sobriety fearing that there really is no real reality.

Have I overexerted myself in the last months? Or did the everyday filter of perception stop for one moment and let the other side creep in? She dances in the universe of possibilities.

It is over. He does not tolerate other gods. Although I suspected that my weeklong vacation would mean the end of my participation in the private classes, I could not bring myself to lie and fake an illness as excuse for my absence.

Chaos reigns on the wooden bridge in the fern gully. It seemed only yesterday that time stood still, lost in the imperceptible cycle of erosion and rebirth. Over night, unobserved or sometime outside of my human time frame, a giant oak on the steep hill side broke in half, beheaded a Sycamore on its way down, plunging across the bridge and tearing the railing with it in its violent crash into the brook.

Twisted prickly boughs and heavy branches arrested in torpid death struggle block the path. Massive tree limbs are scattered like matchwood in the streamlet. A hole gapes in the roof of the canopy.

The silence that hung in the world of ferns broke silently without being noticed. The slow infinite silence burst with a loud cacophony some time yesterday in the fraction of a moment too small to be heard. How else could I have missed the earthmoving equipment destruction only a few hundred yards away?

Chapter Four

The Puzzle of Reason

My mind is aglow with whirling transient nodes of thought careening through a cosmic vapor of invention.
-Hedley Lamarr in *Blazing Saddles,* 1974

Once upon a time long ago in the future there was a princess that lived in a castle. Naturally, all princesses live in castles. She wanted to know what life is. She asked the birds touching the palace walls with their wings. She asked the ants busily crawling around her toes; she asked the clouds shifting form above. But nobody would answer her.

So she decided to leave her palace and wander into the wide world. She vowed not to eat or drink until she would find an answer.

For many days she walked, sleeping at night curled up like an animal. She became very thirsty. And when she came to a river she said, "Oh River, I am so thirsty, may I have some of your water"?

The river murmured, "I am the beginning and the end. I am the water of life and the water of death." When the princess heard this she jumped up and ran away as fast as she could.

47

GABY GEUTER

Like the princess in my story I am looking for the meaning, the basic truth of life. This need for answers drives me incessantly forward. It lures me into the hidden corners, beckons me beyond the horizons, plunges me into the depths.

The witches say that as a sorcerer you sit in the front of the train and you see the world as it approaches you. It does not rush past you while you chase after it.

On the photograph of the three-year-old dressed in a shiny crimson smock with black bows and heart-shaped tassels, you can see in her dark eyes the confusion over the sight of a topsy-turvy world. In the right world the father stays home and takes care of the family, the mother loves him and enjoys being with her kids, the grandmother is a strong wise woman with unconditional love for her grandchildren and not afraid to give answers, the grandfather a trustworthy rock to lean on, the village a community of helpful relatives, the country a covenant of upright, generous and humble people with clear open eyes, the earth a league of nations with friendly exchanges and respectful connections to all life forms, the universe a conscious being. And all would be aware of each other and of themselves.

But it was wrong. It was a mixed-up, distorted world I could not comprehend. I faintly remembered the place I came from. In the cradle of my being we were one, with eyes big as sparkling lakes on which you could sail into other universes. Together we danced, up and down connected with strong lines, slow and quick, like water in the river, like wind in the trees, like clouds in the sky. Joy rippled through our limbs and gigantic exultations rose in comets to the zenith and we all laughed holding each other by the hands of our heart fibers.

Only an aftertaste, a murmur of this dream lingers in my womb. My childhood nightmares were the dreams of an alien stranded in a strange world, confused and sad, waiting for a ship home. Sometimes I came to a place I thought I recognized and hope would surge inside of me that around the next corner, behind the next house, would be my home or at least the farmhouse and my bed. But when I turned the corner in a state of heightened anticipation, I was facing again a senseless and unfamiliar place.

48

In the alien landscape around me I could not find home, only the ignorance of complexity multiplying itself in endless repetition. The search for the true, the root, the original reality, the single beginning, one not satisfied with superficiality, but looking behind the veneer, this enduring search did not let me get caught anywhere.

Like a leaf flowing without resistance down the river, my soul blew me to Los Angeles to sort for years on end through the dull smog, chasing crack addicts from my door steps, pouring out in colorful paintings, dancing its song in ritual performance art until the unexpected meeting with Carlos, the sorcerer, the master of other realities.

He whispers in my mind, "See the open road, the wide endless spaces. There is more out there then what we allow ourselves to see". His answers catapult me to the fringes of the universe, creating space and playroom far away from the mute hamlet where the cows were more eloquent than their milkers, away from the cataleptic, steep-gabled cobblestone rigidity of the Franconian Middle Ages.

At the moment, the latest exclusion from his private classes troubles me little. I'm filled to the brim with undigested thoughts and pictures, breathless with a pounding heartbeat. The experiences of the recent months continue to spool past me like a foreign movie without subtitles. The plot, the actors, the script, are a puzzle of beautiful pictures blooming in the garden of my imagination.

Maybe it is better to assimilate, to integrate the shift slowly, so I don't end up half-crazy in the trees like Taisha. This does not necessarily mean that my association with his teachings is over. He took me back once already without clear reason, didn't he?

Acknowledging my ever-present doubts, I succumb to the influence of habitual sobering deconstruction under which I ask myself if I would have really made the jump. If he had invited me to join his inner circle that is guarded by the witches on constant lookout for the energetic powerhouse, wouldn't I have hesitated?

Something does not feel right. There are too many strange pieces in this puzzle. Even though Carlos' written words accompanied me for decades, and inspired the opening of inner doors that pointed me in new directions, I never dared myself lucky enough to meet

49

someone like don Juan. It seems ironic that after stumbling onto his successor, I'm not sure if I could truly follow him. Did he sense my diffidence? Maybe he knows. In some respect I'm glad it did not come to this point in the crossroads.

But why did I meet him then, what purpose did it serve? A sign. If nothing grows from it, what meaning did our interaction have? Was it not an encounter too fleeting to justify all the decades of preparation for it?

No, the adventure can't be over yet. The door is not shut completely, even if I can't see the crack at the moment.

The crack is opening again. I'm still in the loop. I find out that Carlos is giving a public lecture series at the Phoenix bookstore. It's his way of paying a sorcerer's debt to the magical place that spit the nagual woman back into his reality. A sorcerer leaves no debt unpaid. Otherwise it would tie him down and hamper his exit.

Dodging the heads of the crowd, I spy his peculiar small frame, topped by his silver mop that glows like a metaphor, a symbol of freedom. It all makes sense. I run along his undulating words as if on a sparkling green meadow under a crisp sky with fluffy white clouds.

Deep down inside we face life and death alone. The mysterious attraction is still there, an underlying agreement, the connecting design between all of the pieces of the puzzle.

He is not the sorcerer of spells and voodoo; he's not channeling ghostly voices, or talking to the deceased. His system appears to me as an abstract, almost rational, clean discipline of evolving awareness, conveying thought patterns of austere purity. He shreds the "feel-good-love-everybody" new age philosophy to pieces. His world is somber, a sobering reality of dangers and stark beauty. His is the sorcery of seeing behind the curtain, of seeing the matrix and transcending death.

As always, I listen between the sounds. Sorcerer, shaman, magician, medicine man are all inadequate terms to describe and contain the purpose of his destiny, don Juan had told him. He is to use the expression sorcerer only due to a lack for a better word. How about sortilege? Sorting, divining? Nowadays he would rather call himself a sourcerer, someone involved with the source, the beginning, if this word would exist in English.

Amalia and Humberto sit in the front rows with the members of his inner group. That must mean they still belong to his circle. I know them from the Rim Institute seminar in Arizona in '93 and we had kept in friendly contact.

One time we sat together in the big oak tree growing in the middle of the Indian gravesite. We crawled up the thick elephantine limbs that hung down to the horehound covered ground creating a shady dome occupied by packrats, alligator lizards, blue jays and the occasional perching Red-tailed Hawk. In the cool net of the branches they complained about the ant roads interfering with their enjoyment. They wished for an ant-less tree to practice the detachment from the social order.

Taisha's tree story is curiously devoid of insects as well. This slightly odd piece of urban backyard sorcerers makes me wonder where their universe might be.

Amalia confesses to me during a break that she stopped having sexual relations with her partner Humberto as the path of the sorcerer demands. She takes it very seriously. "She belongs to the Nagual now." Humberto says with tears in his eyes.

The manicured villas with ocean view and the access-denying beach houses fall behind on the way north along the coast. Raw cliffs squeeze the two-lane asphalt snake hard against the foaming blue-green ocean that licks with hungry tongues at the shore. Jagged turns cut off any view to the populated south beaches, reducing the influence of the city to dots on the horizon.

Deer creek, Sycamore Canyon and Point Mugu have remained wild, refusing to be tamed. Behind the harsh naked windy façade, prompting the passerby to drive a scant bit faster, hides the wild. This is where life begins. Here I breathe deeply.

Greg is climbing with me to the top of Mugu, the round hump that juts like the back of a giant turtle into the ocean, to see the Chumash sunset. A wall of fog crawls from the water. This oversized monster spurs us to speed, racing up on the steep well-armed path between the sharp lances of the agaves and the needles of the prickly pear cactus protecting wine-red fruits that stain fingers and mouth blue-red. As the moist fog fingers creep closer, we course faster. It's a contest for the sunset.

The path is a narrow animal trail, barely discernable, but I know it well. The fog follows in our tracks as we hasten to keep abreast. Just before the sun plunges into the ocean we reach the top of the mountain, a collection of rusty baked rocks and wretched looking sumac bushes fleeing from the wind.

Greg heard the news somewhere, and it seems to me unbelievable gossip. Carlos, the recluse, who preferred to pull the strings from the background like the wizard of Oz, who never participated in any of the seminars in the past couple of years, and taught no more than his by invitation-only classes, all of a sudden wants to lead a three-week seminar of magical movements!

"Strange, it does not sound like Carlos at all, advertising and charging money!" I wonder what happened.

Below us the fog pushes against the rough stubble of the mountain. Behind us tower the forbidden looking Bony Mountains with a valley of rolling native grass meadows, coastal brush and crevices lined with oak stretching to the cliffs. The ocean of fog has swallowed the Anacapa Islands.

We tackle the question in our usual ping-pong, yin-yang interaction. "Finally Carlos is getting smart; all other masters are not afraid to charge money for their wisdom".

"But why a thousand dollars?" my social conscience nags. "I can still hear Carlos' mantra in my ears. Don Juan gave it to him for free, and so does he". Carlos did not speak with envy but with dripping disdain about gurus that kept a lavish lifestyle and displayed themselves publicly.

"Don't you remember how condescendingly Carlos railed in the private classes about seminar consumers who only display a leisure time interest in the mysterious?" Mockingly, he hopped around in the typical white man's version of an Indian battle dance. He hammered at us not to become weekend sorcerers.

The fog does not reach us, affording a spectacular view of the setting sun. In my mind, I see the Chumash dancing and singing on this windy outcrop to send the spirits of their deceased on the journey west across the big ocean of time. I throw my shortcomings into their ethereal boats.

The sun, wrapped in a neon pink shawl sinking from the azure yellow sky, - the artist in me keeps wondering how it manages the transition from gas-flame blue to lemon yellow -, dusts the quilted fog with a touch of pink sugar. Then for a short moment she bathes in the pink blanket and hesitatingly glides in.

The remaining half disc gives birth to an otherworldly, phantasmal twin mirroring in the fog in front of her. The sight of the sinking sun emits something indescribably nurturing. Doesn't the glowing disc, hidden in the gauzy fog carry a small hologram of the mystery of life?

"Sure Carlos is worth a thousand dollars, his magnetic humor, his poignant wisdom and the mysterious access to an unimaginable world. But I thought they live by other rules and principles, that the sorcerers are guided by different intentions then money, power and fame. And what happened to the sorcerers' number one rule: Sorcerers are selected by spirit, they don't want any volunteers?"

"You think too much," is considered my downfall.

"I wonder what has changed in Carlos' thinking since the time we were in his private classes! Maybe he moves, like he said, in a flow of energy. And we don't understand the changes from one day to the next. It does not have to constitute an ideological conflict".

A categorical, "Women are forgivers" follows my hypothetical explanations.

I ignore the stab and continue to muse.

"Only if something becomes a business venture it finds acceptance in America. As soon as it makes money it acquires the veneer of legitimacy", adds my sarcasm to the jab. I examine this new misshapen piece of sorceric enterprise with suspicion.

"Maybe the women are getting too expensive", counters Greg with logical Ocham's razor male reasoning.

"I would think he gets enough royalties from his ever popular books. Perhaps he is looking for public recognition. To teach openly in big halls, not like he has been, secretly in the underground."

"Still, it seems absurd to pay money for something that not too long ago we received for free. Doesn't it degrade his precious gift to a plain commodity purchasable by the affluent! Where is the spirit in that?"

I almost liked him better yesterday, when he did not know what was next, how things would continue. When he was standing in front of the wall asking questions, saying there is no plan.

The first stars blink on like diamonds on a blue velvet cushion and we begin the long hike back to the car, avoiding the steep needle-infested trail we took earlier. Night approaches like a thief. Between the reeds, on a dark slope, suddenly something moves. I scent it, an invisible flutter and then a spark. "Where?" "Over there." "Must have been a bird." "A bird cannot create a spark." It was not my eyes that saw in the grainy dusk but a different sense of perception.

For the next two hours we creep forward in the textured darkness. One develops an affinity for sensing with the whole body when robbed of the sense of sight. My feet are familiar with the sandy patches in the path. I orient myself on the smell of purple sage, the pungent sumac, the mugwort and spicy watercress in the cool air near the brook. It helps that I have hiked this path many times before. The kinetic memory that Carlos tries to instill in us during his movement lessons allows us to feel our way along the black shape of the cliffs in the moonless night. Sometimes I think I might expect too much from Greg.

Behind the large barn door entrance of the art studio in Venice I am searching for acquaintances from the introduction evenings of magical movements that the chacmools have given within the past year. The cost for these public sorcery movement classes was minimal, probably just covering the rent of the studio.

On one of those evenings that I attended, Kylie mentioned for the first time a personal pretersensual experience in which the chacmools ran unexpectedly into the nagual woman at Carlos' house. Afterwards they felt very strange, because there was a time slippage and it could not have been the real Carol. That is the only hint other members of the group have given so far about their own sorceric development.

Upon seeing me, Kylie's face softened to a weak polite smile. She must have been relieved that I don't bear grudges. I wondered if they were still looking for the promised electric warrior. I sure wish them luck. Especially Kylie, whose sincerity and conviction I admire.

I expected to run into John at the meeting. After all, he gave me the tip about this group of people practicing the movements that they have learned in the three-week seminar.

Greg and I slip rather shyly into the circle of strangers forming between wooden artifacts and erotic drawings. We seem to be the only outsiders. They stare at us with silent apprehension. Nobody dares to throw us out. Our appearance must have taken them by surprise.

With my previous experiences I don't find it difficult to follow the new movements that are longer and more detailed then the earlier ones, as they are still based on the same principal horse-stance and flat-hand body postures. The system has grown in size. Nobody talks during the pass. The leader position rotates.

Ignoring the wide variety of movement interpretations, I chose an athletic person as a model to copy from. Each student in the circle has his or her own remembered version and believes to have the right one. After the practicing heated discussions erupt about the correct execution.

There seems to be a sort of leader envy in the group, an aversion against "nagualitos", cutting anyone down who dares to rear their head. In the faces of the men and women in the circle I recognize my own enthusiasm, the call of the supernatural, and a certain ambivalence toward what is commonly accepted reality. With this I excuse their extreme zealousness.

At the end of the practice they grill us, wanting to know who we are and what gall we have to turn up uninvited. John's invitation does not impress them. Possibly they don't even know him. Do they feel special, because they paid a thousand dollars for the seminar? Then I would have more reason to be arrogant. Wasn't I chosen by him to be in his class for free without having to buy his attention!

O.J.Simpson is acquitted in his double murder trial. French troops prevent a putsch to overturn the government of Comoros. Where is Comoros?

No matter how large or complicated, in the assembling of a puzzle one starts with the border, the pieces identified by a strait edge. My border pieces of the world of the sorcerers deal with perception. Perception is the prison of the senses, according to Oswald Spengler.

Scientists confirm the existence of sound and light waves beyond our ordinary sensory capacity. The world around us is the product of our own selection. The rational mind can only acknowledge things that make sense. Gathered by the narrow range of our five senses we humans interpret – sort, associate, group - this information into categories of importance. Out of millions of data pieces we choose what we need to survive the situation at hand. Carlos is not the only one saying this.

Not life itself, but our experience of life, is a dream, a waking dream that forms the external reality.

What is really out there? Is everything around me my own creation, my own play? How can I know if someone else sees blue the way I do, sees the trees the same way? My interpretation is only unverifiable mine.

Maybe there is no one else? Ha.

Blind men describe the same elephant, as distinct animals perceived from different positions. What am I blind to?

It haunts me to develop the sense beyond the senses, to know what really is. The sorcerer's goal is to see energy as it flows in the universe.

The ocean reveals itself differently every day. A capricious diva, it laps lead-gray, slippery as bath water, flat with slow river veins, wrapped mysteriously in the silent white fog of nothing. Then it thunders in big foam flakes, spews breaths of rainbows, throwing itself jealously against the land devouring the yellow sand. Dolphins play in the breakers like silver surfers.

Sometimes the sea swells ice blue into the firmament. Or rolls bottle-green humps into white jumping crowns, chasing mermaids. It shivers in jade-green ripples, curls and wrinkles, furrows and tears against the wind.

It washes spilled gold in the evening that slowly expires like glowing steel. It licks the glacial rocks round in the purple evening light. It sees itself in the mirror of the brown pelican eyes that sail inches above the polished waves like glider planes in formation.

It shines pitch-black, sensed only through the absence of light patterns in the drone of the night like a hollow wall. It carries silver moon tears spread on a dark ruffled skirt. It stretches to the sharp rim of the horizon, glimmers with the skyline, kisses and combines in the blue. It towers free into the distance.

Greg makes fun of me, the lost pirate wearing an eye patch and carrying a parrot on the shoulder. Without the ocean on the way to town I could not bear her: Los Angeles, the city of the angels, or the place of many smoking fires, as it was called by earlier inhabitants, due to the fog cover that doesn't move in May and June, held in place by the mountain chain ringing around the basin.

In those days the area was still overgrown with wild rosebushes and a swampy river winding through that transformed the bay into a marsh-lake landscape. When progress came it pinched the river into a plastic choked concrete channel, tarred gray, smoggy billboard-disfigured arteries, drew with pen and square the American dream of the single family home with swimming pool, until it became a Strega mush endlessly spilling over its edges, a hydra without center cowering in the security of its size.

It does not matter where you enter the city; she sucks you up, envelops you, hacks you into little pieces, scatters you, and then forgets you, never to spit you out. Every day thousands get lost in her. You have to look past the grimy sidewalks, the hard-edged replacement buildings, the uncountable turnover of businesses and restaurants, the giant advertisements, the manicured lawns and silent houses, the asphalt and concrete.

Then you might discover the blue triangle of sky between the dark glass towers, and let the gleaming ocean space at the end of the street into the crack of your eyes to capture the smell of wilderness in the alleys behind the orderly single story houses, or a naked human glance between the hissing metal boxes on the gray tar, so you might remember who you are.

It's October, and Carlos announces another seminar, a weekend workshop, here in town. Even though it is cheaper, I still can't overcome the awkwardness of paying for the seminar. Nevertheless, I nurse a certain amount of curiosity and this undeniable secretive longing to be in his presence again, to feel the fresh breeze of the other world, to stand on the cliff of infinity. It is the lure of vacuous space that pulls me there. The lure to hopefully see the complete picture.

A sorcerer has to be patient, sweet, ruthless and cunning, I remember. So he will not mind if I am so cunning to creep into his seminar without paying.

The air in the Culver City high school gym crackles in anticipation. Hundreds of minds and bodies congregate in eager receptivity. Without chatter, they follow Kylie's instructions like well-behaved kindergartners.

She always looks as if she is about to put on a breastplate, grabbing a shield and sword, and go into battle. The precise execution of the movements makes her the superior teacher.

Aricele, the other chacmool from the private classes, does not seem to be with them anymore. So even a chosen one of higher rank can fall out of grace. Or maybe she ran away? The two "cousins", as he called them, have taken the chacmool place. In contrast to the exclusive teaching position in the private classes, here at the seminar, Carlos does not teach any movements at all.

Furtively, I glance around scanning for familiar faces, the ones I want to avoid for strategic reasons. After all, I am not really here.

There is a majority of white, middle-aged men, a few young people, and only a handful of African and Asian features that I can detect in the audience. The dominance of male attendees strikes me as strangely unrepresentative to the members of Carlos' inner group, which are primarily female. I'm accustomed to seeing a vast number of women at similar seminars of a shamanic, dream or Native American nature. According to Carlos' view, men are a novelty, a curlicue in the otherwise female universe. Curiously, Carlos' public teachings generally attract more men, whereas his inner group consists mostly of women.

The concentrated attention of the hungry participants gives the experience the luster of adventure. Or does it emanate from the sorcerers who talk with steeled conviction and irrevocable confidence about their inconceivable worlds? Everybody in the hall expects the extraordinary. Some see Silvio Manuel, a figure from Carlos' books, watching us through the window.

In the evening, the whole troupe appears for Carlos' lecture. Sitting in the front rows, dressed in fancy clothes, freshly coifed and showered, lounge his closest companions, the witches, chacmools and several other women that I remember from the private classes. We sit behind the noble beauties sweaty from the day in our flabby sweatpants like plebeians.

Carlos, the small compact skeleton in his fashionable Armani, with his wrinkled milk-coffee brown face, his grandiose gestures, his self-criticism and presumptuous arrogance conveying humility and insolence at the same time, is the quintessence of a moving contradiction. The energy builds, resembling an electro-magnetic field, as if his hand creates static tension in the air. The insiders call him reverentially "The Nagual", the door to the other world, to me he is still only Carlos in his accessibility and as expression of my affinity, never the distant Dr. Castaneda. The man on stage stirs expectant feelings inside of me that traverse my face like contrails in a virgin sky. No scar from the exclusion and imposed absence remains.

The current of his words carries me down the swifts like a roughly carved pine bark boat on the little river in our village that flowed so low in the summer that we could barely cool off our toes and upside down turned crowns. But sometimes flashfloods would storm from its headwaters stepping over the banks, filling the first stories of the farmhouses and stables and inundating for days our hut of sticks built on the Robinson Island.

The familiar jokes he tells, about the gurus, the moron child, and the poor baby on the cross, the witches must have heard a thousand times. They still laugh. I watch their serene faces from the side and wonder at the background of pervading magnetism that this small man with the South American accent he retained for thirty years exudes over these women.

Relaxed, with soft miens and full attention, clearly beyond polite duty, the women are like loyal wives completely on his side. No cynical down-turned mouth corners, no condescending eye rolling, no blank stares, no masks to detect in their expressions.

My sorcerer maneuver to make myself invisible seems to be working. Nobody pays attention to me. As a precaution I keep to myself. With the borrowed nametag I am a stranger, incognito.

Nobody asks the question why rather suddenly and late in his career he initiated a sorceric corporation that conducts high-priced seminars. I look for clues in Carlos' gestures and facial expression to the surprising change that occurred in his reasoning. Does he believe people will give more weight to his words if they have to pay for it? There is no doubt that he and his group of instructors is taking the presentation of his material more serious nowadays. The organization and execution of the magical movements, their own program has visibly improved now that they are charging money.

The question of general interest, why they decided to go public at this point after teaching for years in the underground, is answered with the story of the unexpected reappearance of the nagual woman.

Apparently, that changed everything. Carol Tiggs, who left with don Juan and was supposed to be waiting on the other side, suddenly surfaced after 10 years of absence. That threw the doors wide open and changed the rules.

Hasn't Carol been back for almost ten years? Are they noticing the open door just now?

The reasoning part of my skeptical mind remembers not too long ago Carlos laughing about the foolishness of the shamanic seminars and the typical participant. Until a year ago, he did not want to convert masses, sorcery is not for everyone, was his credo, he was only looking for the last missing link in his group, the electric warrior.

The new official face of the sorcerer is a toothless sanitized mask behind which he hides his true agenda. They can deceive the unsuspecting sheep, but not me.

The crumbs of his teachings thrown in front of the masses must be merely the tip of the iceberg. His veiled world is an impenetrable thicket whose meaning still slips through my fingers behind the fence of the sorcerer's garden. What is the secret he keeps, interlaced in the hue of saturated generosity that warms and intrigues me?

Greg condemns my sneaking into the seminar. It is only envy. I shirk my shoulders.

"Honesty is not in the vocabulary of the sorcerers. The concept of good and evil does not exist in that world. According to their own rules I did not deceive them, I was merely cunning. Ha! Besides, I did not hurt them."

"One has to have morals." Of which the meaning and origins of it get irretrievably lost in the straight jacket of repetition. "For the sorcerer there is only the female predatory universe and he is making damn sure he does not become prey himself. The sorcerer has no pity, no social responsibility, except the one imposed by spirit. The moral rules of society were established without our consent".

I know I'm strictly quoting the concepts of the sorcerers; these are their premises. I have not swallowed them as a whole, without reservations. On the same token I disavow the profit-driven principles of our larger society with similar apprehension. The world is not only black and white.

The number of people living in poverty in the United States, the richest country in the world, has fallen, according to the result of the last census.

I visit the practice group in the art-studio in Venice now every Thursday, Greg in tow. They have graciously accepted us. The group regulars, consisting of a white-haired businessman, pumped up from weightlifting, a middle-aged female physicist with sparse hair-growth, a ruddy freckled airport maintenance employee, the stylish Venus of Milo artist and studio owner, the flexible Tai Chi teacher with bushy eyebrows and scary twisting body movements, the two innocently shining student brothers from Canada, the three men from South America with broken English, a mathematician with full apostle beard, the tawny girl with big breasts from the Midwest and her hippie friend, the black-haired fast-food business woman, the plump lively geologist that hungers for her and the library clerk, thin as a rail with long braids, have not found a leader.

Maybe they've gained permission from Cleargreen, the company Carlos started for the purpose of organizing his seminars. Most likely they had to promise not to teach the movements. As long as we, intruders, only copy them they are not breaking the rules.

Since many of the movements are unnamed, our practice group attaches memory markers to them, associations with the seminars in which they were taught, or with obvious resemblance to animal behaviors. Handwritten lists begin to circulate.

Only the yelling for intent at the end of practice makes me cringe as it turns something utterly personal into a mechanical rosary bead attempt of group sorcery.

November. The first storms of the season pound the coastline conjuring memories of dreaded mudslides. The sea bellows, streaked with ochre runoff. Another weekend seminar at Culver City High.

Greg wants to participate as well. He might be seeing the glow still clinging to me from the weekend of fresh breezes, afraid to miss something, or to be left out.

This time I pay and register but under a false name. Could be a way to avoid admitting that I have broken down, have overcome my apprehension. The assumed identity still allows me to keep a degree of reticence. At the sign-up, the non-matching face on the friend's driver's license I borrowed does not arouse suspicion. Maybe they are used to discrepancies in the frenzy of name changing that goes on in the sorcerers' world. My earlier acquaintances, Amalia and Humberto, now go by the names of Talia and Fabrizio. Slippery images of changing shapes.

As soon as I am standing in the room, exposed to the intense atmosphere, I realize, to my surprise, how quickly I have forgotten that I paid for this. It does not matter anymore. There is one advantage though. I don't have to hide so much this time. And the group of familiar faces that I spot in the crowd politely ignores the fake name on my tag. Again the predominance of men in the audience is remarkable.

Taisha, with her inverted triangle face cloaked in almost shy demeanor and her familiar low-key sincerity, strings out thought patterns of such clarity and abstract self-affirming logic they dissolve like candy for the brain. What she misses in grand gestures and biting wit she makes up for with deliberations of exquisite almost mathematical beauty rivaling a bubbling brook in the springtime. I could listen to the crackle in her voice forever.

Now she whishes to introduce us to her two friends from the twin world, the inorganic beings Globus and Phoebus that followed her from her apprenticeship in the trees. This promises to be the first magical act the sorcerers are attempting in public and that I am about to witness. The strange animals, the cat-rabbit, the pigeon without feet, the inorganic beings that they have talked about are the unidentifiable shapes on the puzzle pieces I'm beginning to collect.

Taisha makes room on stage for her unlikely companions and says a few words to them. But I can't see them. And I don't sense anything unusual. I am blank. Maybe I am lacking the power to imagine and I can't see them for that reason? I refrain from asking others for their experience, afraid to be perceived as a nonbeliever. Besides, who would give me an honest answer?

Carlos wants questions. I have to borrow a pen. The taking of notes is discouraged at the seminars. We should learn to rely on our kinetic memories. In the presence of Carlos and the witches all my questions vanish. The building blocks of their world line up in perfect simplicity with the unpretentious light elegance of understanding available in dreams. Like a child reading the signs and feelings from the faces of its parents and surroundings, I gage the connections of the structure from their point of view. There is only one question, a basic one that has dug itself into my mind in the attempt to elicit a clue for the position and primary direction of the sorcerer's reality.

If everything around me is the interpretation of my own perception, a matter of assemblage point position, then the perception of the world of the sorcerers has to be no more than a dial on the scale, another point where the energy lines of the universe are interpreted. So what's the difference? Is it of real advantage to operate in the world of the sorcerers, or is it just a switching of props and stage, while the script remains the same?

All questions are written anonymously. I figure this gives my question a better chance. The paranoia of rejection still lingers. From all the well-behaved queries he picks mine as well. Will he detect the wolf in sheep clothing?

Yes, the world of the sorcerer is based on the same principle - he does not refute it! It is the expression of our perspective, but it offers significant and undeniable advantages. In the world of his sorcerers one has more options without the impairing judgment of good and evil, right or wrong. Moral obligations don't exist, neither do social ties. It is a solitary fight. The universe is predatory.

His answer disappoints, conveying nothing more than a regurgitated repertoire of sorceric locutions. Can't he see the fundamental importance of my question? Somehow I expected more in reply to this thinly disguised inquiry for the cornerstone of his teachings, a real difference, a true advantage, and a better system.

Is he again hiding the inner secrets of his path? How can the world of the sorcerers with its loose structure, nonexistent guidelines and missing social connections, survive without the framework of the general world around it? A world without rules that maintain social interactions and without the willing participation of the inhabitants would destroy itself.

The world of the sorcerers can only exist with the help of the everyday world. Does the everyday world need the sorcerers? A conflict that can only be borne through distance. Cognitive dissonance. With the pulling of my inner dueling drives and my recalcitrant attitude no wonder they couldn't use me.

In the beginning of his apprenticeship, in his first books, Carlos described mind altering drug experiences which I never took as prerequisite for myself. Today, answering the over and again surfacing question about sorcery and drugs, he insists it is not necessary to use drugs in order to succeed. We should do it all with discipline and intent. The hard-sodden ones believe nevertheless that Carlos takes drugs even now to access the other worlds. Also in the practice group some people believe in the necessity of hallucinogenic substances.

I want to do it on my own, with my own muscles, to make it in full conscience without drug-induced hallucinations. Make what? To take off like a rocket? No, to know what life is, to find a way home.

Sometimes I fear that my shortcoming is a lack of discipline. The flyers lick the sheen of awareness from our outer energy egg, leaving us with nothing more than the focus on the struggle for survival. Discipline makes us unpalatable. Discipline is the only deterrent against the flyers, not that I'm convinced of their existence. I never got to see the photograph of the flyer. And even if I did, I would have remained skeptical.

We are lacking discipline, Carlos says categorically. Discipline makes the difference. Over and again I get hung up on the issue of discipline. I can't grasp his meaning of "discipline". Judging by his scathing jokes, he does not promote the catholic tendency of self-flagellation, or militant drill, or adhering to pedantic rules and by the clock regulation of daily life. Nor does he seem to imply the complex system of martial arts training.

My reaction to discipline is the same as a bull's to a red flag. As children we were trained like circus animals. At the table there was to be no smacking, slurping, loud chewing, gulping, or talking with full mouth, no talking period, no clanking of eating utensils against teeth, no elbows on the table, hands next to the plate, chewing only small bites, using please and thank you, no unsolicited talking, no disrupting of grown-up conversation (applied at all times), no plate licking, no spilling, no burping, no giggling, no farting, no wiggling of legs. The rules were endless.

Discipline is nothing but a dictate for good behavior, a vice for obedience, the commandment for compliance, the obligation of forced self-abandonment. Everything inside of me screams against this self-enslavement.

Our elementary teacher Mr. Lang had the wooden ruler clapping in his hand parading down the aisle of desks as if he wanted to provoke the opportunity to use it. All the while he was ignoring the raised hands until my bladder muscle gave way and the warm liquid ran down the bench. That was well behaved, civilized, obedient, polite, disciplined. With discipline chaos was avoided, the horrifying dangerous confusion that signifies the end of the world, or was it?

When Winnetou grew older I hid my feelings, my pain over the nonsensical world around me, behind a rigid numbness with empty unfocused eyes. Nobody on the bus saw who I was, nobody could see

65

behind my mask, not that anybody cared to. With vision swimming through a blurred filter, I lived my life removed into a world where only I existed. That was the discipline of survival.

Why does Carlos put so much emphasis on discipline? I do not disagree with his observation of an undisciplined Western society, the forever adolescent, greedy irresponsible consumer mentality. Or my general tendency for laziness. The stressing of the importance of discipline as deterrent and as a tool for success confuses me. As soon as I force myself, I lose my drive, my motivation. Then there is only obedience and pleasing left. But my motor is the wild, the chaos inside of me. Perseverance is the sustained effort in the chaos.

The December seminar in Anaheim is a reviewing of all the passes taught in the seminars this year. Even though that promises no novelty I go anyway. The movements themselves don't have a notable effect on me despite the regular practice. Carlos will be there. It is the moment of exposure to the unfamiliar, the new, that rallies my faculties to a state of full awareness and attracts me like nothing else.

One day into the workshop Carlos drops a bombshell. He wants to get rid of the chacmools, the three women that have been teaching the magical movements until now in the seminars.

Kylie, wrapped as always in the cloak of intensely focused precision, is without a doubt the most qualified of the three movement instructors. She manages to captivate the entire audience, a feat I consider extraordinary. I only watch her on stage. Her bright blue closely positioned eyes, fervidly shirred to a point in the distance, her blond spiky hair, the solid gold hoops in her ears, her toned strong body, and the short precise instructions that are accompanied by clear movements without unnecessary embellishment. I see "Intent" in her, shining like a polished jewel. She retains focus and concentration even in the face of two thousand eyes, which I consider extraordinary.

The other two chacmools often tangle their movements, forget which is the right or left arm and have personal issues that are detectable in their voices.

According to Carlos there will be no more chacmools after this seminar. They fought behind the scenes for the top position and even dared to outshine the master himself. For that they must be punished.

Their egos stretched their necks out like poisonous snakes and now their heads get hacked off.

I'm dumbfounded. Kylie's tremendous effort gives me, of all the helpers of the inner group, the most sincere impression. Is this the last time she will be teaching us? How he could run the movement seminars without her is unimaginable.

Tears steal across her cheeks. From a side view her face appears composed and confounded. Does she regret her behavior, or does she cry out of shame and anger to be humiliated in front of so many people? What trust she must have in Carlos that he does the right thing, knows the right way.

The wrinkles around Carlos' mouth twist into a slight grin, as if he is enjoying the cutting down of the three women. Or is this some kind of insider joke? Is this just a show for our benefit? Another odd piece in the sorcerer's puzzle. I will have to save it for later placement.

The British prime minister says that the widespread fear of the so-called mad cow disease is in general unfounded.

In the crevices and precipices of the canyon I feel complete. Without the protection of the ballast of civilization, naked, one moves carefully. Like an animal sniffing the air around its own body you smell your scent, you feel the sun on otherwise dark places. In this environment you know where you begin and end. You shrink back to a solid whole.

The diverging ravine in Malibu canyon that I named Crystal canyon because of its boulders veined with crystalline teeth, meanders pathless up the mountain in front of me. Clothes hidden in the brush, I crawl on hands and feet, like an ant over rocks, up the slippery small waterfalls, ducking carefully under the thorny Greenbark.

I can sense his closeness. Coyote, the animal helper revealing himself to me while hiking in a savage attack on my senses and leaving his print on the broken tip of a surf board spit from the full moon ocean touching my feet, is invisible, only yards ahead. Shimmering quartz crystals mounted into little signposts mark the branching way and lure me higher.

Reality blurs comfortably at the crossroads of the imagination. Where does the transition begin between the ordinary world and the mysterious? At what point turns the first wordless thought-symbol into the material equivalent of it?

My naked body inches its way to the dividing membrane between hard rock and unlimited possibilities. Reaching the top of the ridge, where the shaggy vegetation stretches over hills and valleys interrupted only by terracotta and pink volcanic rock convulsions, I am hidden in the ocean of leaves and rocks, protected, sheltered, naked like a newborn child. Back to the beginning, the human, the animal, the original.

A woman smelling of dirty clothes has attached herself to me. Her hair hangs in gray greasy strands; birdseed residue is stuck to her teeth. She has come from the former East Germany loaded with a backpack to participate in the women's seminar, the first workshop designed exclusively for women. I take her to the seminar out of nostalgia for my own impromptu travels in the past.

My cautious suggestions to freshen up a bit for the marathon-shower-obsessed Americans in the seminar find no fertile ground. After all, she just took a bath recently in the ocean and soap is bad for the skin.

Even though Carlos indicated a mysterious aversion against water and advised us to take only short showers after people began smelling in the front row, the witches appear well groomed and freshly scented at all times.

The woods-woman believes to have met one of the Mexican witches from Carlos' books. In a letter to Cleargreen she asked for a meeting in Puerto Vallarta. She never got a confirmation as such, but when she stood at the suggested meeting point on the beach a woman approached her and did not deny being Lydia. For weeks she wandered around with "Lydia" hoping to be introduced into Carlos' group. After a while she felt exploited.

I ask her how she can be sure that it really was the "Lydia" from Carlos' books and not merely an opportunistic local woman. I don't tell her that according to Carlos' negative comments he does not have any contacts with the old witches in Mexico any more and that Cleargreen would never agree to such stupidities.

For some reason she thinks I am a witch too. I avoid the embarrassing radius of her seasoned smells that rival the layered stench of an igloo-confined winter, co-existence with fish, seal carcasses and animal skins.

Carlos shows up at the women's workshop. Did I actually believe only the witches would teach at the seminar? Carlos would not miss this opportunity to glance over the mass of women from all western countries and from South America like a benevolent father, obviously satisfied.

Behind his seminar words, behind the movement props, behind his public facade of smiling encouragement hides something else. I sense this intangible substance between his cryptic metaphors and elicited how-to-become-a-sorcerer manual, camouflaged by the notorious guru atmosphere that seems to satisfy most of the people that flock to his talks.

Thinly veiled, yet hopelessly obscured, lies the garden that beckons me. His true world, his true teachings, the true core of his knowledge. The insatiable longing inside of me that turned over all other stones for what I lost somewhere sometime haunts me in the picture of this man.

The energy in the room pulses evenly, without the polarized back and forth of the mixed gender audience driven by the anticipation of new revelations. Surely as always, there are those hoping to be discovered that try hard to catch his attention dressed in wild clothes, striking jewelry and fancy hairdos. One woman in a red long skirt came without panties and does not hide that fact. Others have adopted the uniform look of the insiders and given up their individuality for bristly haircuts, roomy tee shirts, sunglasses and androgynous behavior. Just another facet of the belonging-to-the-herd instinct. The identification markings of warriors.

To my surprise Kylie appears back on stage as one of a group of six female instructors. He calls them the 'energy trackers'. The new women offered themselves after the fall of the chacmools. He can attempt to hide Kylie behind the others; to me she is still the only one of the movement teachers that rallies all her energy.

Lightening-bolt blue-eyed bundled-electricity Florinda gives her provocative emancipation lecture. She is the uncrowned queen. In a tight black top and knee-length black skirt with zipper she looks like a thin bird. Wondering what happened to her breasts that seemed to have shrunk to almost complete flatness in the peculiar boutiqueish chic she is wearing, she obviously does not shop in the average department store; I succumb to the influence of four hundred simultaneously gossiping women's brains.

Florinda likes to shock. The catching of the "wind" with exposed genitals has to be an embarrassment for the average x-sensitive audience. It does not throw the Middle European out of balance, who rips the clothes from her body at the first rays of the sun, runs naked through the wilderness and surrenders on top of the mountains to the airs. Didn't we all play with our genitals when we were little girls? Maybe not in the land of the prude and the free.

Sexuality should serve as a tool for development and not be limited to the release of primitive urges. In the sorceric world woman has the purpose of the evolution of humanity as a whole. A heavy burden. Our uterus allows us to give birth to something new, not merely to reproduce. Every organ has next to its obvious physical function an intangible one. For the uterus, it is evolution.

Wonderful! But how is this supposed to work? The dinosaurs wished to fly and they grew wings. Can they only give metaphorical clues? Only insinuations? Should we invent it by ourselves?

The Blue Scout, the ageless, boyish woman, a couple of years ago still reacting ambivalently towards her role as an extraterrestrial being, has now markedly improved. She reads excerpts from Carlos' new manuscript of memoirs. Lulled by the unaccustomed shelter in the lap of four hundred women, and the monotonous voice of the reader, I slip into a half-waking dream state despite my fascination for Carlos' outrageous stories. The shifting between my borderline dream world and the afternoon shadows of the room creates a strangely distorted effect in both places.

The stream of energy carries me again, rushing past the picture of the young Carlos sitting in a donkey cadaver to catch vultures and the cloud dotted summer sky over the wavering hay wagon. Clear dark blue ponds of clouds wander over the wooded hills. On the worn-out dirt road totters a rack wagon loaded several stories high like a drunk, intoxicated on the sun-drenched fragrant hay. I cling to the beam on top of the vacillating haystack that is lashed with a hemp rope to the wagon shaft. The wooden wheels wrapped with a metal band groan, the whip smacks over the docile ocher oxen, the iron brake squeals in pain. Even without load the slatted wagon seemed unstable harboring wide gaps between the spokes, and only one narrow board in the middle that also transported the top beam. The women in white headscarves mounded the hay with wooden rakes into long rows and the farmer pierced it in big bundles with a sharp four-pronged fork on to the wagon. Dried to a lavender-green, the meadow flowers were indistinguishable, the daisies, the yellow crowfoot, crane's bill, blue bells, lady's smock, red poppies and marigold, that reached between the moist grass up to my children's hip until they fell in flat swaths under the swoosh of the long scythe.

The magical movements selected specifically for women are not notably different from the ones shown to the general audience. And only one is taught directly by Taisha. But we promise not to show them to the men. These special passes could be dangerous for the other sex.

My curiosity and expectation for truly feminine insights and magical revelations remains unsatisfied. They only make intimations, disclose no witches' secrets, tell no new stories. The unsaid gapes in the middle of the room like a drafty block of ice oozing frigid air trapped in the knowing glances between the witches. The minute regurgitated samples give away only surface patterns, obscuring the deeper substance.

What is the secret of the world of the sorcerer? What does the whole picture look like? All I can see is a hollow structure, a magnificent cathedral erected to support the life style of the sorcerer. Where is the "beef"? Knowledge is an effective but fictitious victory over the invisible.

We are told to execute the women's movements daily for one month. It is an experiment to see what will happen when a group intensely practices the same passes. Is the mass now replacing the long awaited electric warrior?

After the seminar I hear rumors that the witches are planning to teach a sorcery class just for women. Maybe this is where they will uncover their inner secrets? The witches have never taught private classes before. It was always Carlos. Obviously they can invite only local residents.

Enthusiastically, I phone Cleargreen to express my unabashed interest. They promise to call me back. A few days later they leave a message on my machine regretting that the women's group is cancelled. But there is another message on the tape, not intended for me, which ended up inadvertently there. The message is an invitation to the women's class for another person.

So they are up to their old tricks, lying to me again. If they don't want me because I'm a known quantity they must still be looking for the electric warrior! For a moment I play with the thought of crashing the class. A friend, struggling at first to overcome the secrecy gag, discloses the place of the planned meeting.

But when I see the invited ones marching into the studio with fresh, proud strides and full of expectations, I don't have the courage to walk in on the class. I console myself with the knowledge of my past opportunity when I spent months in his immediate presence.

Chapter Five

Pandora's Box

See! That was nothing, but that's how it always begins, very small.

-Egg Shen in *Big Trouble in Little China,* 1986

Busty Rachel is standing across from me in the artist studio in Venice where the serious students faithfully practice the newest magical movements learned in the last seminar. Her movements are smooth and effortless without flourish, her posture is upright, and her face is relaxed. I admire her. Guessing her age at barely twenty she could be my daughter. She would be an ideal candidate for Carlos' inner group. Perhaps even a shoe-in for the famed electric warrior position. The younger you are the better chances you have to change behavior patterns, he says. She evades my question when I ask if Carlos has invited her to the women's group.

Joseph pulls me aside showing the twisted tooth-baring grin of a street merchant dealing with forbidden commodities as he whispers that he knows where Carlos teaches the movements to his inner circle, implying that we go there and watch. Why does he divulge this to me? Didn't I tell him that I used to be in Carlos' private classes? Does he expect less indignation from me? Or is he telling everyone, fishing for reactions?

I find this revelation only mildly exiting. After all I know what happens in the private classes. And nowadays we get to see Carlos regularly at the seminars. Running after him would seem slightly desperate and humiliating.

At first I feel no more then a weak curiosity, the kind I needn't act on, lacking the appetite for celebrity adoration. In Los Angeles one runs into famous people every day, Jamie Lee Curtis at Trader Joe's, Arnold at Schatzi's, David Hasselhof on location at the Pacific Coast Highway. My attraction to Carlos is not his elusive celebrity status. On second thought, the knowledge of the current group of chosen ones gains a certain luster, and I agree to join Joseph for a taste.

Is it the fear of stagnation that doesn't let me rest? Do I secretly miss the strong current of the master's energy and the exhilarating ride amongst the rapids? Can't I admit to myself that I long to feel the burning immediacy again, the rush of sitting at the front of the rollercoaster? The taste still lingers in my mouth like blood after a run, the memory of total presence and vivacity.

We are animals driven by instincts, the instinct of our souls.

We meet in the early evening on Santa Monica Boulevard, at the fateful city block where Carlos found his Carol again and walked with her in tears back and forth on the sidewalk, between Fifth and Sixth Street, not able to comprehend her unexpected return.

On this corner the wind blusters around the concrete-steel-glass office buildings and banks. The smell of the Chinese restaurant pervades the alley in a tempting cloud, cars and buses swim by in an endless rhythm of nervous agitation, pretty people stride confidently on the sidewalk to the Promenade, as eagerly smiling Latin valets park cars and blackened homeless sit in shreds begging with heads hanging low. Here a new chapter begins. I am drawn closer, unwittingly caught in the noose of curiosity.

Our tour guide shows us the way through an underground parking structure with elevators that takes us up into a four-story office building currently under reconstruction. From the balcony of this empty and in the early dusk quiet structure one can see diagonally down across the alley into the lit up windows of the dance studio. In those rectangles whirl legs and occasionally the arms of the last row of participants that are invited to Carlos' inner group, in the inaudible rhythm of the new magical movements.

Earnestness befalls me in the shadow of the balcony, an almost hallowed staidness that connects me with the three others that follow the interrupted movements as closely as possible. Seen from a distance there is something rather foolishly innocent and touchingly funny in the efforts of the four dark figures on the balcony, trying to gather snippets of the secret movements with heroic assiduity.

At last the legs in the studio move towards the jackets and bags they stashed near the windows. We pull our shining faces back and race down the stairway into the street. Any moment now the master and his group will be emerging through the door. We are waiting on the opposite side of Santa Monica Boulevard, shyly loitering, feet shuffling and throwing unobtrusive glances toward the exit of the dance studio.

Suddenly the door pushes open and as if on command, they gush on to the sidewalk, surrounding the little man in a cluster like bees protecting their queen. His barely illuminated figure, the small face, his silver hair, his movements between the young ones unleash in me an unexpected flood of affectionate feelings, emotions I was not aware of in the private classes. At that time it was an amalgamation of wonder, respect and careful curiosity paired with skepticism that I brought to him and that kept me at a distance.

Now I feel closer than ever before. In spite of the expulsion and the accepted anonymity at his seminars, depicted in the gulf of the droning street noise that separates me from him and his group, I feel skin close. I stare at the scene as if watching single cell life forms under the microscope, sucking in every one of his gestures, overwhelmed by my emotions.

Maybe it was his generosity that won me over. His ability to be completely accessible and utterly present without holding back.

The parting gestures to his adopted family graze soft strings inside of me. The fibers in my solar plexus vibrate as if touched. A deep space opens up, surrounding me and I can follow the strings running through me until they are lost in infinity. Vague memories of an undefined closeness, trust, and certainty oscillate in the fleeting filaments, images too fragile to be grasped.

If I could only remember why it pulls me so strangely at the heart! There on the sidewalk aroused by his ordinary behavior the longing inside of me wakes up again, the old yearning that cannot be satisfied by anything in this world is chasing me in front of it.

Our furtive glances sweep unhinged across the street while our embarrassed grins engage in mock conversation. Like the children crawling on their bellies under the currant bushes secretly tasting the forbidden fruit, we appease our soul hunger on the bustle across the street soaked in honey colored light.

Promptly Carlos is packed into Kylie's car and they are gone. Sheepishly we separate. He still has this unexplainable attraction for me.

Is it deplorable, shameful, odious, reprehensible, detestable, despicable, low, paltry, insidious and unprincipled - I'm trying to find the right word here - wanting to see the master in secret? Surely our other friends at the Thursday practice group, if they knew, would regard it as disrespectful and irreverent.

We transgressed the unspoken line. One does not follow a sorcerer into his magical world without invitation. And in the ordinary world one does not spy on other people. Regardless, I have no pangs of conscience. My intent is harmless. It did not hurt anybody.

The road leads into boundlessness.

At the border crossing they searched the trunk of our car confiscating magazines and books. But we already knew this. Our real cargo was hidden. Only I could decipher the address I had encoded with an arbitrarily selected bible verse. She drove. If they caught us she would have no idea where we were going. This reduced the risk. I knew the source of our load just as little as she did. In an emergency situation we were told to get in touch with the German consulate.

We drove through the crunching snow of the Czech winter landscape. At a lonely spot we pulled off the main highway onto a narrow and icy dirt road. In the half dusk of early evening I screwed off the rear lights of the car and we started to repack the bibles we had stored in the wall. Several suitcases and bags filled up. With careful glances we looked around, conscious of every change in the snow-covered landscape. Big antennas on a hill stirred our suspicions. But everything remained quiet.

To find a house in the dark, somewhere in a foreign village, often without street signs, without being able to ask for directions, seems even today to border on a miracle. Naturally the people were surprised by our unexpected visit. The bags filled with brand new bibles that had the pages still stuck together were brought into the house cautiously to avoid alerting the neighbors. With a few common words we communicated with our improbable hosts that were very accommodating considering the circumstances by offering us dinner and a musical taste of the saw violin.

In the beginning I traveled by myself with the train, packed with suitcases and bags, heavy as lead, too heavy to lift them off the ground. Fortunately, at that time porters were still waiting at the train stations. Frequently the officials at the border opened a suitcase throwing the whole content over the train compartment. My suitcases were never touched by the border control, even though I made no great effort to cover up the bibles with little clothing in the luggage. God must have been on my side.

Once I arrived in the city of my destination drop I left the luggage in a locker at the station and went on the search for the unsuspecting recipients of my Christian charity. There was Budapest, Budovicze, Prague, H'rovice, Arad, Bratislava, Novi Sad, Timisoara and Prague. Big gray-brown cities, little poor villages, dreary city blocks in snowstorms, hot sticky packed streetcars, miles of shiny cobblestone roads, moldy staircases, and tiny crammed apartments.

I imprinted the map of the city on my mind, memorized the address, did not walk along the same street more then once, did not ask neighbors for directions, and watched everybody that followed me. Precautions. Each time I was aware of the greater danger I could visit upon the bible recipients. After interrogation I assumed I could return to the West. They would have to live with the discovery and deal with innumerable difficulties resulting from it. Pastor Wurm's stories of torture were clearly in my mind.

Some time or other I must have aroused suspicion. It was not wise to continue with the bible transports to avoid jeopardizing the Christians in the communist countries unnecessarily.

Back on Santa Monica Boulevard I'm drawn to the place that he himself called a magical portal, the door to another world. As if drifting in space on a spider's thread I am fishing for my memories of truth and meaning. The last sunbeams illuminate the glass walls. Crisp white seagulls, scissor sharp cutouts, glide over the roofs on their way to the beach. They are coming home from work, I imagine. Blue fingered palm shadows fan in the sundowner wind.

Is it only nostalgia, a piece of lost familiarity, the longing for home that lets me overcome pride, embarrassment and general inertia, calling me to this corner?

The steady stream of tire-humming cars and buses, growling, honking, hissing, squealing and belching flows by like shifting river water tugging at my attention. The biting nasal grip of exhaust riding on the moisture-laden air, the sweat of the ocean wipes around the city canyon.

On the north side of the street the row of shops begins with Council Travel, Hi De Ho comic store, another second-hand bookstore, a barber, is broken by the one-way alley and continues with the imposing beige cement structure of the bank building.

On the south side is Pep Boys, Radio Shack with the Dance Home studio above on the second floor. Next to it runs the concrete alley with several overflowing trash dumpsters, then Lucy's Golden China restaurant, bordered by Deep River books, the coveted location of the former Phoenix bookstore, followed by a vegetarian restaurant, a flower shop with green and lavender neon signs and on the corner, the white table linen restaurant, Jiraffe.

The deep-seated restlessness prodding me on, entices me to seek out the small unreal man and his atmosphere, to breathe his air, to touch his world, to smell the scent of infinity, even if it is just from afar.

Joseph and his girlfriend have evaporated. But even by myself I would be here. Only it would be too obvious standing alone in the dark staring from the opposite side of the street. As a pair one can pretend to be engaged in an important discussion, some personal drama, which I show Greg with greatly exaggerated gestures. He thinks it is funny. Greg is my accomplice, just as my brother used to be.

More then snatching the movement fragments from the balcony I want to see the mysterious sorcerer as if I needed to impress his outline into my subconscious, like the star constellations of the night sky. As if through close observation I could develop a conscious familiarity with the secret, gain a sense of its texture, its habits and sources of sustenance, to track the illusive in its ordinary form, to unravel the mysterious pull.

His lessons in the studio are finished by eight o'clock. From the shadowy umbrellas of the trees across the street we observe the repeating spectacle. The girls, women and men, how they saunter down the steep stairway into the greenish light of the exit, how they wait together on the sidewalk in front of Radio Shack until the master dressed in a red shirt climbs down the steps on Amalia-Talia's arm, how Kylie in the midnight blue Toyota All-Trac manages an illegal u-turn in the middle of the boulevard and stops exactly in front of the door. As someone opens the car door, Carlos, Taisha and Florinda climb in and ten seconds later only the glowing embers of the brake lights remain visible.

Too transitory, too fleeting is the taste, the sample of his picture. The neon illuminated bustling in front of the exit flickers like the dream sequence of a movie, seized and edited by the swooshing river of buses and cars into a temptingly nontransparent episode.

The remaining students linger for a few moments of bottled water sips and inaudible pleasantries. We move to the bench of the bus stop on the corner of Sixth Street to watch where the cluster of chosen ones disappears. Under the neon light we crouch next to a homeless who is absorbed in picking and talking to his bare crusted and blackened feet, paying no attention to us.

I squint with my lowered head at the group as they swim by like a school of fish. If they recognized us it would be very embarrassing. Most of them know us from before. A few shreds of their conversation trail behind them. They did not waste one look at us.

The stigma of invisibility surrounding the street person, and maybe his stench, camouflaged us as well.

On the drive back home we are silent. I don't feel much like chatter. A nearly full moon is hiding behind fog clouds, pulling them like a veil in front of her face and giving us only occasional glimpses. Our newly won friends in the Thursday practice group would not understand our excursions to the Dance Home door, would they? How would Carlos react if he caught us? I cannot imagine. Probably with indignation. Or could he possibly perceive our audacity as estimable?

The impulse that caused me to read his books in my twenties, that lured me across the ocean, far away from Germany, that did not let me rest, and put me into his path, pulls, prods and shoves me gently into a new direction. In the world of the sorcerer there are no rules and this is where I am operating now, on their level, in the shady zone, that moves between elements of the ordinary world, but patterns itself by the design of the unknown. Who knows where it will lead me tomorrow? A sorcerer has no pity, does not complain, or accuse, and most of all, he leaves nothing behind. A sorcerer has no time off. Is Carlos holding the key to the unexplainable attraction concealed in secrecy? If I could only remember!

Eight hundred dollars need a lot of overcoming, thus delaying my sign-up for the one-week seminar until the last day. This morning, waking up on the deck with the first rays drawing silver twirls in the opaque blue sky I decide to go.

The 'Reading of Infinity', a one-week seminar, happens in Westwood on the grounds of the university where Carlos himself studied and lectured. Here on this campus he saw a flyer for the first time and brought his internal dialogue to a halt, seeing energy as it flows in the universe.

In the giant windowless oval of the men's gym, built like a covered stadium with rows of seating up to the roof, we meet for the magical movements taught by Kylie and the new trackers. Kylie's embrace showers me with unusual warmth. She seems friendlier then she acted in the private classes.

Carlos' troop has grown again, even though publicly he maintains they are not a group but individuals that occasionally do things together. A group of six male instructors join the energy trackers. The two that Carlos referred to as his agents, Bruce and Tracy, go by the names of Lorenzo and Julius. The rotund red-hair, who was also a friend of Amalia and Humberto's, getting into the organization that way I presume, has been given the name Grant. Humberto-Fabrizio and two other unfamiliar faces are also part of the new "elements". "Reminiscent of the variable code names ex-CIA operatives receive in the movie Hudson Hawk," Greg chuckles. The rumor, if someone in the group needs renaming Carlos drives around the neighborhood and picks street names, doesn't seem far-fetched.

We notice a person high up between the rows of seats flashing a camera. Immediately Kylie sends out a security detachment to throw out the spy. Any photographing, recording of image or voice is strongly forbidden. When we enter the building in the morning our bags are checked for video cameras, tape recorders and photo cameras that are confiscated until the end of the day. Our bodies get a sweep with the sensor stick.

I wonder if someone has the guts to disobey them, to shoot a picture or smuggle in a small tape-recorder. This much paranoia practically begs for defiance. Up until now no pictures or unauthorized tapes have circulated in the Castaneda fan underground. Carlos erased his past and destroyed every photograph he could get his hands on in a sorceric effort to leave nothing behind that could tether him to this world.

Sitting in the first row next to the stage she wears black lace gloves and is dressed in a hodgepodge thrift-shop style, obviously intended to attract his attention. By now many of us ordinary participants are bringing pretty clothes for the evening lectures, but mostly businesslike dresses and suits. I walk past her to get a closer view.

Her hair is dyed a honey-orange, she wears an odd make-up application that prompts me to linger for a moment. "Nice outfit," I complement her to explain my halting stare and to afford me a longer look. Under the heavy layer of cover-up her face shows smooth

81

patches without pores, stretched like burn victim skin transplants or botched beauty operations. Her unusual get-up and patchy made-up face give her a freakish appearance, strangely alien in the sea of conformity.

The next day during Carlos' lecture this woman suddenly jumps up and yells "You are selling it" and again "You are selling it". He is selling what? Spirit? He is selling his knowledge? I do agree with her, to market the knowledge like a commodity does not seem to be in don Juan's spirit. And I hope for an answer.

One moment the room is startled into breathless silence, then Bruce-Lorenzo, the "agent" gets up and takes the screaming woman aside. With her outburst she crossed the unspoken line. In this world you do not offer opposition. She seems completely overwhelmed by her own impulsiveness. First Carlos must not have understood what she was saying, prompting her to repeat it, then he almost readied himself to give her an answer. His bad eyesight must have kept him from recognizing this woman as Merilyn. The embarrassment is removed.

People wave their arms excitedly as Amalia-Talia - we privately nicknamed her Tamalia - walks through the crowd to pick candidates for Carol's hypnosis trick on stage. My modesty lets me sink into the chair. Greg is keen to experience the ominous black eye of the nagual woman. I don't desire to walk on water. May the old samanas be satisfied with such skills, as Hesse writes so appropriately. Once on stage Greg seems to resist. From my row it looks as if an exasperated Carol has to make him lie down.

During the question and answer session a participant from Greece has the audacity to offer himself to Carlos as an apprentice in front of five hundred people in the audience, pleading to be taken into his group. The crowd momentarily sucks in air, aghast. What boldness and foolishness to gush out with a desire that everybody secretly harbors.

Carlos repeats his standard answer that I knew he was going to give in the face of such haughty innocence. There is no group to join; they are only individuals going the path alone. The fate of the sorcerer is a lonely road. In contrast to these rhetorical assurances is the fact that in the last couple of years the number of people working for Cleargreen and Carlos has doubled.

Humberto-Fabrizio, takes me into a back room to process my credit card payment he had difficulty with. This offers the perfect opportunity for a friendly word with an old acquaintance and maybe even an honest answer to a probing question. He and Tamalia changed their address two years ago and broke contact with me. I took no offence guessing that it was Carlos' program of preparation.

Would Fabrizio with his greater knowledge of the inner workings and in remembrance of our friendship tell me the truth about the path of the sorcerers' apprentice? He says that without the Nagual nothing goes. Without Carlos, without his presence, his intimate guidance Fabrizio-Humberto sees no chance for himself! This is not the publicly staged proclamation but Humberto's personal expectation.

I don't show my surprise. The official version out there for the masses is the lonely individual fight, whose sole success hinges on uncertain, unforeseeable circumstances and can only be fought with discipline and intent, regardless of its outcome, because there is no other way left.

And here Humberto, the insider, close to the core, trembles by the thought that he will not make it without Carlos. Pretty dire prospects for all of us!

Princess Diana and Prince Charles are getting divorced. A blow to my mother's emotional house of cards!

6 p.m. Saturday night, Santa Monica Boulevard. Instead of going to the movies or for dinner to a restaurant or to a concert, for which there is no lack in this metropolis, I am standing again at the doorway to the unknown. First the older plump woman with glasses (that he called Professor Nieto in the private classes I witnessed) drives up in her red Ford, then the two cousins arrive in a silver Ford with a yellow rear-light stripe and park on Sixth Street. Greg and I stay in our car to avoid a run-in.

Carlos shows up with Kylie and Tamalia in the Toyota All-Trac and gets dropped off. Tamalia walks him up the stairs into the dance studio while Kylie brings the car to the lot behind the Santa Monica library. Nowadays Carlos is being chauffeured around constantly. Only a few years ago he insisted on keeping the steering wheel in his own hands.

The sparse view from the balcony across the alley still offers no more than cut-off legs and hopelessly mutilated movements. If only once in a while we could see whole bodies or catch a glimpse of Carlos teaching his students!

To bridge the time until the end of the class we play a game of finding the parked vehicles of the participants. It turns out to be mostly guesswork. I have no memory for automobile details. Greg is better than me. Next time we could write down the license plate numbers to be sure.

To the observant the automobile of a person contains obvious indicators about the financial situation, confidence, self-image and cleanliness of its owner. The inside of the car divulges details of lifestyle and personality, lassitude, procrastination, sloppiness, talent for organization, worldview and mood. Kylie's clean and, except for a plastic water bottle, empty car speaks of admirable discipline and awareness.

From across the inky shadows of the alley we watch once more the unfolding of the now familiar scenario, still expecting something new, a small magical irregularity, a secret overlooked detail like entranced children frequently visiting the Christmas window display of a toy store overflowing with moving trains, flashing lights and dolls.

Just as the glass door of Dance Home swings open and the first bodies spill out onto the sidewalk, a passenger car enters the alley we are standing in. Confused, we freeze like rabbits caught in the headlights, and huddle in the blinding light against the brick wall, to wait for the end of the phone call the person in the car is placing. The cluster on the other sidewalk is swelling. All flock around Carlos.

A tall German towering above the group peers around as if promoted to bodyguard. He glances in our direction. Seen from a distance we might look to him like two bumbling Mexicans with our short statures and dark hair. But if his eyesight is better then ours he might recognize us.

This is uncomfortably awkward. I'm itching to meld into the shadows. I have no need to be discovered, nor do I want to disrupt their lives in any way. I don't want to appear as an intruder. In a rare and undisputed agreement Greg and I committed to a strict noninterference policy, watching but not touching, mimicking the Star trek space exploration directive.

The lanky bodyguard hesitates, displaying irresolute thoughts. But now Carlos slips into the car and Kylie zips off with her cargo into the sparkle of the eastern city sky. In the same moment we turn and dive into the alley black to disperse the disconcerting roaming stares from the other side.

Rachel, the young girl from our Thursday practice group has disappeared. Her friend insists that he does not know her whereabouts. Has she been taken into Carlos' inner circle? Asked to leave her friends and family to live in isolation in a place assigned by Carlos to be trained as apprentice? Perhaps one day we will see her in our secret observations.

The rain has softened the sandstone path, pounded the ochre rock into yellow mud that washes slowly down the mountain to the river and the ocean. A green carpet of edible Chickweed covers the slope. Thrasher gurgles in mellow tones on top of the Toyon bush, and mossy algae powder dusts the branches. Coyote paws with retracted claws leave softer imprints then dogs. The doe and her yearling punched deep well-etched hoof tracks crossing the path in the early morning after the rain. The miniature hands of raccoons reminiscent of stencil patterns on the wall trot through the puddles. When I touch the imprints an invisible connection to the animal establishes itself and draws me without fail into its proximity. Greg laughs, he thinks I'm joking.

Through long and careful observation the hunter gradually develops an instinctive knowledge of the habits of his prey, of its fears and pleasures, its preferred foods and favorite haunts.

If you hunt for Chanterelle you must walk slowly like the deer with the big mule ears, lifting your legs high, stalking them down softly, pausing to smell and listen. Then take a few more steps, blink into the light, all the while searching the leafy ground with the efficient sweep of a metal detector.

The mushroom, clearly imprinted in the mind's eye, is a collage of smell and taste memories. It resides within the overall blueprint of the fungi mother intertwined in the sunny shade dabbled group of trees and the moist slope of oak leaves on the south-facing canyon wall. You can't find her in a straight line. For the rational mind it is a rather aimless meandering, back and forth in a generous zigzag motion of wading, scenting, listening and tasting.

Following the inner impulse you edge closer, engaged in the wordless communication with the mushroom mind image, you recognize the musty leaf covered ground and you know they are nearby. If you don't approach the object of your hunt in the right way it merely vanishes.

But when you track it past the Chocolate Lilies and Miner's Lettuce, between the leafy pyramids of the packrats, in the distant dog barking, behind the morning dew drops twinkling like precious stones green, red and blue, through the pungent scent of the deer pebble mounds, around the still sleeping ticks, under the circling shadow of the red-tailed hawk, you will find them between the naked twigs of the poison oak peeking in orange-yellow virginity and peppery aroma from the oak compost as if they've just burst from the loamy earth.

The same method of finding can be used for forest strawberries, foxes, any lost object, people, or streets. Even though in the city my car usually knows the way better then I do.

The sorcerers say that stalkers use their behavior to change their assemblage point to produce an effect of maximum cognitive dissonance.

My eyes follow the sorcerers into the darkness of the night, after they disperse from the moment of light in which they warm themselves one last time in the stray beams of reflected glory. Sure I know they are heading home to their apartments somewhere in their ordinary life as sorcerers. But it might as well be on the dark side of the moon.

Wistfully, my glance hangs on the red glow worms of Kylie's rear car lights that slowly disappear east on Santa Monica Boulevard. Surprisingly they are still discernable from a long distance moving between the undulating light snakes. Her car has an unusual arrangement on the hatchback of two vertical rows of brake lights that float above the lights of the other vehicles.

This car would be the only one possible to follow. A tempting thought appearing out of nowhere dangles innocently between Pinky and the Brain, how we call ourselves in frequent self-mockery. To chase after the sorcerers! That would be a challenge!

Would he let us? Are we allowed to? In the realm of the sorcerer nothing is as it seems to be, nothing is for certain. Inconsistent as quicksand and unreliable as sand dunes whose forms blow away by morning, the magical world twists with tornados and opens up sudden craters.

And then there are the fear inducing monsters that serve the sorcerer and guard his border. "That didn't help the old Mexicans against the Conquistadores," Greg appropriately remembers. Maybe because the unwitting Conquistadores had no inkling of the local traditions and therefore did not believe in monsters, we explain to ourselves. I don't fear tricks of the mind.

Realistically, what chances do we have against the sorcerers? They are in every way superior to us, so he said. They have a razor-sharp awareness that lets them see things normal humans don't ever notice. There is also the obstacle to consider, if by trailing the sorcerers' car we are actually stepping over our self-imposed threshold. Would it change our position of peripheral observation to an actively intrusive participation?

I don't think so. It would still be nothing more then watching. Didn't he tell us to look deeper, beneath the surface appearances? He told us to see the shivering fabric of life in the shadow play of the leaves, in the sand pattern, in the naked rhythm of the pool water, to see energy as it flows in the universe.

And didn't Florinda herself, during her apprenticeship forgo the "verbot" and secretly walk on the trail of ashes to the small hut, driven by her unstoppable curiosity and characteristic audacity? Obviously, rules are there to be broken. This pushes the next hurdle out of the way.

Regardless, a certain hesitation has to be overcome, next to the acquired inhibition to spy as adults on other people. After all, respect, admiration and affection towards Carlos should not suffer. It is not the thrill of stalking the master stalker, but my curiosity and the commitment to the path that began so long ago, to find out where it ultimately is leading. This path that restlessly meandered from an alienated childhood through this earth in the search for the truth, that does not shy away from hardship and pain, and that pulled me into Carlos' magnetic spell, it now seems to glimmer behind the brake lights of his car. The challenge lies in front of our feet like a glove thrown into the dust. Should we accept?

His fur was midnight black, as shiny as my hair. His amber eyes contained pupils deep enough to fall into. They shimmered with the luring adventures of the impenetrable world an energy strutting jungle cat disappears into for weeks. There he was king. A part of me strolled with him through the tall grass, chased in moonless nights after the marten, conquered with heavy paw strikes his competitors.

He came and went as he pleased. His massive head surrounded by a thick bristly ruff gallantly bowed over the milk bowl I presented as an offering and slurped the contents without disdain. He did not depend upon my generosity.

The unshakable bond that brought him back from his roving to the paltry room was a bond forged in the moment when my unexpected appearance prevented the premature death of the sickly kitten in a throw against the barn door. His red brother was already dead. He, the black one, survived. Tenaciously, he grew from a diarrhea-ridden hairy skeleton into a gigantic Tom. In his thick short hair I smelled the world. Outside in the garden, in the meadows, in the barn or the chestnut hedge I never ran into him.

One day he resurfaced with only one eye. His left one hung from the empty eye-socket in a dried up string. Politely he lapped his milk, making no fuss, no sound over his condition before he left again.

The pain over the loss of his impenetrable yellow eye knotted my stomach and became at once the grief of separation. I knew he would not be able to hunt anymore and his animalistic wildness could not be locked inside of a house. So he left, forever to hunt in the big nothing of the cat world. I learned more from this cat than from all the grown-ups around me, so it seems.

So far, every time we watched the Saturday night class, Kylie drove east on Santa Monica Boulevard. If we attempt to follow her it is better to start a few intersections further east on their route, not directly in front of Dance Home. It will be less conspicuous.

We come prepared on this Saturday night. The darkness has already swallowed the last hues of the day, leaving us in the sea of streaming lights. We make sure the class for the favorite ones is happening as usual, then we wait two street corners down the road.

The headlights of the oncoming cars all look alike. How can we recognize Kylie's car in time? It is pure luck. Impatiently, I peer through the binoculars along the street. Bad planning! We are too far away to see the exit of Dance Home. For some moments we flounder in the crack of nothingness. All we can do is wait blindly.

"If they stick to their punctuality they should appear any second".

To the minute, Kylie rushes on. Only when they pass us we confirm the characteristic rear lights and jump hastily into Greg's car.

The chase is on. A fortunate red traffic light slows her down long enough to guarantee us a position a few cars behind the Toyota All-Trac. They are still heading east.

Kylie drives fast and smooth. Too fast! At the lights she slithers through yellow-reds, threatening an early abortion of our pursuit. "As if she knew!" "No" I reassure us, "they only see our glaring headlights in their rearview mirror, they can't see any details". The shadow of Kylie's head pops up; Carlos' hides behind the neck rest of the front passenger seat. Now we are directly behind them. The new shocks in Greg's empty truck make the ride jumpy, just as we are, a bucking horse with throttled reigns. We see Kylie's look into her rearview mirror and shrivel in our seats.

At Federal she suddenly turns left, too quickly for us, since we are only a few feet behind them. As we continue across the intersection I catch a glance of her blinking right turn indicator reaching the next corner.

Los Angeles is an unbelievable geometrical grid drawn with a ruler. Where I come from streets grow like twisting vines over centuries yet seemingly changing direction at night. "Turn left on the next light," I press the driver, who only on rare occasions heeds my advice. "If she continues to drive in an easterly direction on the parallel street, Ohio Avenue, we should be able to catch up with her there." Theoretically we should not be very far behind her, driving at the same speed.

Luck is on our side again! As we charge onto Ohio the backlights of Kylie's Toyota shine like two glowing signposts only a street block ahead of us. Greg steps on the gas, closes in and we hang on to her bumper. Quickly we cross Sepulveda together as if connected by a tow rope.

Ohio Avenue now narrows down, becoming a side street with less traffic. Is it conspicuous if the same headlights stay on their backs? Better to leave some distance between the cars. Maybe the energy for the chase is draining from us? Have we not had unbelievable luck up to now to be able to follow them such a distance?

The street runs through a dark residential neighborhood. Jerking dips in the pavement make us slow down even more. Kylie's brake lights disappear further and further ahead of us. She knows her way. One more time I see her turn left in the blackish distance, and then they are swallowed by the neighborhood. Somewhere in the unreal magical garden they arrive at their sorcerer's home. Or did they trick us? Maybe they felt our presence and took us on a wild goose chase through town and are laughing right now over our pompous gullibility? Florinda's familiar ripping laughter echoes in my ears.

My rational mind calculates. Generally they drove east, in a straight undeterred line. After that they turned south for several blocks, and then continued east again. The unswerving direction of this line does not point towards a trick. Logic concludes that we have to be very close. It amazes me how relatively easy it was and how far we could follow them. This I did not expect. It fell into our laps like a present.

"I know what we are going to do next," I tell my visible and invisible audience, as if he didn't know. "Next Saturday we will wait right here where we lost them at a quarter past eight". If fate determines, and the sorcerers agree, they will take the same route again. I have touched their tracks, their intangible strings. Can I pull the superior sorcerers closer like the animals in the wilderness?

One week later. 8 p.m. The night pulls a lead colored veil over the neighborhood creeping from the crevices of the sewer gullies and the thick canopy of the jacaranda trees like a black jaguar. We are sitting on the corner of Thayer and Eastbourne under a streetlight with my engine turned off.

"What if they don't come," Greg thinks out loud. "Then it is not meant to be" is my answer. They will come. I can feel it. The lamp above us buzzes on darkening the city sky into an eggplant colored tent. The jaguar out there lurks in the shadows. I remember the unlikely jaguar from Carlos story that hunted Carlos and don Juan through a bristly desert. He smelled their tracks, swam in the subconscious of the collected psyche reading their thoughts, chasing them for fun; a symbol of the nagual, the unknown.

Does Carlos know that the eater of souls, as he is called in the Amazon, has been sighted recently in the Baboquivari Mountains in Arizona? The jaguar is known to travel five hundred miles for food and mate and his range still reaches from the South American jungle to the spurs of the Sierra Madre. Now it almost seems this symbol of the unexplainable prowls the shadows of Los Angeles and has followed him home.

Fifteen minutes past eight. If they don't show up soon, it will be too dark to recognize them in time. Minutes drip in sticky blobs. Suddenly as if spit from a black ink jar, Kylie's car jumps toward us and turns a few feet in front of us onto Eastbourne. The telltale backlights remove any doubts. Immediately I start my engine, turn on the lights and follow. A small hill going up Eastbourne blocks our view momentarily, but they can only be a few hundred yards in front of us.

91

"Hurry up, Kylie is a race car driver," Greg sputters, his voice hoarse from excitement. My few Hyundai horse-powers can't make it up the hill quickly enough. On top we don't see them until we get to the next crossing. Turned to the left, Kylie is standing more or less on the corner with her foot on the brake pedal. Is she stopped in front of a door? Is she waiting for a parking spot? Or did the sorcerers see us and are waiting to catch us in the act? Only half a second to make a decision. Spontaneously I continue to drive straight, as if we had no interest in them. Then I circle back to the corner of Pandora and Eastbourne. Kylie's car is gone.

Again they have eluded us. Maybe the sorcerers do have a superior sense of awareness and surround themselves with an impenetrable wall, the yellow fog from his books. Carlos does not want to be a celebrity haunted by reporters. He is not listed in the phone book. Nowadays contact is only possible through his company that operates through a post office box. Obviously they don't want to get overrun by wannabe sorcerer's apprentices.

Kylie could have parked her car out of sight in one of the underground parking structures. Frustrated we wander along the street. Eastbourne between Thayer and Beverly Glen consists on both sides of apartment buildings several stories high. In the lit entryways of the houses we search for familiar sounding names. Most of the names on the signs seem to be of Middle Eastern origin. No Spanish ones behind which the sorcerers would hide. Somehow I cannot picture Carlos living in an apartment building. In the covered parking areas visible from the outside we cannot detect any familiar cars either.

Pandora Avenue runs north south crossing Eastbourne. There are single-family houses with pretty front yards planted under a thick canopy of magnolias and Chinese elm trees. On the corner of Pandora and Eastbourne, where Kylie stopped for a moment, sits an older Spanish style building complex with several one story apartments surrounded by big conifers and an unusual, well-trimmed hedge taller then a basketball player. A rusty colored metal garden gate in the hedge opening on Pandora gapes a foot wide, opening to the inside.

Greg snoops into the front yard. I whisper to him to get out of there. "This is certainly not the sorcerer's house. Carlos can afford a better place. Do you believe he, the elusive recluse, does not have a burglar alarm and no motion detector lights on the outside like most of the houses in this neighborhood?"

Greg mumbles something about Pandora's Box. For today it is enough. They are close, I can feel them. As the musty odor of the leaves on the ground betrays the presence of the mushrooms, I can smell the sorcerers.

One week later. Again it is Saturday night. We leave the car and slowly stroll along the sidewalk of Eastbourne Avenue. The anticipation makes us giddy especially Greg. The street is empty. With every passing car our expectation jumps higher. This time it will work! Or it is over for good!

The night falls in dark-blue. The lights in the apartments bloom brighter. Music blares from somewhere. A soft evening breeze rustles through the leaves. I play nervously with the fragrant blossoms of the star jasmine. Occasionally I check my watch.

Fifteen past eight. Almost in disbelief, my eyes fasten on the blue-black car with the familiar row of brake lights that passes us in a precision of habit I didn't dare possible. If they would have stopped somewhere for an errand, or if they would have taken another route, or if Carlos would have wanted to see a movie or go to a restaurant, everything would have been over. It would have been the omen for me to stop; the wink of destiny to end our hunt gracefully. But now she is driving past as if being served to us on a platter.

For a few seconds the surprise jumbles my limbs into disarray. Once they collect themselves we run hastily behind the car to the corner of Pandora. Here we come to a sudden stop. Past the banana bushes, in the blue dusting of the approaching night hovers the feverish glow of Kylie's double-parked brake lights.

In the pink glimmer the car door opens and the small figure of Carlos' emerges. Slightly hunched forward he walks the few steps to the gate and disappears with a hasty gesture of good-bye into the gap of the tall dark hedge. The clicking sound of the closing door, after

Kylie has driven off north on Pandora, accentuates the final goal of our chase. Greg was right.

I can't believe it. My mind keeps rewinding the ordinary display of the slender lonely figure exuding a slight vulnerability as he walks through the hedge into the house. The secrecy enshrouded home of the master sorcerer lies exposed in strange blackness in front of us. Behind the hedge that divides light drops like a lace curtain, grows the magical compound, quiet, modest, unobtrusive, and imperceptible. Like Pandora's Box, it guards its contents with eyes hidden behind a veil of inconspicuousness.

Somehow I can't comprehend it. On this seemingly ordinary level, without exceptional talents and abilities, we found the house of the sorcerer, the one who sees more then the majority of humans that live in total unawareness.

Obviously it can't be the result of our meager talents. It is a present we graciously accept. It is the validation of my inner pull.

Chapter Six

In The Bowels Of The Twin World

Don't call asking what the object of the game is.
Finding that out is the object of the game.

-News reporter in *The Game,* 1997

Astronomers say the universe is so big that one has to know what to look for in order to find it in the vastness. The desires I hurled into space unraveled the chain of events that is propelling me down the rapids. Is my longing connected to the immense power out there, that he calls Intent, leading me closer and allowing me this visceral view from the periphery, opposed to the self-absorbed abandonment in the center of his group?

I will keep the wonder about this tacit endorsement untouched like freshly fallen snow or like a just windexed pane of glass on a crisp spring day. It is a delicate arrangement. It nudges me, rides on my shoulder, tugs at my heart, takes me hostage and pulls at my stomach. I don't stop to ponder where it will take me. I'm a nomad in the no-man's-land between reality and imagination, the place of transition where from the first wispy strands of thought manifest the ethereal beginnings of its physical twin. This shifting point of birth fascinates me.

The longing to watch Carlos teaching his chosen companions cavorts in the recesses of my mind through unexplored pathways. Not motivated primarily by the speck of private satisfaction of being able to execute the new movements in the next seminar as if I had dreamt them, but to come one millimeter closer to understanding the riddle by watching him long enough, by imprinting the fleeting image of his being. In the sorcerer's gestalt appears to be another silent voice calling me, reminding me of something long lost. The secret. And he holds the key.

Dance Home on the second floor looks from a long row of windows across the abyss of the alley to a brick building that is supported by the crutches of a rusty fire escape winding like a skeleton to the third floor. We speculate that the large hallway windows function as access to this precarious emergency exit.

"From those windows one would have a perfect view into the studio on the other side", we imagine. A little risky, considering the grandiose lighting in the hallway and the close proximity to the dance studio windows. Like water searching for a way to the ocean my mind runs through the three-dimensional blueprint of the buildings for an opening. "Let's see how far we'll get!"

In the already familiar underground parking garage that serves the offices and restaurants on the boulevard we pass through a metal door that leads to an Eiffelesque steel staircase on which our soft rubber soles scrape in mute compliance. In this gray din of murky filtered light, of hushed traffic noise accentuating the hollow clinking of my metal wristwatch against the rail and the breath robbing musty smell of trapped air, it occurs to me that we left the ordinary world of busy pleasure seeking people behind, that we are now traversing the cavernous bowels of the mysterious world of the sorcerers. There are no rules in this world that recreates itself each second anew.

Following my unfailing sense of direction, we head left where I deem the brick building. A gray locked fire door blocks our way. "Maybe a level higher," I whisper. On the next floor the door is open and we quietly enter the hallway. Even the inner chatter slows. Forest green carpet swallows our steps; only Greg's sandals squeak. No sound breathes behind the office doors. Nobody works overtime. At the end of the hallway awaits the promised window, beckoning us like a big screen TV. Carefully I close in on the dusty pane covered by a film of rain patterns. With only one eye I dare to squint around the frame.

Dangerously close and only minimally obscured by the crisscross of the fire escape, the row of green-framed studio windows appears to be no more than two feet away. In the brightly lit opposite rectangles I see the participants of the private class in full view now and between them Carlos, a gesticulating figure walking back and forth in pantomimic monologue. Discernable are the backs of the students in the last row, the mirror reflection of the faces from the first row, and Carlos turning towards them offering us mostly his back. With weak knees I realize that the people in the studio could see me just as clearly, a silhouette in the lit-up hallway, a head with binoculars growing out of the window frame.

Once in a while roaring laughter blows across the alley. Otherwise the spectacle in the studio evokes the silent movie days with its half tones and wordless action accompanied by a piano player. From our vantage point the street sounds, the hissing brakes of public buses, the steady flow of swooshing cars and honking horns, the clatter of dishes in the Chinese restaurant's kitchen below us and the drifting voices of sidewalk traffic play the background music.

The whirlpool of their shared cheerfulness tugs wistfully at my insides. With all my imagining faculties I am over there, on the other side of the alley, bathing in the light of the room and his high voice. It is the peephole of strained attention, my longing that dissects the movements, adding the stored knowledge of gestures, stories and grimaces that transports me into the room on the other side.

A mountain lion in British Columbia kills a woman who was trying to protect her son during a horseback trip.

At first glance the city has only two obvious seasons, the one when you can see the snowcaps of the San Gabriel Mountains in the distance behind the high rises, alternating with the season of smog that hides all reference points of a natural setting. But standing still, watching the same frame over long periods of time, you notice more.

Every year the jacaranda season washes over Westwood Village, the month when the blue blossoms fall from the sky under the trees, inundating the grass carpet as if a painter slopped blue-purple over the sidewalks, neighborhood streets and lawns.

Greg and I are sitting in the car on Pandora, a few houses north from the sorcerer's place. Punctually at six Carlos strides with liquid grace through the gate in the hedge. Behind the row of parked cars only the top of his head sticks out, a fuzzy mop in the binoculars.

He climbs into Kylie's waiting car. After a quick u-turn Kylie speeds down the hill to Santa Monica Boulevard. Taisha and Florinda's heads bob in the backseat like balloons. They have all gone to the practice at Dance Home.

This time we will not follow them. The witches' house, so seemingly ordinary on the corner, lies dormant behind the wall of green in the subtle hues of sunset. The perfect opportunity to look at the place from up close.

On the Pandora side the lot begins with a cemented driveway and a thin hedge of yellow hibiscus that separates the property from the neighbor's. The painted wooden gate on the driveway offers no cracks, no view into the backyard patio that is surrounded by a stonewall reaching past our heads. The evergreen hedge, at places ten feet tall and squarely trimmed, borders the street. We stick our noses into the front yard. The garden gate is open.

In front of three maroon doors that Carlos uses as his entrance, grows a thickly trunked tree with an unusual bulging root lump. Next to this monstrosity lies a rolled up garden hose. The faded vanilla yellow stucco of the house walls could use a new coat, as do the brown wooden frames of the windows that are covered by fly screens and iron bars.

A gravel path leads along the green hedge dabbled by quarter-sized peeking holes. In the corner tower two cedars that dangle their blackish green-covered arms like giants in the evening breeze high over the street lamps. Their roots are methodically circled with smooth fist-sized river rocks. Somebody labored with love over this. Behind the hedge wall breathes a protective silence. Under the cedars rest two abandoned composting bins.

On the right side, past the steps to the entry grow dwarf fruit trees, Kumquat, Apple, Peach, Tangerine, beneath them someone placed an open Have-a-Heart trap armed with bait. Rosemary climbs on a trellis around the window, hiding a living room, kitchen and bathroom. A flat roof covered with brown tar shingles gables low over the structure. Everywhere I see the caring touch of its inhabitants offset by an overall tarnish of wear and neglect left behind from the Seventies.

The Eastbourne side of the corner property has another garden gate and a second entry door. Do the witches live on this side of the house? The hedge is slightly lower here. A big lemon tree planted next to the house wall must provide cooling shade on hot days. Echinacea and aloe plants grow here. Next to several concrete steps that lead to a hallway between the main building and a separate garage, a luxuriant fig tree resides. Above the garage there seems to be another living space with two open windows. The property ends with a small cactus planting that Greg amusingly calls the "Sonoran Desert".

The whole complex, a square on the corner of Pandora and Eastbourne, possibly consists of several connected apartments with a secluded backyard. The people living in the four-story building next door have a direct view from their balcony into the backyard of the sorcerers. "We should befriend the neighbors," Greg jokes.

One can assume with some certainty that Carlos, Florinda and Taisha live more or less on a regular basis in this house. A check-up with public records confirms the last title change as of 1973.

The punctuality and antithetical regularity of the sorcerer's schedule becomes our unexpected advantage. Similar to knowing where to find the deer grazing in the morning, or the prowling coyotes at night, his routine makes it easy for us to catch him leaving his house, watch his arrival at the studio or see him return home.

The neck straining with binoculars in the office hallway unfortunately is only tolerable for a few minutes at a time, and then the fear of discovery shakes my limbs. No, I'm not playing with the subconscious desire to get caught. I'm not secretly pining for acknowledgement. The view from the other side is too direct and the lights in the hallway of the office building cannot be toned down. Two rows of neon lights along the ceiling brighten the narrow space like daylight. An added disadvantage is the glaring white walls.

"If one could meld into the background like a chameleon!" I'm thinking. "Or disappear under a cloak of invisibility." Suddenly a solution presents itself in my mind. The astronomers are right.

The image of a white figure in front of the white wall in the hallway takes form. She could stand for hours in plain view and go unnoticed by the students that concentrate on Carlos' instructions. All I need is a white sheet with two prepared eye-sized holes.

The sheet rolled up in a shoulder bag we trek as usual through the empty labyrinth of staircases and reach the hallway window that seems to be a little more transparent after our last cleaning attempts. The class in the studio is in full swing. Shadows flailing arms, light puddles with earnest attentive faces, Carlos weaving back and forth.

In the corner out of sight I pull the sheet over me and adjust the eye openings. Then I creep slowly, step by step along the white wall. Quick movements attract attention; gradual changes go unnoticed by most people. Standing upright close to the wall in front of the window, the studio in direct view, slightly dissected by the metal rafters I can now theoretically watch comfortably for hours with my binoculars.

Greg interprets my genial disguise as a joke. Or does he suddenly realize the advantage it offers? I feel his body close behind me, and then the hard metal of his binoculars on my head. Too fascinated by the tremendously clear picture in front of me I shirk my irritation about his hindsight adaptation and don't rag on him for not bringing a disguise of his own. Things are heating up under the cloth multiplying body temperatures and trapping my steaming breath. Or is it Greg's proximity?

As children we stayed under the bedcovers until the sweat dripped from our faces and we almost fainted from oxygen deprivation. That substituted as heating in the frosty bedroom. The warmth under my sheet is getting unbearable. I don't know how long I have been standing there suffocating. Every sense of time is melting away. Suddenly a view from the outside of my dress up pops into my mind.

Seen from the dance studio, in the brightly-lid window of the hallway hovers a ghostly apparition with black eye caverns that has a second pair of insect eyes growing out of its head. That image lets me laugh out loud. Bowled over I drag myself into the background of the hallway.

It seems without effort and planning that Greg and I spend every Saturday afternoon now in front of the witches' house in the shade of the magnolias that drop their waxen blossoms like giant tired tears. Maybe without this sounding body, this extra pair of eyes I would have given up by now. Just as I, he can see the irony of the whole project: us lingering around the periphery with the zealousness of innocent amateurs hooked by a pact with the unspoken, the magical, while the sorcerer figures play their game of shadow puppetry without noticing us.

Greg's playful indiscriminate humor makes me burp with laughter as much as his impulsiveness irritates me at times like worn out Velcro. The space we occupy together is growing in the endless hours of squinting. I roam the borders hunting for the thread; he delves in practicality.

Greg cannot sit in the car without snacks. His stomach is trained to get hungry while sitting in traffic. He packs strong handled paper bags from Trader Joe's with his favorite finger foods. His apple-cookie-potato chip crunching is a welcome respite from the trickle of the usual inane exchanges between us.

Resembling a comical movie surveillance scene the dashboard becomes the serving tray, which we use to dunk the mini pretzels into the mustard lid turned dipping dish. Unlike agents in movies we occasionally need to visit the restrooms at McDonald's around the corner. Often times a portion of fries follow us to the car. This bridges the long intermissions of stillness in the empty glare of the open sun.

The neighbors don't seem to notice us. Neither do the visitors of the corner house we regularly train our binoculars on. Sometimes I wonder about that. Does Carlos' energy on a certain level agree with our closeness? Maybe without his conscious knowledge? I can't explain the course of events otherwise.

101

Nevertheless we keep the distance that is condoned by spirit. Close enough to see details and personal habits but without influencing their daily lives.

Illuminated by the afternoon sun, reflected in the windshields of the row of parked cars, the Saturday rolls off with timed regularity. Around one o'clock Kylie or Tracy bring take-out from a restaurant or home cooked food to the house and deliver it to Florinda, who is already waiting behind the hedge at the Pandora gate alerted by her cell phone. The mailman makes his round from house to house, but consistently has no deliveries for Carlos. Obviously he also uses a post office box.

After that it gets quiet. During the occasional brief walk-by, we dare not run into one of the inhabitants, Carlos' high voice in Spanish and music pieces seep through the hedge. Shortly before six Kylie drives up in her Toyota All-Trac, parks on the Pandora side in front of the gate and waits in the car.

Exactly at six, with the punctuality rivaling the Munich Glockenspiel on top of city hall, the hedge spits out Carlos with Taisha and Florinda in tow. Kylie, the champion of creative u-turns, makes it to Dance Home within ten minutes. All students are already waiting politely. Most of the time the class goes until eight. After that Kylie drives him back home. We have never waited until the lights go out.

Clinton is reelected for a second term as President.

In the garden I found a rattlesnake. In all the years of roaming the back trails and off trails of the Santa Monica Mountains I have met very few rattlesnakes. Not more then one per year. She lay curled up like a garden hose under pressure on the bare dirt. Her gray-brown diamond markings were subtle, not at all terrifying. She was a young one; about three years old as the rings on the rattle gave away after I poked her softly with a stick.

For a while I hesitated, after all I'm still on the side of the wild, but then the image of stepping on the snake one day inadvertently with sandals helped me decide to catch her. Young rattlers are supposedly more dangerous and aggressive. She only lay there taking a nap and warming herself in the morning sun. Before she realized what was happening to her, I shoveled her into a plastic bucket with lid.

Nowadays, the firemen kill rattlesnakes if they are called for removal. I did not want to kill her. So I brought her far into the park. When I let her out of the bucket she was not stressed out, but instead crawled slowly, tongue tasting from the bucket as if she had adopted the plastic container as her new home. I don't imagine she eyeballed me to thank me, but her hesitating slowness prompted me to encourage her with words. After that she slithered easily into the dry branches whose colors she wore.

On a dark evening in Westwood, after watching the group of apprentices depart for Dance Home, Greg and I stroll along the alley behind Sisterhood bookstore where I first met Florinda years ago. Here live the blue scout and a few of the other trackers. We make one last circle around the block before we take a break at Lucy's Chinese restaurant next to Dance Home altering our routine.

Steeped in whispering thoughts with glances plumbing the night shadows out of nowhere a female figure crosses our path just a few yards in front of us. She looks quite familiar in shape, color and movement. I stare after her wondering.

"That woman, doesn't she look like Carol to you?"

She staggers, almost faltering as if she is very tired or intoxicated. "This cannot be the Nagual woman! Impossible! She is supposed to be at Dance Home practicing".

The shadow woman stumbles further on the sidewalk of Rochester Avenue. Transfixed, I gape after her. "If she takes the steps up to the apartment complex on the right side where the young trackers live, it has to be her" we murmur. In front of the ivy covered yard she turns abruptly and climbs the steep concrete stairs to the apartments.

We run like suddenly released wind-up toys to the other side of Rochester to see what apartment she will enter. The mystery woman opens the first door on the left and disappears inside the building without switching on any lights. Medicated, drugged, drunk?

The question, if it really was the Nagual woman, who alone, drunk or under the influence of drugs struggled up the steps, keeps rummaging through our minds. Does she have a double life besides the loyal participation in the classes? Can they really be in two places at the same time? Or does she have a twin? Or did our eyes play tricks on us! A mysterious piece of the puzzle. One would have to see her in decent lighting and in undeniable company to ensure her identity.

A focused attempt at solving this riddle finds us one week later standing in a dark space between the apartment buildings. Shortly after eight the small group of four women, Carol and trackers, return from movement practice to the well-lit patio through a narrow walkway from the alley where they park their vehicles.

We wait in the shadows immobile like the stiff bushes until they pass us. Our eyes glued to their backs follow the procession to the last apartments of the complex. The women stop in front of two doors lying opposite of each other. Carol is the only one entering the left apartment door, the same one the staggering woman went in a week ago. This confirms her as the tenant but it does not explain her strange behavior.

Weekend seminar in Pasadena. Carlos does not leave the Los Angeles area anymore, he declares after getting sick during the last workshop in Oakland. He surely belongs to the dreamtime of Los Angeles, the fabric of creation, where stories and images, brilliant as Inca gold, are woven and unraveled in one night. Here is the seedbed for his flight into infinity.

Here he will not deny his funny lectures to the crowd of hungry loners. The mass he despised not long ago, now supports him, is good for him. So he tells us. Perhaps it is nothing more than a compliment aimed at taking advantage of accumulated hopes and dreams! I still think there are other reasons. Or has the mass supplanted the need for the electric warrior? The mass in the large seminars props him up in the exploration of the twin world.

Sometimes I feel as if I am living in a double world myself. Next to the mundane everyday is the heightened sphere of the seminars and practice groups and then there is the riveting secret world in which I track his energy. Or am I stalking myself?

Rumors are circling that Carlos' adopted son C.J. has come to the seminar to show him the manuscript his mother wrote that describes her marriage to Carlos. He gets turned away by Cleargreen' employees. Their cautionary measures are increasing. Upon entering the hall we are frisked for weapons and metal objects, airport style. Our bags are ransacked for cameras and tape recorders. Their distrust seems to be growing with each seminar. What are they afraid of? Until now, we have seen no sign of threat.

Does it irritate me because I secretly follow him? My knowledge poses no real threat. Under no circumstances would I give away the location of Carlos' house. I can restrain my bragging impulses. And in the seminar I am no more then a drop in the sea of participants. But I still wonder if none of the other eight hundred or so workshop attendees feel provoked by their paranoid behavior.

During the evening lectures, the entourage admires him from the front rows as always sweet smelling and dressed nattily. He is without a doubt the main attraction. In a cool anthracite Armani suit, one must always wear ones best in the case of sudden energy transformation, he gesticulates with the charm of his Latin heritage. The combination of challenge and tender knocking bundles my attention as well. We love him on stage. His sweet and putrid words of inner freedom from societal and physical restrictions awaken endless escapist dreams of other realities.

I told him once in person that I loved him. He shrugged my words off his shoulders like dandruff. He did not take me seriously. According to him we are not capable of real love. What we call love is merely a bartering for favors. We are only on the take. The sorcerer gives a blank check of affection without expecting a return. Does the disappointment over failed relationships lie behind his theory? Don't the witches love him, as he sometimes teases them in public? In spite of his gloomy judgment I feel the ability to love with abandon within myself. The relationship to my daughter is proof of that.

What I meant and was not able to express clearly to him, is that I love the example he provides for me, the direction he points to, and the hope that once and for all I will solve the riddle of life.

Carol's talk on stage sends my mind roaming. As always, I have difficulties following her disconnected thought patterns. Then rather surprisingly one of her sentences penetrates my thicket as clearly as if spoken to me alone.

A WOMAN IN WHITE IS FOLLOWING CARLOS! They don't know what the apparition wants. He forbade the group to look into the mirrors at Dance Home because this is where she appears. This energy being has attached itself to Carlos. A strange smell resembling watercress surrounds her. My eyes furtively search for Greg, who is sitting a few rows in front of me. His simultaneous look is heavy with meaning. It conveys the same explanation that is forming in my shaken mind. They are talking about us!

Any moment, I sweat, fingers will be pointing at us exposing us for what we did. I crawl into the hard plastic of my seat. The 'woman in white in the mirror' is me with the sheet. The similarities are too striking.

For some time now I have a strange smell surrounding me, something unidentifiable, not related to dirty clothing, bad body hygiene or ethnic cuisine. In my opinion it does not smell like watercress, but rather musty. Even Greg can smell it. Somehow Carlos must have felt us, except he has come to the wrong conclusion.

Or could it be that my longing, my concentrated focus, has collected itself into an ethereal figure that visits Carlos even at his home at night? Has something else grown between us, a third element in the equation? Has our intense observation caused the appearance of this phantom? Could it be that the invisible I am reaching for is reaching back at me?

Noninterference! Our Star-trek directive of noninterference has been breached on an energetic level not anticipated. I'm only millimeters away from the decision to confess. Do they want us to surrender on our own? Would he understand the phenomena and appreciate it or will they banish us like lepers? No sign comes. No knowing glances into our direction, no inviting opportunity. And the cup passes.

Maybe it was a shake-up to heighten our awareness, to sharpen our inner eyes, to take note of the web of energetic connections growing between the sorcerers and us.

The princess of my story who searches for the secret of life, refusing to drink the water of death, arrived now tired, hungry and thirsty at the foot of a tall mountain that blocked her path. She complained, "Oh you steep mountain, don't make my road so difficult. I'm thirsty. I'm looking for water."

"What," the mountain replied, "did you not see the water in the river?" Oh, yes," she answered, "but I only want the water of life." This made the mountain very angry. He started to rumble loudly, his whole body rattled and shook. Then his head exploded and flew off into the air and he threw rocks and hot breath at the princess. She turned around in fright and ran off head over heels, as fast as her legs could carry her.

Until she sank into the grass completely depleted of strength. Again she heard the murmur of the river. "I'm the water of life and the water of death. I'm the beginning and the end". Exhausted she looked at the water flowing by in endless motion.

What am I looking for? The unified field theory? The secret. Theirs, mine, the secret of life, the secret of the universe. Or just a way back home.

Maybe it is only the search, the adventure that captivates me, the hopeful anticipation of finding something precious? The hunt, the process of searching rivets me on a deep level, a level onto which I train the muscles for a still unknown function. The energy body? He says that our energy body is miles away from us.

I feel as if I could almost touch this other body in the search for answers, and in the activity of secret observations that serve no practical purpose in my daily life, similar to don Juan's not-doings. For easily excitable Greg it might be primarily entertainment. If he has a motivation beyond the quarrying of the moment for every ounce of its comical value, it escapes me. For me it is more. I find distraction in nature, in a neon green kayak on the waves of the ocean.

The concentrated force in my navel area reaches with energy antennas into the playroom of the invisible.

Chapter Seven

Digging For Bones

"I say, we get a look over in those garbage cans".
"Well, call me overly cautious, but don't you think that's a bit
suspicious. The three of us going through their garbage at
eleven at night in the middle of a rainstorm!"
-Art and Ray in The Burbs, 1989

On the mountains in the distance behind the phalluses of downtown Los Angeles shimmers the virgin white of freshly fallen snow. The neighborhood around Pandora, the square hedge, the tree shadow voices, the front yards of bobbing blossoms, every inch of this place feels familiar, touched and listened to like the inside of trouser pockets or the fillings in my mouth.

On a Saturday afternoon sitting in the car at the crossroads of Pandora and Eastbourne, next to the fire hydrant and a red curb, packed with provisions and binoculars, bundled in inner silence and outer chit-chat, when I almost fear that we have slipped into a bland routine conjuring questions of doubtful justifications, a new door opens up, unexpectedly.

Taisha appears from the hedge with a plastic bag, walks along Pandora, and crosses Eastbourne in front of us with her head lowered to the cemented sidewalk. Instinctively we duck. The plastic bag hangs heavy in her hand. What is she carrying away from the house and on foot, no less?

A sudden surge of curiosity propels me from my seat. Now Taisha is turning left into the alley that runs parallel to Santa Monica Boulevard. Uttering, "I have to know where she is going," I leap from the car.

On soft running shoes I am in no time at the corner of the alley and espy Taisha next to the big orange dumpster of the grocery store. With a deliberate force she throws her plastic bag in it. Then she returns the same way she came.

Greg remains in the car. Stunned we watch Taisha passing by and the questions mount on my dashboard. What did she have to throw into the trash so far from the house?

Luckily for us, her discarded bag still lies on top of the garbage. Our quick examination produces raw red meat cubes, old, not stinking yet, probably just thawed. Looks like they emptied out their freezer and didn't want to throw the meat into their own garbage can to let it rot until the day of collection. The tossed meat itself is no startling revelation, but suddenly a new sphere rises on the horizon on which threshold we find ourselves without preparation. The question, "what do the sorcerers throw into THEIR TRASHCANS" opens up another level.

A new dimension appears, an uncharted landscape waiting to unfold in front of me. And it promises a panorama of unending possibilities that will lead me into the inner workings, the bowels, the digested, the discarded world of excrements that gives insight, like the mittens of refuse at Wupatki provided archaeologists a picture of the culture of the Sinaguas.

With those details a scientist pieces together the diorama of a culture. Not only will the scrapped materials assure me of a more complete picture of the sorcerers' lives that admittedly will still be fragmental, yet to a certain degree reliable in the systematic evaluation, it might also give us access to their plans for the future.

There it is again. A new card dealt to us by the game. It is not over, not stagnating. As long as this invisible energy net draws us closer, I will follow its direction. When the game becomes stale, it will be the sign of the end.

Tuesday evenings the inhabitants of Westwood Village put their trashcans out on the street. After ten o'clock Pandora Avenue is quiet. Like pedestrians walking an imaginary dog, we stroll along the familiar streets talking in soft voices, the car parked around the corner. Motion detector lights and sprinkler systems wetting the sidewalk are the only moving life in the swath of late night news time.

In front of Carlos' hedge is a line-up of four big black trashcans and one green container for yard clippings. China clatters in the lit-up kitchen. No familiar cars of visitors who could surprise us are parked in front. The sidewalks and the streets are empty. The occasional car lurching through the neighborhood night does not make us shiver dressed in expedition polar tech.

On our second pass we diverge from the path and cross the grass strip to the edge of the street. Listening for the sound of voices, moving shadows and car motors or the telltale cones of headlights we lift the trashcan lids. Like two homeless people looking for recycling goods we grab a selection of different sized bags.

If they throw another bag into the containers over night are they going to question the strangely half-empty trashcans?

Loaded with bags like my mother after shopping in the city we slip with our anti-consumer goods into the safe shadow of the canopy on the other side of the street. Any moment I fear the wrath of the enraged sorcerers spilling from the hedge opening. A slapping hand on my back, a kick into my calves, a knuckle on my head. Nonchalance or experience, no determination pushes me on. Nothing happens as we quickly round the corner through the gulf of livid light to my waiting car.

After a short drive the car begins to stink unbearably. We race home with open windows, hurrying to keep up with our decomposing spoils. The retched smelling treasure would be hard to explain to a traffic cop.

Full of anticipation we dump one rescued bag after the other onto the plastic cover we hastily spread over the floor. What are we hoping to find? What are we looking for? Anything unusual and ordinary.

Secret messages, the inner mechanics, the true attitude of the sorcerers, an accurate picture of their lives, miniscule clues of the extraordinary that can only be detected by looking closely. What else? On our knees we sort through the portion of household trash.

One thing is immediately obvious: the sorcerers don't recycle. Plastic Pepsi bottles, glass vodka bottles, paper and kitchen garbage is clumped together in an unconscious mix. When one is preparing to leave soon for infinity, does one not need to worry about the degradation of the environment on this planet anymore?

Between chicken bones, eggshells, tomatoes and advertisements stick envelopes addressed to Anne Marie Carter at a post office box in Beverly Hills. Yes, that was a name Taisha Abelar mentioned at a seminar as one of her stalking identities. Apple peels, tomatoes, grocery receipts from Gelson's drenched in barbecue sauce. The sorcerers seem to stick to a hunter and gatherer diet, primarily meat.

A bathroom bag contains Q-tips and Light-Days sanitary pads, and small bundles carefully wrapped in paper towels. Greg does not hesitate to dig around in this undeniably female bag and unfolds one of the packages. He reveals a nest of cut mousy gray hair. The other bundles contain hair in different colors as well. This must have been a grandiose hair cutting session at Carlos' house. He snipped each woman's hair and conscientiously swept up the clippings, collecting them into clean heaps without mixing it with the hair of the next person.

We muse from which heads the hair bundles might originate. Kylie and Florinda are candidates for the golden blond. Gray-blond could be the blue scout's; a blend of dark and gray could be Talia's; the medium brown and gray points to Carol and the mousy gray mound to Taisha.

To summarize our findings we can confirm that the sorcerers are meat eaters, they don't bother to recycle, some of them still menstruate and that they save on the expense of going to a beauty shop by cutting each others hair. In the end nothing is left of our hoard but a few scraps of paper and the hair bundles. Uninteresting advertisements disappear into our hungry stove, plastic and glass ends up in the recycling can.

FILMING CASTANEDA

Only then I notice a manila envelope addressed to Toltec Artists. Wasn't that the company Kylie worked for years ago? Their offices used to be in West Hollywood. The location on this envelope is on Santa Monica Boulevard in West Los Angeles. Could it be that Cleargreen is in the same building? Not far from the post office box they are using?

Now I remember an aborted car chase on New Year's Eve when we followed the group packed into Tamalia's Ford to a spot on Santa Monica Boulevard. When Tamalia turned left unexpectedly, and we did the same one street further down, we lost their vehicle amidst the valet-parked cars of people celebrating at the restaurant. We could not see Tamalia's car anywhere. We assumed they had gone to dinner at the restaurant since the neighborhood seemed otherwise to be an unlikely place for the sorcerers. Instead they must have gone to their office, as this envelope is revealing.

Nobody is in the building after business hours, situated on a lifeless strip of Santa Monica Boulevard. The ground level harbors a mediocre furniture store. The underground parking is accessible from the alley behind the structure. I follow the trail marked by intent to the hidden offices of Carlos' new company. As if any detail I might miss could be the decisive revealing piece of the puzzle!

Using a crammed little elevator that rattles slowly up to the third floor Greg and I end up in a mint-green hallway. The creamy white plastic lettering of the register on this floor unabashedly displays Cleargreen's name. The hallway in its murky greenish tint takes on the dreamlike quality of a futuristic mystery movie.

As often as we unsuccessfully bumble blindly through a labyrinth, following threads presented to us, once in a while we end up at a door. This door of shiny-brushed steel more polished than a kitchen sink, looks strong enough for a bank vault. A small vertical window next to it made from darkened glass with wire reinforcement does not offer any view into the rooms inside.

In contrast to Carlos' house we can assume that this place has a burglar alarm. Like a fortified castle it conceals the interior. None of the other office doors in this building are as substantial. What do they

113

have to guard so heavily? From whom do they have to protect themselves? "From people like us," Greg notes sarcastically.

On the roof terrace that surrounds the top office from all sides, we are able to peek through small cracks in the blinds of the windows. We notice the usual office stuff, computers, desks and paper stacks. The movement posters confirm to us that they operate their business from here. But other than adding to our knowledge of the sorcerer's web, their offices seem to be a dead-end. On our way down the outside staircase we come upon the big trash dumpster in the alley. And here we realize the continuation of the thread. The container reveals itself as an easily accessible source fed by a constant stream of carelessly deposited trash. The Matt Drudge syndrome is spreading.

At night, usually after ten o'clock, when we pick up the trash, slipping from the orange golden ponds of the streetlights into the shadow of the magnolias, I believe to see his tail dancing across the concrete sidewalk like a shadowy branch whipping in the wind. There are moments when the mirrors on the cars parked on Pandora reflect the sheen of his pupils, and I anticipate the smooth curvature of his velveteen purple back gliding over the front lawns. My black cat has become the jaguar. From the cat universe and the Baboquivari Mountains he prowls through his new range in Westwood Village.

Did I bring him here? He comes and goes as he pleases. He does not need my permission. The jaguar is circling the sorcerers of Westwood. When they are out practicing and the house is empty, he pushes his wide bristly neck like an evening shadow through the crack in the hedge. His heavy paws gently crunch on the gravel paths. His muscular shoulder edges the door to the interior patio open. Like a phantom, he slips over the brick walkways, snuffles at the metal frog figurines and peers into the open windows. Under the group of fruit trees in the darkest corner of the garden, next to the wooden gazebo and the cow-pie-sized quartz crystal, he waits for their return.

Patiently he watches the shadowy figures in the lit up windows until the lights turn off. The white datura blossoms shimmer iridescent in the moonless night. In the darkness he breathes in what the sorcerers breathe out. He guards their sleep. Do they know he is so close to them? Early in the morning with the downy shadows of the fleeing night he noiselessly leaves the patio. Where he stays during the day I'm not sure. Maybe he lounges in the tangled branches of the cedars in the front yard.

In all the months of secret observing Greg and I have not come across another person that follows the master discreetly. Someone like us would immediately attract our attention. Contrary to the sorcerers, we change our approach pattern often, vary the observation position and witness any change in the surroundings. Only once I notice a guy loitering in front of Dance Home, a familiar face from the seminars. Kylie intercepts him; everybody else, including Carlos, is already in the dance studio.

The pantomimic scene plays out as the intruder asks for permission to enter the studio, is turned away by Kylie with a consoling brief hug and sent on his way, disappointed, with slumping shoulders around the corner. Kylie watches for a few more seconds shooting her disapproving glower after him.

Out of view behind Pep Boys the rejected apprentice amuses us with an exaggerated effort of the decision-making passes we learned recently. He looks like an escaped mental patient. What nerve to show up uninvited expecting to be taken in! I wouldn't dare to make such an approach. I know too well that the sorcerers have to be prompted by inexplicable random omens or their own hunt.

Once the Carlos' fan leaves we visit the window in the office hallway again for a short taste. The thick carpet swallows our muffled sounds, no words pass between us. Everything is familiar. Only on the wooden staircase connecting the third and fourth floor I hear creaking. Already poised to turn and flee, the door opens and to our surprise the face of the guy from the street pops out. He also discovered the hallway! For one moment he hesitates, snared in the sudden confrontation. We stare silently at each other.

This could become a sticky situation if he tells on us. Or if he would want to join our sortie! The thought flashes through my mind. Then it occurs to me that he reacts as if we caught him in the act. Possibly he thinks we are a Carlos' patrol. I send him a sharp look just as he turns around to walk back down. For our own protection I don't want to alter his misinterpretation of our presence in this hallway. We don't see him again. Have we unintentionally become Carlos' outer guards?

To navigate the unknown one needs pedantic practicality, limitless sobriety and guts like steel, the sorcerers said. I want to add an iron nose. We are sailing through a new landscape spread out on the carpet in front of us, chasing the unknown in the indomitable garbage. Like the pariahs of homeless and poor in many countries of the world we have become accustomed to the sticky smell on our shoes after hopping into the dumpster, learned to identify bags with promising content quickly, and lost almost all repulsion. This is the science of garbage information retrieval.

Over time we accumulate heaps of information, sorted by importance and meaning. We form separate stacks on individuals. Taisha's pile contains Anne Carter's graded UCLA Spanish exam from spring '97; a plumber's estimate for replacing the garbage disposal of the sink in Carlos' house; she must be managing the everyday problems of the household.

There are catalogues of specialty clothing like J.Peterman, Peruvian Connection, The Territory Ahead, fashionable but practical; possibly she does not buy anything from those catalogues. A letter from Teme, regretting the end of the Sunday classes. The class is still going, only they have excluded her. A customs form without date reporting the import of three candles as part of a business trip with Mexicana Airlines, as address she gave her post office box, as a birth date she wrote 8/25/1945. That would mean she has an official passport with her sorcerer name Taisha Abelar.

Flodo, how Florinda calls herself, has a more animated life. She shares the appetite for expensive clothing, or what I consider expensive. There are receipts from Neiman Marcus, Barney's N.Y., DKNY, Adrienne Vittadini, Anne Klein and Nordstrom's totaling over 3,000 dollars; a catalogue of Tiffany and Co. summer collection '97, empty blue velvet jewelry boxes from Tiffany and Co. Judging from the sizes they contained bracelets, rings and necklaces; skin tightening cream from Sothy's Paris; advertisements of 'how to fake the darkest tan'; hair dye; birthday cards from Aunt Suse and Aunt

Hanni from Germany, hoping that Regina, under which name she is known to her family, has completed the extensive dental work.

Calendars with dental appointments for Dr. Robert Weinstein; a Blue Cross insurance card from 1996; bank deposit receipts from City National bank; torn credit card checks; Josef Schmidt chocolate bar wrappers; Theodor Schober chocolate boxes (Florinda told the story of getting sick from chocolate over-consumption to the point of seeking medical help; at that time she also met Kylie who was giving her massages); a receipt for a California Drivers license number SO618520; car insurance for a Toyota Tercel '91; movie ticket stubs for Fool's Rush, Shine, Smilla's Sense of Snow, Father's Day, Nightfall, Lost World, Larry Flynt. Their choice in movies seems indiscriminate without obvious preferences. The many movie visits are nothing unusual for the majority of inhabitants of this movie town. But somehow I expected less worldly distraction from the sorcerers residing in the disciplined spiritual realm. My misconception.

Clothes, cut and torn to unusable shreds come from the garbage cans at the witches' house. A black Calvin Klein bikini top, black cashmere sweaters, good quality, Calvin Klein panties. Do they cut their dresses to prevent the accidental garbage collectors enriching themselves on the energy that is still clinging to the witches' clothes?

Sometimes unexplainably a whole still undestroyed piece slips in between. There is a black, slightly worn soft leather jacket, made in France, a short black silk dress with mother of pearl buttons by Anne Klein, creme and beige striped towels in good condition, two black stretchy pants by Armani Xchange, in my size! I don't have a habit of picking my wardrobe out of other people's trash, but with these special pieces I make an exception. My environmental conscience forbids me to waste perfectly good clothes.

Carlos' pile is smaller, his personal waste harder to identify. We wait for a seminar when all the witches have left the country. In such a week there is considerably less garbage in the cans at the Pandora house, with bags containing primarily chicken bones and eggshells.

Several notes with large lettered phone numbers point to the fact that Carlos can't read small print anymore. One time we find a pair of his famous sunglasses with a broken strap. Greg, the handyman, repairs them. A page torn from a notebook with the words Sao Paulo

Brazil, Dec. 25, 1931 in Carlos handwriting (could that be his real birth date?), a deposit slip with his City National bank account number, check copies with royalty payments, contract copies with his signature. A Profit and Loss statement for 1996 shows next to other miscellaneous income royalties of about $130,000 from his books. But his expenses were almost twice as high, including a $60,000 tax audit and $20,000 for rent.

A poignant letter from France written by a ten year old girl is asking Carlos if the stories in his books are true. Well, Esme - we all would like to know!

A note from "Annie" to "Joanie" for leaving her outside light on all night tips us off to another woman living at the compound with the name of Mary Joan Barker. She never participates in Cleargreen activities, seminars and classes. But she generates a copious amount of paper trash with a wide interest in local archeology and anthropology. We have only seen her once leaving the house for a walk.

Cleargreen's trash lies easily recognizable in see-through plastic bags with knotted ends on top of the heap in the container they share with the other tenants of the building on Santa Monica Boulevard. Greg stocks up on scotch tape. They can attempt to rip their papers in ever such small pieces; challenged to a contest we reassemble them again. Often, to my surprise, we find all pieces of a torn page.

In a focus typically reserved for life threatening situations we pedantically look over every piece of paper that like a puzzle might contribute a part to the total picture. With the meticulousness of archaeologists or paleontologists we pick through the collection of bags. I hunt for discrepancies, for traces of the realm of sorcery.

Greg wonders why he can't detect anything magical, like the cat-rabbit of Kylie's description. We just have to look closer, read between the lines, peek around the corner of the eyes, practice patience, perseverance and persistence. They don't eat their hamburger buns.

Before the establishment of the present corporation Carlos wanted to set up a nonprofit religious organization, the Chacmool Center for Enhanced Perception, the religion of Dreaming!

Tamalia's discarded complete list of phone numbers reveals all twenty-four members of the inner circle, sorted by importance, including Carlos' private numbers. Currently Cleargreen has fourteen permanent employees on their payroll, as well as fourteen shareholders. There is a cable TV bill for a residence on Manning Street. We wonder, who lives at this address? The street is not far from Carlos' house. A new thread to explore.

Often we find the standard reply of "Dr. Castaneda is currently out of the country" given to pesky people including journalists, which elicits from us a hooting, "Wrong! He sits in Westwood Village, we see him there all the time." What we don't find is also interesting. There is no indication of Carlos owning property in other places, for example Mexico. Other than Cleargreen's connection to Verde Claro the selection of trash shows no phone numbers, no correspondence with a witches' house in Mexico.

In a Toltec Artists' plastic bag stuck between movie-industry information inconsequential to us, we stumble upon a printout of Tracy's weekly schedule. On every day of the week a certain time is marked, including Saturday evening. We know where he is on Saturday evenings, practicing movements at Dance Home. Could this mean that Carlos teaches a class every day? There is no location given. But that is not difficult to check. By now we know all vehicles of the regulars. So even a quick drive-by at the marked time confirms the information on the schedule. I'm impressed by the fact that Carlos teaches a private class every day of the week.

Slowly an outline of the sorcerer's lives develops in front of my inner eye. Connected with the behaviors and gestures observed from the periphery and the interaction at the seminars, the details from the trash flesh out the texture and depth of a slice of their every day lives. Their dietary and hygienic habits, the status of their physical and financial health, their health care providers, the source of their clothing, their leisure time entertainment, their moods, individual peculiarities, practical living arrangements, their vehicles, ages, former names, relatives and social interaction between the members make up the facets of their total imagined lives.

On the surface it seems the sorcerers are ordinary people, doing ordinary things in an ordinary way. Reading "The Taylor of Panama", watching every other movie, drinking cappuccino, talking for hours on the phone, pedantically controlling their schedule, shopping for pleasure. Carlos determines the position of everyone within the group. He answers to no-one. And he is enjoying it utterly.

But where is his magic, the magic that imbues his words? There is no trace of it in his refuse. Is it only tangible on stage, in front of people? Do we, the audience, draw this magic out of him? Is our desire eliciting the miraculous from this otherwise inconspicuously living man?

Granted we only take a certain selection of trash and watch them primarily on Saturdays, many particular details may elude us. Nevertheless it is an outer skeleton, a visible scaffolding of the lives of the sorcerers that is growing spread out on the tarp on our floor.

In rare moments of satiated satisfaction, shared only between the two of us, Greg and I indulge in the fleeting relieve of comical scenarios.

"What, if we'd order an item from their catalogues for them?" "Oh yes, and pay by phone with THEIR credit card" - "And then have it delivered to their HOUSE by UPS! That would make them doubt their own mental faculties!" An imaginary poking with a stick into their anthill.

"Or what, if we called Carlos on his unlisted private number at home and whispered in a somber tone: Hi Carlos, this is don Juan. How are you?"

"A call from the netherworld. That would surely weird him out."

But of course these are only ruminations for our occasional entertainment. We are committed to non-interference and leaving the future to the thread that keeps unrolling in front of us. We never forget that we are not spying on normal people, not on the neighbor sitting on his balcony on the other side of Pandora reading his paper, not on the couple who meets at night secretly on Pandora, crawling into the darkened SUV for half an hour to then drive away in separate cars, or the newly arrived Armenian neighbors who fortify their house with bars on the windows and fences. All these details I catch inevitably as part of the net that surrounds the center, Pandora's Box.

Carlos is not a notoriously famous celebrity idolized blindly by the general public and trying to defend an image by hiding his private face. No, Carlos is a sorcerer, as he says, one that is twenty-four hours a day nothing but the same slippery non-human that disappears into a twin world. Is he not?

Chapter Eight

Back From Hell with Trophies

If only you could see what I have seen with your eyes.
-Roy Batty in *The Bladerunner,* 1988

My annoyance with myself multiplies as I realize that I've never held a video camera, let alone filmed pictures. Incredulous. And now is no time for practice. Under pressure my self-criticism gains overwhelming access.

The winter rains left a floral pattern splashed into the dust that clings to the window of the office hallway. Greg props the lower half open with a short piece of wood conveniently found lying there. A clear view at last! My colleague at work did not give me an instruction booklet for her video camera, only the advice not to change the automatic settings.

Switch the on-button! Does "on" mean at the same time "recording" or "pause, standby"? It's pathetic. I should have taken the time earlier to examine the equipment. A hint of fear that with too much preparation the sorcerers would be alerted of our intentions sidled around the periphery, wrapped in the quiet thought that the connection might run both ways.

Up until now the idea of filming Carlos has never entered the realm of serious possibilities. I don't own a video camera, not even a functioning photo camera, I'm sorry to admit. Our secret undertaking lasting for more then a year is not driven by my conscious strategies, but by the fortuitous pointers of a force that conducts the course of events from behind the scenes. We only approach where the doors open without pushing.

It was just as unforeseen that the girl at the office agreed to my spontaneous request to borrow the video camera she had brought to film the male stripper we hired for our boss' birthday. Suddenly I am holding in my hand the formidable, overwhelmingly unique, almost mythical opportunity to catch the sorcerer on film, or at least attempt to. A risky operation, considering the special powers the elusive master has at his disposal.

You have to grab the opportunity when it presents itself, he said.

Strung like a kite I creep towards the window and push the camera lens slowly past the frame to focus across the alley into the window of the studio on the other side.

Just hope I'm not recording a lot of extraneous shots! But I can't let myself get distracted by that now. Maybe the slippery sorcerer will only offer a second to capture no more then a frame of him before his guards energetically scout us out and sick their patrol on us.

My excitement and inexperience with the camera jumps in shaking pictures back and forth like a scared chicken. The automatic focus lags behind my movements and sharpens the figures in the studio in slow motion.

Between the shadowy backs of his students Carlos scurries from one window cutout to the next, revealing himself only for fractions of a second before disappearing again. A cat and mouse game! With the dusty peek hole of a window, the curtain of steel rods, the palisades of backs hiding him and the unfamiliar instrument in my hands alone, it is going to approach a miracle if anything worthwhile will appear on the tape. And aren't the sorcerers capable of magically erasing their picture?

I have to put everything on this card. It might be the only chance. Out on the fire escape one would have a better view forgoing the crisscross of the steel structure.

With a quick and measured step I bend under the window and climb out onto the metal platform. There I press my back against the dark brick wall. Greg has blackened out the camera light in foresight, only the dot-sized red recording light glimmers. Totally in the open, suspended above the alley illuminated in dreary orange, with the rough bricks hugging my back and the smell of burning oil from the restaurant in my nose, my eyes sweep unhindered into the row of windows across the way.

My agitation yields to a practical calmness. My senses surrender to the task, finally free to combine thoughts and movement into one smooth process.

In the milky yellow light of the studio the arms and legs of the participants dangle back and forth, fluttering like windmills. I'm searching for him swinging the lens from one window opening to the next. There is Taisha! And Carol scratching her scalp gracefully with a pointed finger in the thick hair. A short break. My breath stops.

Carlos walks through the picture and stands still, posing unknowingly for my camera. He admires Carola's new gold earrings, and then he glides like a ghost behind the columns. Only his white sleeves swings forward as if illuminated by a spotlight. The automatic focus of the camera is overtaxed. Too late to learn another setting! My thoughts punish.

There is his hand again with Ellis. He tells jokes, rolls up his sleeve; Ellis throws her head back and laughs. Another ballet begins of whirling arms and kicking legs in which Carlos' bright hand whizzes by in rhythmic swimming motions immersed in eerie white light. After a few minutes he calls another rest period with head scratching, gesticulation and laughter. He wanders between his chosen pupils bathed in gleaming white. My breath hesitates as if less air would draw less attention.

How long have I been standing here, suspended on the platform, pressed against the wall? I do not know. It seems a thing of absurd improbability to catch the mirror reflection of the sorcerer through the dirty windowpanes with an unfamiliar apparatus. But I must have captured at least a few good shots.

Now in contrast to the previously hidden faces of the students moving forward, the figures in the studio slide parallel along the window wall like puppets. I can see their expressionless miens as close as if I could touch them. What if they notice a silhouette on the brick wall and the red recording beacon? I hope my partner keeps an eye on the triangle of street visible from the window. Despite the wintry temperatures I start to sweat.

Carlos is standing in front of Kylie. An unlikely pair, she is solid as a poplar, heads taller than him, while he appears next to her small, silvery, and wiry. Locked in a medieval dance they harmoniously push together to the right and then back to the left. Horse stance. Once in a while a fleeting smile scurries over Kylie's face. The roaming eyes of the practicing students make me feel queasy. Maybe my adrenaline reservoir is exhausted.

During a break as their backs are turned towards me, I quickly slip back into the security of the hallway. My arms are stiff from holding still. The exertion of the concentration and fear of being discovered is evident. My limbs shake uncontrollably.

Greg wants to have a go with the camera. But he refrains from standing on the platform outside the window. More vocal then me in his agitation he struggles with the difficult light conditions, vilifies Lorenzo for obstructing the view of Carlos, and curses the roaming camera auto focus. I watch the sidewalk and the alley below to make sure nobody approaches the office building unnoticed.

In case of a detection we have prepared a getaway plan that would first lead up to the next story and then have us crossing over the balcony to the adjoining building. At that point we would separate to confuse our pursuers and exit through different staircases down onto Fifth Avenue or the alley. As soon as we can be sure that we've lost the troop we would meet up at the car. A good theoretical plan that does not appease me in the least.

Finally the tape is full. "More likely with pictures of bricks, light bulbs, pant legs, carpet patterns then a decent shot of Carlos," I comment in my under-appreciated glass-half-empty attitude. Feverishly, we leave the place and hasten without detour back to our waiting car.

Nobody is following us. In the dark one-way alley we would notice a pursuer right away. In fact the eerie quietness of the empty side streets seems strangely disconnected from the tumultuous moments on the fire escape, as if I'd never hung up there on the platform, five feet away in the open, recording the multidimensional sorcerer.

A pronounced distortion, a dreamy quality sets in as we pace along the shadows. At any moment I anticipate the grip of a ghostly hand on my shoulder that would shake me back into the waking world. It seems inconceivable that we are getting away with this. At the truck our tension brakes. "Let's leave quickly. We don't want to offer them another chance with our trance-like dawdle".

The drive back home into the canyon can't go quickly enough. An unspoken fear prevents us from voicing the possibility of the self-destruction of the tape. As if our words could be the trigger! Then the moment of truth is near. Will he be recognizable? After a few attempts we manage to find the rewind and play buttons on the camera.

Hypnotized, I stare at the images. Bricks, carpet, white stucco wall, jeans leg in close-up - obviously we experimented with the recording button. More blurry light bulbs and shadowy heads. The automatic focus hobbles behind the camera movements.

But there is a white arm, lit up; it flutters like an excited seagull. Then his slender frame walks between the extras, back and forth. A little fuzzy and harshly lit with unbecoming shadows, but clearly recognizable.

He did not make his image invisible! His mop of silver hair shines blue-gray; his poised hand ready to scratch hovers in the air. Often there is only his back, as if he means to tease us, occasionally his face flashes in profile, and sometimes he offers a fleeting grimace from the front. The witches' images, Florinda, Taisha and Carol, are recognizable as well.

Carlos teaching private class

Carlos admiring earrings

Carlos and Ellis

Carlos and Kylie

Nobody disappeared magically, destroyed the film, and overexposed the pictures. Nobody noticed us and followed us, or did they? I listen to the night world of the canyon. Outside in the cedars next to the house resounds the soft triple hoot of the long eared owl. A breeze jingles the chimes in front of the windows. The wooden walls creak, in the ivy the rats rustle, the possum creeps in the branches of the orange tree, and the swimming pool gurgles softly. Maybe another rabbit has fallen in. I hear no crunching steps, no harsh knocking, no whining car engine interrupting the lull of the night. Nobody comes to rip the video from our hands.

A euphoric realization sets in sweeping me up like a tsunami wave. Somehow we accomplished the impossible! The video that contains unique pictures of a sorcerer living in seclusion did not destroy itself! Greg jokes that we should print Carlos' picture on a T-shirt with the saying "Back from Hell with Trophies" and wear it to the next seminar. It was not hell we escaped from, but it feels as if we've received a trophy.

Blue Pyramid Seminar in Long Beach. Unexpectedly, Greg and I get work-study. Our previous requests have been dismissed by the Cleargreen office with even regularity. Many familiar faces from the private Sunday class make up the bulk of volunteers. My job is to help at the sign-in tables. The most coveted positions are bookstore sales and the security detail, the guard troop. For that we consider ourselves especially qualified, but nobody knows our secret. The sorcerers, as far as we can tell, are unaware of our double involvement. The time for confession has not yet come.

Early in the morning we walk into the blue pyramid before anybody else. But we don't consider for a moment to bring a recorder to tape Carlos. The mass has clearly replaced the electric warrior. Now Carlos shrugs when people dare to ask him about the discrepancies between the lessons in the previous books and his current teachings. Forget the books, is his answer. Now is now. What is that supposed to mean?

For myself I could explain the contradiction of his belated memory recovery as follows. When he says that he "remembers" more of what don Juan told him, he means that his understanding has grown, has taken on a different dimension. He draws from an ever-changing current, and any glance backward seems inappropriate. It could also imply that he makes it up as he goes along.

The magical movements have expanded with the number of new teachers on stage into a complex structure and suddenly available explanations. Now one can almost grasp the idea of an actual system, that four years ago seemed nonexistent. They have rescued the passes from the moldy past, dusted them off, named and reorganized them for the average consumer.

Despite the fact that my body enjoys physical activities like rock climbing, kayaking, dancing and mountain biking, I still see the magical movements as a momentary interlude, a distraction for the mind that I gladly tolerate. Beneath it though I listen to the vibration of the strings in the universe, to trace my connection, to make sense of it all, to reduce everything to the smallest denominator. The attraction, as it always has been, is the feeding of my mind and soul that conjures the sensation of speeding towards an exceedingly important answer.

He is standing on stage; his small figure stretches, expands and takes in the whole room all the way into the tip of the pyramid. Extending his arm he points with his finger into the sky like an arrow. His eyes are fixed on the point in the ether and he says, "Don't look at me, look to IT". We should not see him, admire and adore him, but seek the connection to IT, to the indefinable all-present power out there.

Bypassing my frequent reservations and ever lurking sarcasms he manages again to address the deepest desires in me, to formulate truths that carry me away in rapids. My thanks to you, Carlos! I don't hear his vulgarity, his incessant criticism anymore, or the million times repeated jokes and anecdotes, the formulaic sounding sorcery explanations, the contradictions: only the small truth that touches me. The entirety of his eccentric behavior becomes nothing more than the shell, the container for the pearl inside that takes me on a journey of infinite dimensions.

The princess of my story, looking for the meaning of life, not minding hardship and pain, sank completely exhausted into the grass at the river's edge. Again she heard the murmur of the river, "I am the water of life and the water of death. I am the beginning and the end". Tired, she watched the water flow by in endless motion.

The river said, "Come and drink". She leaned over the edge just a bit to scoop some water with her hand when she lost her balance and fell head over heels into the river. Slowly she drifted down the stream, losing consciousness and filling up with water until she was so full that she sank to the bottom.

March 26, 1997. Thirty-nine people calling themselves Heaven's Gate commit suicide. They were waiting for a spaceship, supposedly hiding behind the comet Hale-Bopp.

The video tape they made before their deaths displays the bright-eyed intentions about the planned suicide, imparting a surrealistic incongruity. The outward appearance of the men and women, in short haircuts and asexual clothing, mirror an aching similarity to the androgynous look of Carlos' inner group.

Greg, carried away with the tsunami wave of our previous success, surprises me with a new video camera. He takes the ball and runs with it, meaning that we will continue to film but also at the same time that Greg has the finger on the control button. My only hope lies in the editing room.

March 29, 1997. Saturday, 2 p.m. First filming in front of Carlos' house on Pandora Avenue. Florinda, looking as if she has just been peeled, crisp and dewy in her white shirt and pants, drives off in a bile-colored Chevy truck. It must be Carlos' old truck that he doesn't drive anymore because of his bad eyesight. We had noticed this truck parked in front of the house from the beginning, but we weren't able to connect it to the witches until now. So Florinda's assertion of having sworn off driving, after the bittersweet incident of her red new sports car ending up in a ravine, is not to be taken literally. It makes one wonder what else they are lying about?

It is obvious that Florinda uses this vehicle to run errands in town, and does not limit herself to the occasional parking of the other witches' cars, as she has told us in the seminars. And since she has to be part of the private classes that happen every day, she has no chance to leave town for a longer trip.

Florinda coming back from shopping

Kylie in 'sack uniform' delivering lunch

March 30, 1997. Sunday, 12:40 p.m. Kylie arrives in the Toyota All-Trac. Tamalia gets out of the car and carries dishes into the house through the Pandora gate.

3:45 p.m. Florinda, or Flodo how she calls herself in personal correspondence, arrives driving the Chevy truck, then she parks and exits the car with a brown shopping bag that she carries into the house.

4:24 p.m. Kylie comes back and lets Carlos out of the car. Tamalia kisses Carlos on the lips. He wears sunglasses and carries a roll of papers in his hand. He quickly moves through the gate in the hedge. Carola follows directly behind him.

4:30 p.m. Last drive-by. Everything is quiet.

April 5, 1997. Saturday, 11:43 a.m. Corner Westwood and Rochester. We decide to document the location of Carol's apartment. Carol does not live in Carlos' compound on Pandora but occupies a one-bedroom apartment, near the Sisterhood bookstore where I first met Florinda. In the apartment next to her are Zaia, Darien and Carola, and in the adjacent complex lives Nuri, the Blue Scout.

12:15 p.m. Pandora Avenue in front of Carlos' house. Wind in the trees. 2:11 p.m. Tracy drives up in the old yellow truck, parks it and walks to his own vehicle. Flodo exits the house, opens the passenger side door of the truck, rummages around in the cab and locks it up.

4:57 p.m. In the horizontal evening sun Tamalia, Darien and Aerin crawl on top of Carlos' roof, armed with hammers and work gloves, as if they are searching for something. I assume for an animal under the rafters of the roof that makes noise at night, maybe mice or bats. Or perhaps loose roof shingles. Why don't the handy men of his group, "the elements" take care of this?

Tamalia's rosy-cheeked face and her self-assured smile give off a happy impression. She is the only one that blossomed noticeably after she was taken into the inner circle.

6:01 p.m. Carlos comes out of the gate on Pandora, dressed in a dark-blue golf jacket and a red shirt, Taisha in tow. We never see him using the other door on Eastbourne. For a moment they are idling on the sidewalk with their faces pointing north. Until Tamalia arrives to pick them up in her metallic Ford Taurus and they pass in front of us. "Duck, quick!" Our reflexes are as jumpy as they were in the beginning, never taking our luck for granted and still expecting the end or the sudden discovery of the constant sidewalk visitors armed with binoculars and camera.

6:48 p.m. Inside Dance Home. Tamalia, Nyie and Carlos wear long-sleeved red shirts. He touches Tamalia, who is one head taller than him, gently by the elbow as if showing her off, then he embraces her from the side and kisses her heartily on the cheek. Everybody laughs. Even Fabrizio standing opposite of them. Sometimes he looks directly into the camera, but his face is only a mirror reflection enraptured by his attention for Carlos from which he is not allowed to waver.

8:17 p.m. On the street in front of Dance Home. Fab, how he calls himself in office correspondence, Bruce and Tracy are the first ones out on the street, and then the women appear in small groups.

Finally Carlos shows on Zaia's arm with a large department store shopping bag. The palisades of students obstruct his small figure.

Only his grinning head pops up between them. Then he glides, his profile illuminated by the neon flooding from Radio Shack, to the waiting car. Kindly he embraces Tracy by putting his head on Tracy's shoulder until it is Fabrizio's turn. Now he is standing in front of the car. He gets in and hands his paper bag towards the back. Tamalia, the driver, takes off. Bruce and Fab march together past Pep Boys.

Carlos and Taisha in front of Dance Home

Heartfelt hugs

April 12, 1997. Saturday, 11:59 a.m. Pandora Avenue. The red car of Margarita is double parked, waiting in front of the house. Florinda comes from the house with a small paper bag; she sits down in the passenger seat, keeping the door open. They talk for a while, then

Flodo says goodbye with a kiss in the open car door, readjusting her wedged panties. With a last wink she retreats back into the hedge.

12:57 p.m. Tracy shows up in his black Lexus and waits in the car. Florinda steps out of the house to receive the covered bowl and aluminum container from him and takes the food inside. Their faces glow in the reflection of the foil. She comes back out of the hedge; they kiss each other on both cheeks and talk some more. The wind moves her golden polished hair. She looks toward us. Greg twitches.

Maybe she mistakes my dark-blue Hyundai for Kylie's Toyota. From a certain distance there is a similarity in the front. But, no, she turns away. She did not see us.

1:12 p.m. Florinda in a black T-shirt and pants crosses Pandora to put a brown grocery bag into the parked truck. Then she returns to the house.

1:16 p.m. Kylie drives up and stops in the middle of the street due to a lack of parking space in front of the gate. She carries a bowl of food. Florinda is expecting her. Kylie kisses Florinda's cheek. Two gold-blond heads glimmer in a Hollywood fairytale sheen in the bright sunlight that bounces off the parked windshields.

After Kylie hands over the food she caresses Florinda's spiked hair with a tender gesture and kisses her gently on the forehead. The expression on their faces is not discernable in the blaring reflection. A final tender touch of the golden spikes and then Kylie steps back into her car, while Flodo disappears through the garden gate carrying the food. The open tenderness, the generous signs of affection, displayed for no audience - they don't know we are here and they keep no contact with the neighbors - are endearing to watch. The sincere amity in their gestures is undeniable. It shows an admirable respect and love for each other.

Without being able to catch the words that pass between them I depend upon an interpretation of their gestures. In contrast to words, gestures are less likely to be consciously manipulated. People are mostly unaware of their body posture and behavior. The silent movie in front of us, playing without subtitles, demands greater vigilance and concentration then a multi-sensory experience. Everything depends upon the eye.

5:57 p.m. Kylie parks in front of the Pandora gate and waits in her car. 6:00 p.m. Florinda steps from the hedge, followed by Taisha wrapped in a jacket and a shoulder purse. Flodo runs back into the house.

6:06 p.m. Carlos appears in the hedge opening and takes a seat in the front of Kylie's car. Kylie u-turns on Pandora and drives off without Florinda.

8:12 p.m. In front of Dance Home. It is already dark. Kylie's car waits on the curb. Tracy and Bruce are standing on the sidewalk. Fabrizio yawns. We are on the other side sitting in the car the camera lens trained on the exit of the studio. At last Carlos appears on the stairs. Fabrizio receives a hug from him, Tracy gets a pat on the back; and then Carlos is stuffed into the front passenger seat. Tamalia takes the back. With a glance into the side mirror Kylie speeds off. The others stand around in the clucking of embarrassed chatter until all of them on some invisible signal move and walk away like birds on the shore.

Carlos after the class at Dance Home

Carlos in front of Dance Home

Sometimes I wonder why they don't notice us. Even ordinary people unconsciously notice a gaze that is placed on them. I have tested this hundreds of times in a bus or a restaurant. It is a deep-seated primate recognition. In the vocabulary of gestures a long stare is interpreted as hostile behavior. Without thinking, the observed turns around to reassure themselves of the harmlessness of the look. Averted eyes immediately disarm the provocation. That the sorcerer and his group don't feel our prolonged stares is very strange.

Carlos "Onassis" in front of his house on Pandora

Timothy Leary's ashes are shipped into space by a rocket launched from the Canary Islands.

April 26, 1997. Saturday, 12:30 p.m. Carlos' house. Tracy waits on the corner of Pandora and Eastbourne in his car. He kisses Florinda on both cheeks and gives her a container wrapped in aluminum foil, which she carries into the house.

1:30 p.m. Flodo opens the passenger door of the puke-yellow truck, digs around in it and locks it back up. She is only one car length away from us. Then she enters the compound through the driveway gate with the hibiscus bushes.

Our position is dangerously close, close enough to touch the curtain that separates us. We move. I don't want to provoke an unintentional discovery. A crow sits in the middle of the street and picks around on the pavement. Carlos or don Juan? We joke in the boredom of the lazy street.

5:49 p.m. Taisha comes out of the Pandora gate in a loose black tee-shirt; she walks around the hedge to Eastbourne and continues on that street until she is out of sight. She carries only a wallet in her hand. Where is she going so close to the beginning of the evening class? It can't be very far. Five minutes later she reappears holding a covered paper cup. This time she enters the compound on the Eastbourne side.

5:56 p.m. Kylie parks on Pandora. She squeezes herself with elegant verve into the smallest parking spot. Her superior sense of practically applied space becomes very obvious.

5:57 p.m. We all wait for him. Kylie throws little pieces of paper out the car window onto the street. The wind plays with the shreds as if they were cherry blossoms.

6:04 p.m. Florinda, tucked in a light pink blouse, flirtatiously holds the gate open for Carlos who strides onto the sidewalk in an open black shirt and his Onassis-look sunglasses. He takes his customary place in the front seat.

After they leave I collect Kylie's discarded pieces of paper from the playful grip of the wind. Is it a secret message she threw away without concern for the environment? The note contains an order for a "little strong decaf café ollete" and strawberry jello. We laugh.

Florinda and Carlos at the Pandora gate

Shadow Carlos leaving studio   Florinda and Carlos

May 3, 1997. Saturday, 5:40 p.m. Pandora Avenue. Darien walks to her red compact car and drives off.

5:59 p.m. Kylie arrives, parks and waits in her Toyota. Flodo comes to the car in a white shirt blouse. Intensely focused, we wait for the wiry figure of the master as if it were the first time. Like the Hopis watching their repetitive rituals to understand the message behind it. The hedge gap yawns open like a crack in the juicy green wall. From our particular vantage point we cannot look inside. We see the sorcerers magically manifest as if they are being spit out onto the sidewalk from the nether world. A sorcerer trick.

6:57 p.m. Dance Home. Clapping and laughter. We can hear it clearly. It lures from across the alley with ghostly fingers, pulling me to greater attention. With the mirror image of Carlos' back turned towards the camera his arms and hands describe every syllable he speaks like Punch and Judy in front of his audience. Gently he touches Tamalia's face; everybody smiles. Then, as if to repeat the lesson, he touches her cheek and head with his outstretched arm.

They adore him, the Nagual, the one who brings freedom, abstract and total freedom. What a feeling this must be for him, surrounded by friendly faces, eyes dripping with love, admiration, respect, total devotion and commitment. He is the absolute solo-act, the conductor of his orchestra, and all are pleased with themselves in the role of the chosen audience. Naturally, we can't hear any of his words as hard as we try, but the miens that surround him speak volumes.

7:25 p.m. His speech continues.

8:00 p.m. In front of Dance Home on the street. The light conditions are bad. Somebody turns off the green light of the stairway prematurely. Carlos steps to the car in the turmoil of the gray fuzzy dusk. Even the night sensitive setting of Greg's new camera can't manage decent pictures.

Carlos 'entertaining' his students

May 10, 1997. Saturday, 8:08 p.m. Exit Dance Home. We grab a parking spot exactly opposite from the door. Today each member of the group carries light-blue rolled up mats. For floor exercises? The not-doings of the next seminar? Kylie stops her car, blocking our view of the door. If Carlos wasn't so small! Despite the many hours of filming and watching so far we have gathered no more than a few clear minutes of the master. It's as if he wants to tease us by letting himself be seen only in small doses. So we don't lose our appetite? Only half of Carlos' head leans on Tracy and Fab before finally diving into the vehicle.

Tamalia receives a letter from her parents that she threw unopened into the trash. My diminished Spanish language skills decipher the despairing request of her parents not to sever all connection to them; how sad and confused they are and how little they understand what has gotten into Amalia.

The pain and love speaking from these lines touches me deeply. I almost decide to write an anonymous letter, reassuring her parents not to worry, that sooner or later Amalia-Talia will get in touch with them again. Florinda still seems to keep a loving relationship to her parents, judging from their correspondence.

But a letter from me could be regarded as an intervention and we are committed not to meddle with their lives.

There is also a sticky note for an appointment at the Beverly Hills Superior Court with time and date, in regards to Castaneda's adoption of Nuri and another woman. Greg misses the hearing by minutes, but is assured by the bailiff that the hearing took place.

May 17, 1997. Saturday, 7:43 p.m. Exit Dance Home. Kylie runs like a valet driver to get her car, her hair flapping in the wind. It seems to be longer then usual. Did they realize their similarity in looks to the Heaven's Gate members and let their hair grow? Bruce and Tracy are waiting in front of the door. The shadows in our car interior are not pronounced enough to conceal us. Anxiously I push down the door button. If they discover us they can't rip the door open in the sudden fury of anger.

Kylie parks her car next to the exit. Carlos comes out of the hallway, embraces Bruce who rests his head on the masters shoulder like an oversized son on his little father. Then Carlos pats good-byes on Tracy's back and gets into his ride. Good close-ups.

Somehow it seems as if we are collecting the precious seconds of his appearance like the moments of accumulated silence needed to see energy as it flows in the universe. What will we see in the end?

Sometimes I fantasize of mingling between the members of the group in front of the studio exit, disguised as a homeless beggar equipped with the typical assortment of dirty clothing and pushing a shopping cart. The running camera could be hidden under the garbage in the cart.

Greg imagines himself hiding under the heap while he films and me pushing him around in the shopping card. A pair of mentally disturbed stalkers? There is no doubt it would be a fascinating episode, a definite adrenaline rush, a tickle for my appetite for adventure. But despite the effort there is no guarantee that this outlandish maneuver will yield better pictures.

Kylie and Talia pick up   Carlos in front of his house

May 24, 1997. Saturday, 8:08 p.m. Overcast blankets the L.A. basin. This could be considered another unnoticed yet legitimate season. The season of fog, when the moist hand of the ocean binds the air in little droplets like strands of wet spider's hair for weeks on end until people wish for the sun.

The light bulb over the exit of Dance Home has burned out. Bad chances for filming. Next time we will bring a new light bulb with us, and Greg will replace it.

May 31, 1997. Saturday, 7:21 p.m. Pandora Avenue. Reni, baptized Blinky by us because of her incessant lid blinking, gets out of her silver Ford in a knee-length dress with flowing silk scarf and runs affectedly into the house. That does not look like a practice class. What is going on? Others from the inner group arrive. Could this be the mythical Sorcery Theater?

In the dark of the night we cautiously approach the sidewalk in front of the gate. The roaring laughter, squealing and raucous bawling extends beyond the block.

Through the gaps in the hedge thicket one can spy into an open door that is covered with a bamboo shade for venting heat. The vertical stripes between the bamboo slats create an intriguing shadowy display of figures jumping up and down and wallowing in ripping laughter. During a break a vertically fragmented Carlos screws a new light bulb into the ceiling fixture with a tool extension. With all the young men attending does he have to do it himself?

The few word scraps that reach us destroy the illusion of an otherworldly performance, exposing them as rather amateurish skits but still admirable in their exaggerated zeal of execution. The hysterical laughter, the fun that they have with each other is catching. It must be a group thing. The conviction and energy it took to pull this evening off and the weeks of preparation for this elaborate event, just to entertain the group, is nevertheless remarkable. The average family does not spend that much effort entertaining each other.

In the replay of the video our rudimentary skills reveal something unexpected. Seen through the shifting black-yellow slit pattern of the curtain the seemingly ordinary performances receive a touch of magical surrealism and change the awkward pieces into an unexplainable view of the fabric of mystery.

June 1, 1997. Sunday afternoon 3 p.m. Dance Home. The participants of the three week August seminar from 1995, our friends in the Thursday practice group, are the chosen members of the Sunday class. In the garbage we find a list with the currently invited ones and the scratched out names of the excommunicated.

On Tamalia's arm Carlos emerges from the dark hole of the staircase stepping into the gleaming midday light that bounces vertically on to the sidewalk. On his way to the waiting car he stops, caresses the head of the orange scout like a benevolent patriarch. The woman waited for him leaning against the house wall near the exit. He exchanges a few words with her, embraces her and kisses her goodbye with pursed lips on the mouth.

With a friendly smirk he gives the thumps up of encouragement for everybody in range, and then he disappears into the car.

The overpowering light bleaches all colors and throws deeply contrasting shadows. The risk of getting caught in broad daylight also is much greater. We entrench ourselves behind the columns of the bark colored bank building standing diagonally across.

One person from the class waits separately, lost on the side. Unnoticed by the other sorcerer students that mimic their master in the exchanges of momentary kindness and pecks of kisses, and with raised noses indulge in their shared fragile fortunes, wrapped in sunglass loneliness. And then they go home by themselves, renounce sexual relations, don't talk to friends, if they still have any left, and ignore their family. All in the true warrior spirit.

Carlos in front of Dance Home

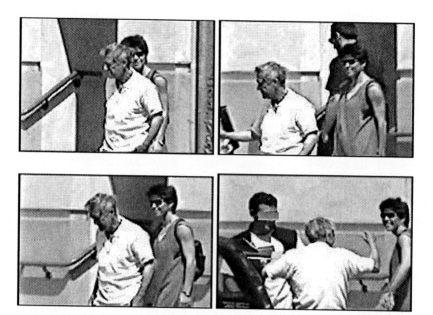

A program of the "Theater of Infinity" event from May 31st falls into our hands, rescued from the garbage. During the intermission the group had a 250$ feast of Gelson's barbequed ribs.

June 7, 1997. Saturday, 6:11 p.m. Pandora Avenue. Taisha, Tracy and Haley admire a forest green Ford parked in front, which seems to be Haley's new second hand car. Taisha looks tired and exhausted. Actually, she always has a pale complexion. Maybe it's the June overcast. Flodo joins them to inspect the new purchase from the front and the back. She nods with satisfaction.

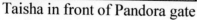

Taisha in front of Pandora gate

7:55 p.m. Dance Home. Bruce or Enzo how he calls himself in private correspondence within the group, comes down the steps from the studio and walks away instead of waiting in front, as is his usual behavior. Tracy props the door open, Fab and all the others appear with blue mats. Carol scratches her head waiting for Kylie. In the greenish yellow cast of the staircase Kylie has a surprisingly serious and concerned expression that is almost sad. No Carlos!

This is the first time since we are watching them that he missed the Saturday class. The group walks together to the corner of Sixth Street; there they mingle with each other like sheep without a shepherd. Kylie participates out of halfhearted politeness somewhat forlorn in the chatter, still carrying her weighed down composure. The others behave as usual, not particularly subdued. Who was leading the class? Who taught the movements? Is Carlos okay?

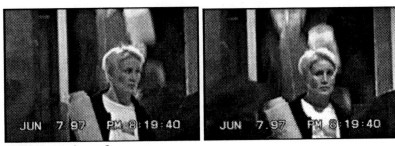

Kylie's serious face

June 8, 1997. Sunday. Pandora Ave. 1:55 p.m. Taisha emerges from the gap; Florinda holds the gate open for Carlos. He is alright! A little ashen maybe, but perky as ever. His disheveled hair remains uncombed like the bad hair day of a neglected doll. Greg thinks that they must keep him in a box. To me he looks as if he has just been in a dryer on high heat without wrinkle guard. Maybe he had another bout with the fungus problem he fought in Oakland. Or perhaps a cold? In the private classes I witnessed in 1993 he was very prone to catching viruses.

3:45 p.m. Dance Home. Kylie gets her car. Carlos comes out of the studio door by himself, without attendant, dressed in a brown jacket and sunglasses. With a smooth, almost imperceptible movement he takes the teeth out of his mouth and puts them into his

145

trouser pocket. Then he looks around, waiting until Tamalia, Taisha and Florinda join him. Together they get into the ready car. Enzo waves a goodbye from the studio door before he closes it again.

Bad hair day

Taisha and Carlos at Dance Home exit

June 14, 1997. Saturday, 5:56 p.m. Aerin and Darien wait in front of the Pandora compound holding their purses. Kylie drives up in her Toyota and leaves for Dance Home.

6:45 p.m. Sorcery theater performance, magical movements disguised as dances. Aerin dresses as a man with hat and jacket and wiggles in front of the line up of witches, Taisha, Carol and Florinda, who enthusiastically clap their hands and smile approvingly. Two men in masks perform scheming sorcery movements that remind me of uneven martial arts passes. Taisha rests her head in her hands. A girl with a fan performs a hectic and highly stylized dance. Tamalia and Kylie show their knife passes.

Carlos, in a red shirt, visible only in profile due to the strong outside light of the summer evening, claps and walks around. I consider it an admirable feat to learn the movements, remember them in sequence and execute them in harmony with a partner.

Dancer in Sorcery Theater   Carlos orchestrating event

Rare line-up of all three witches

June 15, 1997. 3 p.m. Sunday group. Ron is the first one coming from the studio. That is unusual. He hastily walks away without the customary lingering in front of the door. Margarita waits in front of the exit by herself. Her hair gleams in the sun. She pulls over her black sweater. A transit bus puffs by. Others slowly emerge from the hallway and also walk away unceremoniously.

Then a smiling Carlos appears on Tamalia's arm, scratches his head in the characteristic gesture and shakes his fist in a call to arms. Miles holds the car door open and Carlos gets in while the remaining Sunday group watches.

Carlos leaving Dance Home

We retrieve several scripts from the trash, sketches from the Sorcery Theater that seem to focus on the superficiality of love, the flatness of Hollywood society, and the over-identification with gender.

Two versions of the 'The Danger of Being', 'A Lesson with Master Buhdda', 'The Jewelry store', 'Duet with Strings' and the interlude with Cleopatra. There is a survey taken with a few Sunday group participants that gush in "wows", "blown away", "funny and clever", "impressed".

Then why did it sound so amateurish to us?

June 21, 1997. Saturday. The fog is still clinging to the morning hills. Over night delicate small spider webs hanging in the chamiso brush caught the mist from the ocean like sticky sieves, until the weight of the droplets transformed the webs into baskets filled with tiny perfect glassy pearls.

Each one crafted like a piece of art, slightly bowed, with transparent pearls sorted by size; on the outside the pin head sized, in the center the ones as big as a baby's fingernail or a lizard's eye;

carefully arranged like liquid crystal; each one surrounded by the thin circle of a two day old crescent moon.

Gathered under the glassy droplet bowl arches a double floor fashioned from the tiniest pearls. Above the bowl floats a structure of delicate pearl filaments, strung in all directions that convene to a point of connection. In the moist breath of the wind the crystal garlands vibrate softly. I can almost hear the tinkling.

12:24 p.m. Pandora Avenue. We are parked on Pandora opposite of the hedges and his gate, driven from our favorite corner next to the fire hydrant by a yard sale. Carol's Ford Contour sits only a few yards in front of us. We should have expected that she would walk out of the gate sooner or later. She crosses Pandora to her car and fumbles with the key. Lucky for us she is so engrossed in her cell phone conversation that she doesn't see us. Or is she ignoring us? Our position is untenably close.

Carol too close for comfort

June 22, 1997. Sunday, 12:47 p.m. Pandora Avenue. Kylie picks up Carlos, dressed in a black leather jacket. They pass in front of us, as we duck with twitchy reflexes. Should we follow them? We know they are going to Dance Home, even if we lose them we can always catch up at the studio. Greg agrees.

Kylie's Toyota swims not too far ahead of us on Santa Monica Boulevard. We charge closer. Carol's round head bobs in the back. Carlos' is shrunken behind the neck rest of the front passenger seat. I'm in the lane next to them, but driving diagonally behind their car to make use of the blind spot. Kylie's eyes might spy us while concentrating on the surrounding traffic. Our unsuspecting quarry and Greg's jumpy attempts of videotaping turns this short intermission into a funny chase episode. Different than our quiet hours of waiting, we glide behind them in the steady flow of traffic. Approaching a red light I sweat with indecision. Cautiously I stay more than a car length away from the line in spite of my usual boldness and Greg's insisting for a better shot. He can't possibly expect me to stop next to Kylie's car with my open window, then look casually at Carlos and wave politely, with Greg pointing the camera at them? I shirk from this unnecessary tempting of fate. I don't have a hidden desire to be discovered. I don't need this kind of attention. My self-esteem does not rest on the laurels of our success that needs recognition to be satisfied. The steering wheel sticks in the noon heat. It is only a game.

Black leather Carlos

The chase on Santa Monica Blvd.

Hanging close

Before the kiss

3.00 p.m. Dance Home. We are positioned in the one-way alley across from the door. This time it is my turn with the new camera. Ellis and Margarita line up waiting for Carlos in front of the entrance. Five more minutes go by in silent anticipation. The tape in the camera has only a few minutes of recording time left. If I stop now to save space the camera shuts down and it will take a second or two before the recording resumes. I might miss the crucial moment of his emergence. We are still wresting images from the grip of chance.

Suddenly the dark hallway spits him out. Ellis steps into his path. His face enters into the vertical midday light, stretches forward, lips pursed for a kiss on Ellis' cheek, showing a distorted monkey expression. Then I run out of tape. My luck!

June 29, 1997. 2.05 p.m. Sunday group. In the studio the group is bedded down on blue mats. Carlos is lying on the floor within our field of vision, dressed in white socks, dark top and pants. He shows slow movements on his back. A horizontal Tai Chi? In between are short resting periods.

These must be the new not-doing passes he promised for the upcoming seminar in August. They don't resemble any of the not-doing actions described in his books. The not-doings of walking backwards, or hanging fruit and vegetables on your naked body, have been adapted to flipping your feet while resting on the floor.

Carlos doing 'Not-doings'   After the class

From the trash we retrieve Kylie's printed instructions that she left for Reni during her absence while running the seminars in Barcelona and Berlin. One paragraph is noteworthy.

In regards to Carlos' libel lawyer Kylie has several pending issues that should not be discussed with the lawyer openly. The Nagual is keeping a delicate balance with the things he has her do for him. And whatever happens, under no circumstances is Reni to speak with the Nagual about it.

Translated it means that Reni is not supposed to know certain things, neither is the lawyer, and as a general rule nobody should know what the other person knows and above all Carlos should not find out. Everybody is on the no-need-to-know basis, a technique of control and faith.

They purchased insurance for the European seminars against the event of the nonappearance of the advertised celebrities. The personal information on those forms makes Carlos and the witches ten years younger. I wonder if the insurance is valid with wrong birth dates.

July 5, 1997. Saturday, 8:11 p.m. Dance Home exit. Grainy blue evening light washes across the street. Fab, Aerin, Enzo, Miles, Reni, Nyie, Darien and Tamalia line up to build a pathway through which Carlos' diminutive figure floats like a pontiff in street clothing. For a few moments he lingers in the warmth of his flock, his face displaying the impish grin he is famous and adored for. Then he walks through the alley of people, lifts his hand, and with a quick thumbs up he disappears into the waiting car. Excellent pictures despite the muted light. The quintessential Carlos!

Impish grin!

Taisha and Talia

July 6, 1997. Sunday, 3:19 p.m. Dance Home. At the end of the lesson Carlos and company come down the stairs. Curiously, the group now consists primarily of women. All men must have been excluded. Carlos, dressed in a sky blue shirt, scratches his head in a gesture of temporary bewilderment, confusion or maybe to provoke thoughts to bridge a pause of indecision?

He turns around to talk to a girl right behind him and walks her along the display windows of Radio Shack. He leads her gently on the elbow away for a private chat. What a great photo opportunity! He offers us so very few. The young woman, age about twenty, as tall as him, with short thick brown hair, most likely is one of the Argentineans. The conversation seems to have a serious topic. Carlos' face shows no teasing smirk, only sincere attention.

He stops her next to the trunk of a tree and hides behind it. Obviously, only from our line of sight, from the alley where we are sitting in the car. The girl engages in a conversation with the tree bark, swiping her hand across her forehead to move her short hair growth back as if she wanted to wipe something heavy from her brow. Carlos' hand appears like an appendage of the trunk, stroking over her hair in the opposite direction, rectifying in a tender gesture the embarrassment or frustration presented to him.

Then together they walk back to the others. Carlos scratches his back irritated by the clothes tag. In front of Margarita he makes an abbreviated Buddhist bow, nods in greeting to another woman, and approaches his waiting transportation.

Exit Dance Home

Talking to student

What are they talking about?

Attentive Carlos

Smiling for fans

It is the collapse of hope for Emmanuel who in a letter to Kylie, fished from the trash, laments the end of the Sunday classes. The thought that Carlos could leave at anytime now produces panic and fear in him, because he knows that without the Nagual nothing goes - all bets are off!

July 12, 1997. Saturday 8 p.m. No class at Dance Home. What is happening? Are all other classes, besides the Sunday session suspended as well? For more then two years he has stuck to his schedule of instructions like an atomic clock and suddenly he stops? Or did they switch to another location? We drive to all the places of the sorcerer's crossroads.

Nobody is at Cleargreen's office. Carlos' house is quiet. No tracker car parked out front. In Kylie's apartment on Rochester Avenue the lights are burning, but her car is not on the curb. It could be stored in the garage. Carol's place is dark without activity. Where are they? Did they leave us in the dust?

July 13, 1997. 1 p.m. No Sunday class. The busy Dance Home portal is deserted. Is Carlos canceling the classes on grounds of illness or is this one of his cyclically reoccurring outbursts of disappointment?

July 19, 1997. Saturday, 1:34 p.m. Pandora Avenue. Flodo drives off in the Chevy. Taisha follows not much later in the van that was parked in the Pandora driveway.

2 p.m. To our surprise Carlos comes out of the gate and walks north on the sidewalk along the hedge to the driveway. An unexpected opportunity! He wears a bright fuchsia colored shirt and seems physically well, energetic, and full of determination. We have never observed him in front of the house alone, without his entourage. From our position on the southwest corner of Pandora and Eastbourne we are not able to see into the driveway niche.

Spurred by his unusual behavior I start the engine and pass the property in a slow but steady speed. There he is, half obstructed by the hibiscus bushes, with Darien who is holding a small metal ladder. Parked on a side street diagonally across we observe Darien climbing up a few rungs on the ladder to clip several twigs off the bushes that are touching the wall. Carlos watches her from below and scratches his neck, his v-spot, wrapped in thoughts. The vulnerable dent that we are not supposed to be touching, I giggle to myself.

2:19 p.m. Taisha returns from shopping, and parks in the Pandora driveway. Two mockingbirds attack in dive bombing fashion, harassing the crow that sits in the top of the fig tree gorging itself on the early fruit.

2.35 p.m. Florinda returns with a shopping bag and purse. She moves the van from the drive and parks it on the street.

3.14 p.m. Flodo and Carlos stand in the driveway. Aerin assuredly leans the metal ladder on the outside wall surrounding the compound. Carlos climbs up a few steps and bangs with a hammer against the upper edge, his aim invisible behind the low hanging branches of the magnolias. Again he tantalizes us with a view so accessible and still he manages to obscure himself. Determined I jump from the car with a "Give me the camera".

Under the cover of the parked row of automobiles I shrink even smaller, stopping next to a leathery gray trunk opposite of the activity in the driveway. I kneel in the grass that grows around the gnarly roots able to see now even the top of the wall, the center of their attention. The magnolias are dropping their shiny seeds that look like red coral beads. The zoom unveils the mysterious activity.

Darien hands a piece of lattice to Carlos and he attaches it to the top of the wall to extend the height, protecting the inside from curious eyes, I assume. He uses quite a number of nails, hammering more then 15 minutes. Even when he has to stretch to reach the higher corners he does not climb to the next steps and still holds the hammer in an unprofessional way too close to the head. Carlos, the carpenter!

The wind moves through the bushes waving oscillating shadows across his body. His red shirt flickers as well. Again we wonder why none of the capable men in his group assist in the repair and maintenance of the building compound.

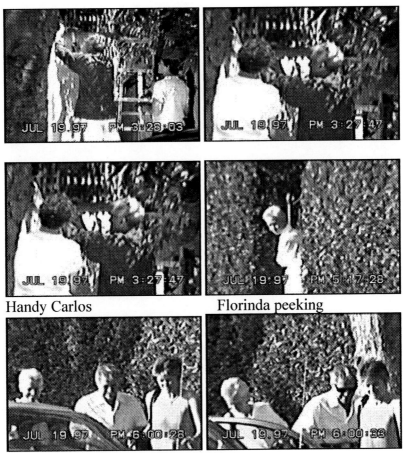

Handy Carlos   Florinda peeking

Going out for dinner in Westwood

5:02 p.m. Tamalia and Nuri come from the hedge gate with blue mats and drive off in the Ford. Carlos must be teaching the new movements now in his house to pairs of visiting trackers. Is it an energy conservation method or a temporary group punishment?

5:17.p.m. Flodo peeks like a bird out of the hedge dressed in a white bathrobe.

5:20 p.m. Taisha returns with a bag from the bagel shop around the corner.

5:48 p.m. Carol parks in front of the Pandora gate with her Ford Contour and waits in the car with the driver's window rolled down until Flodo waves her into the house from the hedge opening. She is dressed elegantly in an anthracite pantsuit with a lime green sheath.

6.00 p.m. Carlos, Carol and Flodo together step out of the gate, Carlos gets into the back seat. Where are they going dressed up in fine clothes unfitting for exercise classes? To our knowledge they have not had any classes in weeks. We follow the golden Ford Contour north on Pandora, then turn west moving over hilly side streets with stop signs. The distance between our vehicles increases and as feared we lose Carol's car on the first traffic light on Wilshire. Considering the direction and their appearance, we assume they went for dinner in Westwood.

August 2, 1997. Saturday. Another subtle season in the city appears when the asphalt on the street bubbles in the lick of the sun oozing a smell utterly place specific. The season of millions of air-conditioners humming to crank out frigid moldy air while opportunistic vultures circle in the foothills.

5:34 p.m. Florinda drives off in the Chevy and is back within ten minutes with a shopping bag. She wears sunglasses, a crisp white shirt blouse and white pants. She pushes the garden gate with a spirited kick of her foot. When she turns around to close the metal frame, she glances into our direction. For one moment fear sears through my body that she might mistake my car for Kylie's Toyota. But she does not return. Is she calling Kylie now to check if she is parked across the street? These potentially close calls keep us on the edge, sharpen our awareness, and help us determine the permitted distance. It feels like touching the membrane of energy barely separating us from the sorcerers.

Another shopping moment

6:13 p.m. Flodo and Taisha leave the house equipped with the female armor of a shoulder purse. Florinda has changed into black pants; Taisha wraps herself in a tan knitted sweater. They wait on the sidewalk looking around occasionally, but mostly facing north on Pandora. Then they wink. Haley and Carol arrive in the forest-green Ford. An unusual excursion! Without the regulated outings of the movement classes the witches now have extra free time.

This lends itself to a rare chase tracking their new interests. Haley, the driver strives toward the Santa Monica freeway. Easier then I imagined we are able to keep on their tail until the green car turns off on the Fourth Street exit directly into the bustle of the Saturday evening traffic.

Guessing, from their attire and purses, a movement practice rules itself out. I'm forced to stop at a red traffic light on Second Street watching helplessly as the witches are swallowed by the hundreds of cars heading north. What now? Continuing in the momentum I drive along the parking structures that line the right side of the street. "Maybe they are heading for Third Street Promenade!"

Arbitrarily, I turn into the last parking entrance and squeal around the levels to find an empty spot. Suddenly, as if a hatch to the other world opens up, as if I had voiced the silent wish in a dream, we meet the witches again. They are just about to get out of their car. We feign disinterest as we slip by. Blood pumps quickly boosted by the recovered opportunity. It takes us at least three more minutes to find a parking spot and run down the urine-infested stairway to the alley. But no speck, no shred of the witches is left to see.

Indecisively we halt in the pedestrian zone of the Promenade, staring at the carnival of people, sounds and smells. The short musicians with flutes and braids from Peru dancing in circles, the fake human statues, the plastic bottle drummer girl, the Chinese juggler playing to haunting Chinese opera music, all compete with each other for the favors of the twirling mass that gushes like a river around us on the way to restaurants, movie theaters or just to be seen.

Where are the witches? Their tracks are still fresh, the imprints sharply defined. Their smell signature lingers in the air. We divide. Greg stays at the entrance near the parking garages, in case they return. I run like a hunter in the forest between the human trees in the search for the deer after their scent.

Still they are nowhere to be seen. Perhaps they went into a movie theater! Should I buy a ticket and search in the dark room for them? Maybe they are shopping inside a store, invisible from the outside. I could go into all of the stores. Irresolute, I turn around, with the capillary trickle of doubt seeping in and without searching any further I walk back to the waiting Greg.

In a moment of unguarded thoughtlessness I digress to wander spontaneously into the Midnight Special bookstore. Unraveling the tension, I aimlessly meander through the aisles of bookshelves until I come to the back, where a man arranges chairs. In a short while there will be a lecture. The tiny thought slips into my mind that this might be the reason for our witches' outing.

Outside on a bench I tell Greg of my hunch. While we are discussing our chances I see in the corner of my eye the approaching gaggle of witches, a surprisingly familiar troop, dressed in light colored summer garb with scarves whispering around their uniformly short hair cuts.

Within the ethnographic hodge-podge of the Saturday evening audience of the Santa Monica Promenade they stand out like the strangely homogeneous appearance of an alien life form. They flaunt past us without noticing. We are nothing in the field of their vision. Then they disappear into the bookstore. Just as I thought!

The lecture held by a literary circle announces readings of several members' works. In the first row of the audience sit Florinda, Taisha, Haley, Zaia, Darien, Carol, Nuri and Aerin. The only man present from the clan is Enzo. I pretend to absorb myself in the section of book rows with rock music history so I can listen in. I don't dare join them. My appearance would be more than suspicious. Or could this moment offer another opportunity to present myself to them as if by accident, manufacturing an omen?

Finally Zaia approaches the podium. So that's what they came for! To support Zaia. She reads about her feelings and thoughts during the translation of the diary of a Jewish Czech woman under Nazi occupation. Her voice has a sad leaden tone appropriate to the theme. None of her lines hint at her life as a sorcerer's apprentice.

Occasionally the women in the audience smile at each other knowingly.

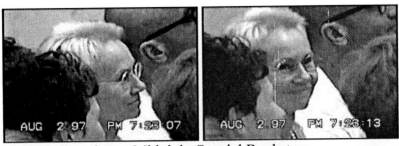

Florinda listening at Midnight Special Bookstore

Carol clowning

Midnight Bookstore outing   Florinda and Nuri

Greg climbs on the pedestal of a lamppost in front of the bookstore to look over the heads of the assembled crowd. A black Rastafarian inspired musician plays catchy tunes for the circle of swaying onlookers.

Aerin and Carol dance in the doorway of the bookstore like silly teenagers edging each other on, while Florinda purchases something from the bearded cashier. Their gold jewelry glimmers in the cool evening blue as they step together from the store engrossed in the atmosphere of momentary independence like students on recess or children without supervision.

Neither the witches nor the crowd surrounding us pays any attention to Greg clinging on the lamp with his camera or me on ground level observing. They are so close. And we are invisible. Again this curious fact surprises me and causes me to wonder.

Are the sorcerers really able to see more? Or have we become integrated features in their surrounding landscape no longer perceived as an infiltrating threat? Is the mysterious force, he calls "IT" on our side? Or are they just as unaware as the majority of people, wrapped up in their world of thoughts without seeing anything?

In the last scene of our capture the group of witches wiggles away to the beat of the music with the amoebic cohesion of a singular life form through the passageway back to the car. We don't follow them any further.

August 16, 1997. Saturday, 1 p.m. Taisha walks through the gate with a rod in her hand. Ten minutes later she drives off in her van.

1:26 p.m. Tracy parks on the Eastbourne side to unload boxes with cakes and platters. Haley's green Ford stops in front on Pandora. She and Nuri bring a crate with fabric into the house. It's beginning to look like a party.

4:11 p.m. Carlos comes home from lunch at the restaurant.

4:19 p.m. Taisha returns from her errands.

4:45 p.m. Aerin and Darien arrive dressed in Chinese silks and shiny satins.

4:56 p.m. Rich, wearing a summer suit and a sky blue shirt, walks around the corner of the hedge to the Pandora entrance, hesitates for a moment, then changes direction and enters the house through the gate on Eastbourne.

Kylie drives up in Carlos' old Chevy truck, talks a few moments with the tall German who has just arrived as well dressed in a light colored suit appearing to offer his help. Kylie wears an elegant black evening jacket with slacks. She embraces him quickly and then sends him away. He also enters the house from the Eastbourne side.

5:01 p.m. Enzo parks on Pandora. The tag of his jacket is still hanging on his back. Kylie while talking on her cell phone waves him away, prompting him to walk around the hedge to the Eastbourne entrance in his typical one arm-dangling gait, lurching forward to reach the gate in a hurry.

Greg repeats his speculation that besides Carlos, no other man is allowed to use the left entrance of the building, the magical Pandora side. Today the behavior of the participants certainly strengthens this view. In all the time, more than a year, that we have been sitting here on the weekends next to the fire hydrant we have never seen another man enter or exit the house through the gate on Pandora. The resident women and female visitors, on the other hand, seem to be using this gate exclusively. A curious idiosyncrasy?

Kylie has been waiting for Tamalia; together they schlep a double wide black coffin through the hedge opening. In the process they have to turn the coffin sideways to fit it through. When we run the video backwards it looks as if the two elegantly dressed women nonchalantly transport a dead person out of the house. Carol and Haley carry bags, boxes, flowers and a plastic devil fork inside.

The night roars with laughter.

Carlos returning from late lunch

Kylie and Talia carrying coffin into Pandora gate

Props for Sorcery Theater   Talia and Kylie

Chapter Nine

Caught in Westwood

Well, I don't think it's quite fair to condemn the whole program because of a single slip up, sir.
                    -General Turgidson in *Dr. Strangelove,* 1964

Gingerly his arm inched around my shoulder. I did not look at him. My eyes pooled over the green slope resting on the tip of the church tower in the distance. We were sitting on the grassy embankment of a roadway hollowed by centuries of oxen drawn wagons where the sour cherry hedges grew.

A strong wind whipped from the Ellinger heights, ripping in gusts over our heads. After what seemed a long time his head moved timidly towards mine. The space between us gradually diminished. I ran off with the wind in my mind, and he followed me like Siegfried, the Germanic hero, who chased after Brunhilde to prove his strength before he could win her.

We raced across the golden wheat fields, orchards and rutted dirt roads to the dark trees lining the hill. In the gloomy conifer forest too dense to permit entrance for any sunbeam you could hear only the roar of the wind in the high treetops trickling down to the pillows of the soft needle floor.

Forget-me-nots and spearmint were growing in the road ditch in fleshy summer green. The cracking of the wind trapped and separated us from the outside world, encapsulating us like an upside down glass shade. He was from Nuremberg visiting a relative in our small village during summer vacation. I didn't think he was particularly attractive, but definitely more interesting than the rest of the unmarried village bores who only under the influence of severe alcohol consumption attempted furtive finger fumbling advances.

A recent unfamiliar desire rising in my meager chest demanded to be played out in the stadium of puberty yielding to hormonal pressures. The bra my mother had given me a few years earlier still did not fit properly without sock inserts, but that did not worry me much, since all of the women in my family bend forward from carrying heavy attachments. Sooner or later mine would fill out as well, or so I believed.

The wind tore sounds to shreds, gathering them rapaciously to carry them off like hostages it never meant to release. We spoke little. I only sat there, feeling the warmth of his skinny adolescent body next to mine and waited an eternity for the first kiss of my teenage life.

In the forest Siegfried caught up with Brunhilde, overtook her and captured her in mid-flight. His breath, hot from the chase, blew passionately over her cheeks. His flashing eyes searched for agreement in hers. With the flicker of consent in Brunhilde's black pupils he pressed his lips on hers. The kiss burned like hot sand. Then he loosened his grip slightly to allow for his prized catch to melt into his body. Brunhilde's lips softened to moist velvet and his chest felt like a feather pillow. All locks burst open, sluices broke and unexpected rivers gushed from warm reservoirs.

Time distorted, washed away in the tearing wind, in the hot breath and the moist exhale of the green earth, until any sense of time and space collapsed completely and only the slow warm pressure of his arm on my shoulder remained. Siegfried's grip held on to Brunhilde's waist like a young tree trunk, tenderly strong. He wrapped her in the glowing heat of his arms, gently kissed her hair, her eyelashes, and the curve of her neck before closing her inviting lips with a moist seal.

Just as I was about to turn to meet his flushed face a sound bellowed on the bluster of the wind lunging at us with ferocity. The Gruner farmer on his tractor appeared in our wind bubble. He was already too close for us to move apart nonchalantly. Torn from the entropic world into which I had drifted imperceptibly, I felt caught in the awkward attempts of first touch.

The tractor rattled past, the farmer did not acknowledge us. But there was no doubt that he had seen us. Siegfried and Brunhilde drifted away on the wind in a tight embrace whispering love affirmations. My cheeks blushed crimson from the gale, the embarrassment and the suddenly uprooted unfulfilled fantasies.

It seemed as if the whole village had watched us - in a rare uninebriated state - and like the grip of harsh frost this image tore all tender buds from the sprouting tree of love.

By the time the bells where ringing for the evening prayer, everybody in the village knew about it. Especially the diligent pub customers extorted their unbridled imagination. When the news reached my mother, delivered by my vindictive stepfather, our harmless thwarted attempts of tenderness had become complete sexual intercourse without any effort on my part.

She was standing in the kitchen, in front of the stove on the eternally cold tile floor under the ever burning lonely light bulb, cooking. Maybe she remembered her own first awakening of love. She foamed with rage, slurring insults calling me a whore, the usual ungrateful pack, raising her wooden spoon as if she was about to hit me and kept on cursing and wailing. In me she fought her own insatiable sex drive that swept through generations of ancestors resulting in early and numerous pregnancies.

Brunhilde meanwhile bathed in rose water, combed her black hair with jasmine oil, crowned her head with a wreath of fragrant violets and lily of the valley, and dressed in a shimmering gown of green silk.

If my mother hit me I did not feel it. Her words, her distrust, burned in my heart like hot tar. She believed those sharp-tongued gossips in the dull village more then me. She did not bother to ask if it was true. Maybe she thought to smell in me a rival, one that

167

threatened her imaginary place in front of the mirror as the most beautiful and desirable woman.

She screeched that I would have to go to the doctor for an examination. I stood there with hanging head, choking down my tears, unable to counter her attack, which she might have interpreted as an admission of guilt. Her mistrust gave me the last blow.

My heart clenched in a tight lock and turned away from her for good. This was the final stroke. Years of disappointment eroded my hope for an understanding mother, one that could share the joy of first love like a friend. No, I did not expect compassion, sympathy or pity anymore, only an ounce of common sense. But she even lacked that. She did not know me; she did not know who I was after fifteen years. The accumulated weight from all previous experiences grew into an insurmountable clot that stuck in my throat.

Quietly I interjected that I did not need a check-up from the doctor. She did not believe me or pay attention. But after a while her eruption fizzled out and she gave up yelling. The feeling of being a good-for-nothing, extraneous, bothersome, despised impediment, a hindrance to her happiness whose only way out was death, invisibility or running way would not go away anymore. A few weeks later I left home.

Brunhilde and Siegfried played their game of love for many years without my notice.

The young red-shoulder hawk that sat on top of the telephone pole squawking all summer has finally gotten his adult plumage and takes off to hunt for himself.

On a cool summer night steeped in jungle black the dry magnolia leaves, cupped like beggar palms, burst and scrape over the cement sidewalk under my carefully placed steps. The sound of the cracking leaves echoes in cries through the sleepy neighborhood.

Our voices are muffled as usual. Actually we talk very little. It is not necessary. With acquired routine we stroll along the side streets like a couple on a walk to get fresh air. Pandora lies deserted in the first lull of night dimly illuminated by cones of yellow light that act as beacons in the inky shadow pools.

On the corner we run into the woman with the Pekinese. Nothing new. Also the two cars belonging to the energy trackers parked in front of Carlos' house don't concern us much. It would not be the first time we quickly and efficiently pick through the containers while there is still activity in the house. One only needs thirty seconds, not more than a decently sized earthquake.

Still sweaty from the practice group where we did the magical movements he taught us in seminars, I'm thinking how ironic it is that we are standing now like thieves in the night in front of the master's house to rummage through his trash.

Julio Iglesia's music seeps through the walls. The garden gate cut into the tall hedge gapes as always open to the inside. In sorcerer terms this could mean an invitation. Or oversight? Some windows glow. No indication to break off our intended objective. Softly we continue along the hedge. The lights in the room above the garage are burning.

Looking at the empty street canyon of Eastbourne Avenue a faint taste of flatness, an almost stale familiarity trickles in, as if the flow of discoveries has slowed to a stagnant eddy, to a windless lull or a river that seeps slowly underground.

Maybe we are losing the thread, the connection to the indescribable power out there. Maybe I made a wrong turn somewhere. Maybe this is the end of the road.

Just as I am poised to turn around to complete the goal of our nightly excursion I notice a strange movement in the merging shadows of the front yard bushes ahead of us. My eyes discarding the common from the new register the unfamiliar like a starving bobcat.

Carefully we approach the commotion in the bushes. Glowing iridescent eyes, rustling, scratching, tittering clumps of shadows peak my curiosity further. Getting closer the squeaking smirches become a family of raccoons, a mother with three half-grown young.

True, raccoons are not on the endangered species list of the Westwood neighborhood but up until now we have encountered none in the course of our nightly wanderings. They waddle up a staircase like wound-up stuffed toy animals in a badly lit Disney film. The smallest one, dragging a round belly, cannot make it up the

169

impossibly high steps; his front body too weak to pull the heavy back he squeaks with frustration. The bigger animal returns and with the unwavering patience of an experienced mother she nudges him with her friendly nose to try a little harder. Amused we watch them only a couple of feet away. They don't seem to mind the audience at all.

Almost thankful for the lighthearted diversion we follow as the group continues to romp through the yards. In this moment I completely forget the reason of our outing. The plump youngster lags behind a little. Hindered by his extra baggage or out of curiosity he sometimes turns his head to look at us. Without hesitation, as if they're at home in the yard with a trap waiting under the fruit trees, the raccoons crawl through the fence into the shadow of Carlos' fig tree. We hear them rustling along behind the hedge.

At the Eastbourne gate we catch up with the straggler that stopped to gaze through the bars with unflinching intention, almost formulating a question. In his eyes shimmers the starlight, reflecting pools of deep mysteries.

He stretches a delicate miniature hand towards us through the iron bars. A coaxing invitation or plain begging for food? For one instant the balance on the scale of reason tips precariously to rampant intuition conjuring fun house mirror distortions in my mind. Could these adorable raccoons be in cahoots with the sorcerers? Is their magic calling us? There are four raccoons leading us to his yard and there is one master with three witches in the house.

And then, as if to confuse me even further, from nowhere a gigantic black moth wobbles silently in front of my face pausing in midair before it enters through the gate to be sucked into the shadows of the sorcerer's yard. The touch of its velvet wings fans my disorientation. Night moths are the messengers of sorcerers.

Am I losing it? Are these omens an invitation to enter the gate and knock on the door to confess? Hi Carlos! We have watched you secretly for more then a year, observed your everyday moves, witnessed your follies and displays of tenderness, searched through your garbage and videotaped your comings and goings. The amber warmth of the room floods over me, and in my imagination I smell the cleaned away dinner, my eyes skim the barren walls, the immaculately clean wooden floors, the ascetic furnishings and their surprised faces.

But I can't envision their reaction. Would the sorcerers appreciate the pull and guidance of this strange unexplainable force that allowed us to get so close to them, or might they perceive us only as despicable intruders into their private lives? No other sign comes. And I cannot bring myself to test the delicate balance of the web. Maybe the moment for truth has not yet come.

The sentient tempter retreats behind the hedge hiding from our eyes. Around the corner on Pandora there is also no trace of the raccoons as if they vanished on the left side of the magical compound.

Unsettled by the images of the unusual encounter with the incongruent animals I walk on cottony legs to the row of trashcans to fall back into the comforting routine. With a few practiced movements we fish through the cans to make a selection of mostly lightweight bags hopefully containing papers and mail. Then with swift strides we begin our diagonal crossing of the street into the safety of the shadows under the magnolias.

Out of habit or in a senseless trance I move my head from side to side checking for cars, a superfluous gesture at night when their approach is obvious. Almost incidentally, I notice from the corner of my eye peeking over my right shoulder the fleeting glow of a dirty white image in the gap of the hedge behind us. It can't be the stucco wall that is obscured in the square rift of the hedge entrance. Just as we dive into the velvet black puddles I hear the faint crackle of a voice coming from far away, as far away as another universe.

"Hey! Hey you!" a female voice sounds. Is she calling us? Our feet keep moving forward like toy soldiers'. The voice insists. I glance once more over my shoulder. Sure enough, a girl from Carlos' house is following us.

The trees swell, taken by a mysterious night wind, dropping rustling leaves like projectiles. The wet lawn steams musty sweet, its scent mingling with the intoxicating night blooming jasmine and the heavy perfume of the magnolia blossoms. No doubt she is talking to us. She clings to our tracks like a little dog.

Should we drop our smelly bags and run off around the corner, split up and return later to the car when it is safe? Our steps accelerate imperceptibly. Or maybe it only seems that way. Unclear is also if we are actually talking to each other. Definitely not in complete sentences. Our thoughts seep and mix with each other freely in a telepathic state or hypnosis that erases the boundaries between thought and spoken word like a dream. Considering our usual bickering and miscommunications this is a miracle in itself.

"Maybe it's one of the new girls, a tracker who does not know us personally," my thoughts are saying, "we can pretend to be recycling homeless fumbling about in the trash."

I begin to experience the scene from a distance like a movie, sometimes in a camera angle from above, sometimes from behind, from a neutral uninvolved position, as if the story is unfolding all by itself.

Seen from 20 feet above, two trash pickers steadily strive towards the next street corner, and then pass through the suddenly glaring light of the soda street lamp. A detached calmness comes over me, a feeling of acceptance of circumstances and consequences.

"Hey wait," it rings again behind our backs, to which my feet don't heed. Her steps are louder and faster now. Just past the light, my car waiting in the shadows, the pursuer outpaces us and passes me on the left. Hands on her hips, she blocks my way to confront me face to face. Even in the twilight zone of the dimming light circle I recognize her.

It is Nyie, the cousin, former chacmool, now tracker who knows us well from the private classes and personal interaction during the seminars. No doubt she will identify our darkened faces even in the blinding halo of the sulfuric light.

She stares at me for a silent gasp. Finally she spits with a vibration of scathing indignation in the tone of her voice, "What are you doing?" No use of hiding behind the anonymous trash recycler role anymore, I stammer lamely, "But ...but... it's only trash".

My words brake the petrifying phase of her shock. She dives towards me like a hawk after fluttering, and rips the smelly plastic bags out of my limp grip. On her next lunge she passes me and attacks Greg's load, who has come to a halt just a few paces behind me. Then she runs off clutching the trash triumphantly to her chest. From the corner under the streetlight she yells, "You will never get close to us again".

Already in the echo of her voice I try to make sense of her words. One thing is sure: she recognized us. The half shadows did not protect us. In her instinctively spontaneous gesture of garbage rescue was something hilariously comical. She acted as if she prevented the robbery of the English crown jewels. Aren't the bags full of refuse, of garbage that they threw out?

Now physical awareness begins to slip back into my legs. The Hyundai is only a few feet away. My heart beats wilder as if to make up for the moments of disassociation and slowly I watch the implications of the last seconds trickle into my frontal lobes. A scenario, feared for months and played out in my mind many times has come true. We've been caught in the act.

Without losing another moment, I drive the car away from the place of discovery. The spilled anger on this corner and the upheaval growing in the house hidden behind the hedge is like a monster sitting on my back that chases me down to Thayer Avenue. Are they already following us? Furious thoughts thrash back and forth searching for wordless escape.

We hurry past the green and red traffic eyes, the neon glow of advertisements, the snaking pink-red rear lights. We hasten by the moon wrapped in fog shreds, pass the lapping ocean that slaps soft breakers in slow rhythm onto the polished rocks, to sink into the blackness that falls like a blanket around us, our dark canyon, the star studded coyote-howling world.

The road lined with strands of hairy eucalyptus branches digs a path into the thighs of the mountain, keeping the creek and its black alders company. Even in daylight the California laurel forest creates a dark impenetrable wall. Guarding the entrance to the narrows where the canyon becomes a gorge of volcanic outcroppings that tower straight into the triangles of sky, where puny shrubs claw into the rock of slick cliff faces that in spring transform into raging waterfalls, but now are reduced to trickling tear stains, standing at this place, a ghostly sycamore stretches its flecked limbs pointing fingers. In the fall the rust tinged leaves reflect in the mirror of the creek. Stone gray thumbnail sized frogs hop over algae covered rocks.

173

And hidden in the abyss below rot in mute concentration the skeletons of technological dinosaurs. Like strange red and blue fruits rusting car carcasses hang in the trees, the latest eagerly swallowed additions, pushed or fallen in drunken frivolity from the road that jams against the cliff.

After a ten-mile distance my thoughts begin to catch up with the rest of me. At home in the dark bedroom we stare at the white ceiling tiles that have an occasional brown water stain, and paint in detail the worst case scenario.

Brain is confused, Pinky afraid. "Are they on their way to us? They know our address." "At night without streetlights they will have difficulty finding the place." "They are plotting revenge." "Sorcerers are ruthless and cunning." "What will they do? Interrogate us? Sick their horrible beasts on us? Burn our house, threaten, and or kill us?"

Sorcerers have no scruples. Morals in the general sense they don't possess. Brain carries a heavy load. "Kylie will have to go to the office to get our address." "If she had caught us with the trash bags we would not have gotten away that easily. She would have chopped us to bits with her amazon knife movements."

"We have to stash the videos at a safe place. And hide the stacks of paper gleaned from the trash." "But where? Not at home! Maybe in a safe deposit box! They could not get to it."

Can they know what we really did? The extend of our yearlong endeavor? "All they know for sure is that we picked the trash once from their containers".

The darkness and the warmth of the blanket enveloping us give me a temporary feeling of reprieve, a fleeting comfort in a world that suddenly feels like crashing down a waterfall or a raging current without a kayak.

The minutes in front of the Pandora house play through my mind in constant repetition.

Why didn't we run off when we heard the voice? A riddle.

Why did we go ahead instead of waiting for the visitors to leave Carlos' house? Flipping arrogance or waning awareness!

Everything is over now, that is certain. This is the end of our adventure. Snuffed out by our own negligence and overconfidence.

The raccoons teamed with the moth unsettling my equilibrium of repetition posed a strange omen. Did I misinterpret it? Still, it appears as if the course of events once set in motion ran off by itself, unavoidably. Even my characteristic self-chastising can't undo the sudden avalanche that reduced me to a mere passenger. The raccoons, the moth were extraordinary signs. And the calmness that overtook me and gave me a perspective of removed compliance without thinking of escape, was like the movie segment in a video game in which the player temporarily is unable to manipulate the characters.

For hours we chew on the rubble of the sudden change and tremble with agitation until dawn wakes us. The morning comes in the deafening quiet of the first calm day after a storm. No loud knocking, no threatening voices, no smoke, no crackling fire, no collapsing beams. Did it really happen, the scene in the shadows of the street corner? Or was it just a bad dream? The scent still clings to me like a night in a smoky bar. What will happen next?

Since nothing seems to happen I go to work as usual. Pretending that it was only a rip in the fabric of time, a suspenseful movie segment, a scary dream that will heal by itself.

But then there is a message on Greg's answering machine. No, it will not be forgotten. The rocks we knocked loose are hitting the ground now. Kylie says in a businesslike tone, "Greg, this is Kylie. Call Cleargreen tomorrow please. Thanks very much. And be sure to call in the morning. Bye." "What should I tell her", Greg queues me on the phone. My suggestion powered by confusion is to let her stew a bit.

Shortly after comes the next, more pressing message, "Greg, this is Kylie again. I'm afraid that you're going to have to talk to us. Your registration has to be cancelled, you're going to be refunded your money, and the incident has been reported to the police, ah... you are going to have to explain, so you have to call Cleargreen, ah... there is just no way around it, and ah...you have to explain, not only to us, but also to the police. And ah... again you have to call because you have to know that the registration is cancelled. Bye." Kylie is the bulldog they've set on us. Possibly because she knows us the best? Greg has been writing her over the past years to describe his dreaming experiences. She never answered him, but we also never found his letters thrown in the trash (like so many others).

The third call from Kylie comes from her car phone. Her voice sounding desperate, creaking with hurt shows her private feelings, "Greg, how could you and Gaby do this?"

What did we do?

Is this the moment of truth?

Greg resorts to calling Kylie back after he is followed by an undercover police car to his work place. He recognizes the specific car type sporting prominent hubcaps. At my office I can't make dramatic private phone calls with my boss sitting right behind me.

With his phone call Greg manages to calm Kylie down, telling her that we weren't sure if it was Carlos' house that he had stumbled upon, accidentally driving by, until we resorted to searching the trash for confirmation. Only Nyie's overreaction gave away the importance of the inhabitants. Greg promises to keep the knowledge of the location to himself.

I'm astonished. I did not believe he was capable of such a cunningly reduced and minimalist confession. Usually when I ask him to avoid a certain subject in public his thoughts keep circling around the secret until sooner then later he spills it unintentionally.

Kylie is worried about my reaction though. I wonder why? Is the revenge of a woman more vicious? In contrast to me she might not have forgotten how they got rid of me in the private classes. Or maybe it has nothing to do with me personally and she reacts to ugly incidents they endured with others?

I would call her but she is most likely wrapped up in preparations for the next seminar in Pomona that is only a couple of days away, the yearly seminar in our area I definitely planned on attending. There is no question now that we are expelled from participating. This is the minimum punishment we can expect. I'll write Kylie a letter hoping it will convince her also of my harmless intentions.

Dear Kylie and Concerned,

Since I did not have an opportunity to talk with you on the phone I want to express my intentions in writing. I don't want to harm you,

Carlos or anybody in his group; neither do I intend to undermine his work. At the moment I have little personal contact with people in the practice groups. When we stumbled around the neighborhood and ran into the endearing raccoons, a mother with three young waiting for us behind Carlos' gate, when the moth fluttered in front of our noses we fell under a spell.

Still, we did not have the courage to follow the mysterious animals, ring the bell and confirm the identity of the inhabitants. So we succumbed to picking trash bags from the containers. We did not react when someone called and ran after us. Only when Nyie confronted us and ripped the trash from our hands it dawned on me that we really might have found Carlos' house. This realization was like a shock. I could not believe it. I'm sorry we disturbed your privacy. It certainly was not my intention. Sincerely.

Kylie promised to send back the check Greg mailed to Cleargreen for the seminar. It seems that they don't want to anger us, only punish us a little. And at this point it occurs to me that our knowledge effects a guarantee. They are afraid we could tell the whole world where Carlos lives and tomorrow tourist buses will drive by with the tour guide's voice on the microphone saying "and here lives the famous sorcerer of Westwood..." And camera lights for the press will go up in their front yard.

We are safe as long as they don't know what we really have.

Diana, princess of Wales, dies in a car crash in Paris. I can't fathom the reaction of my mother to that tragedy.

For days, even weeks we are uprooted, nervously looking over our shoulders for spies or intangible shadows following us. I almost wish they would have dug up the depth of our endeavor and the secrecy would be over. Only slowly my fears wear off. As the dust from the rockslide we caused settles, I realize, we are still intact.

In the aftermath I wonder why we got caught. Did we get cocky? Did we mock Intent with an unwittingly acquired attitude of invincibility? Or was it only a random turn in the universe of possibilities? Was it a warning from the power that granted us the access in the first place, a knock on the head to get our attention? We grazed a possibility.

It is inconceivable that the sorcerers believed us when we trivialized the extent of our undertaking and it is a splinter of disappointing negligence under my skin. In their place I would have talked to the transgressors face to face to find out what else they know and how they found Carlos' house. It equals a dismantling of their proclaimed superpowers, and it makes them smaller, more ordinary, and more human. On the other hand it saved us. We came close to losing everything, our collection of papers and the videos.

Now the path that seemed to end in disgrace continues after all, the door is still open a crack minus the mar on the shield of innocence.

During the daytime we stay away from the Westwood neighborhood as Greg promised. They know our cars and license plates by now and will have notified the private security patrolling the streets to look out for us. Realistically there is not enough proof for malicious intent to get a restraining order from a judge, which I'm sure they've checked with their lawyer on retainer.

The witches' ingenious move of holding back the trashcans until the morning of the pick-up was to be expected. Our access to that flow of information is now diminished, but there is as always the container behind the office building and all the other apartment locations. We will keep a light finger on their pulse.

It turns out Carlos did not participate in the weeklong seminar in Pomona. Greg is happy he didn't miss anything. It is unusual though. Carlos never used to let the opportunity pass to address a seminar crowd here in our county. Did our detection shake him up so much to cause his withdrawal from the seminar? A twinge of guilt nags on my stomach.

In the office trash we find a fax dated from August 14, with a schedule of the recent seminar. Even then, weeks before our discovery, Carlos was not included as a speaker. So we can be pretty sure that our transgression did not keep him away. I'm glad about that. I could not stand the guilt if we caused an illness or his missing of the seminar.

During the seminar Florinda supposedly revealed the shocking news about Carlos' ongoing sexual activity. The Sunday class was crushed by his revelation in June and subsequently he had to abandon the Sunday class project. That explains the sudden end we observed months ago. Funny, he never seemed sexually attractive to me on account of his age and I never considered his sexual overtures in class as actual pick-up lines, viewing them as rather sarcastic in their crudeness. And yet looking back over the time span that I have known Carlos and his interest in women, it seems not surprising. For myself I took his advice to test his veracity but not to blindly follow any one of his rules.

My fairytale princess looking for knowledge about life, that fell into the river and floated downstream to sink to the bottom, disintegrated slowly. She became green like algae. Tiny pieces drifted away settling on the stems of water lilies to be swallowed by frogs and fish to nourish plants and insects; her molecules danced on the waves reflecting the blue sky, caressing the slick rocks, playing with the petals of flowers to burst into sun streaked waterfalls.

Occasionally, in the evening, we slip by Carlos' house without stopping. Just to check if there are any other changes, if our exposure caused larger ripples in the pond of the sorcerer's dimension. That they neglected to follow up, that they did not "see" what we really did, this unexplainable turn, left the door ajar. The small sliver of light squeezing out of this door, this crack winks like an invitation to continue.

In one week the roof of his building is being resurfaced. Are they planning to sell the house and move? The place has been in a slightly neglected state for years. It certainly needed a new roof.

By October it becomes too cumbersome for the witches to get up early on Wednesdays to take the trashcans out to the street. The garbage is back outside on Tuesday night lined up like cans on a supermarket shelf. The sorcerers don't seem to fear us anymore. They have forgotten about us. Good.

The streets are empty, and the traffic lights shine for us alone at three o'clock in the morning. With the city in deep sleep not even the witches' dream thoughts bother us. The trash remains our only link to the river in which the sorcerers swim away. The air smells of changes.

In the full moonlight you can see your shadow in a silvery pale world. With little effort we peek over the wall on Pandora into the backyard patio. Maybe in the past the sorcerers of old jumped across this wall into infinity! Brick covered walkways surround a small empty dirt square that is meant for planting.

Next to the garage is the little house with washer and dryer that Flodo mentioned in a talk. Along the main house runs a ledge lined with figurines of metal and clay. Dwarf fruit trees grow next to the wooden gazebo. In the leaves under the trees sits a big flat quartz crystal and a bench. Through one window we can see Carlos' desk where we assume he wrote his latest manuscripts.

The copies of correspondence and faxes from the trash reveal that Tracy, Carlos' agent, pushes the publication of a new book "The Active Side of Infinity" through Harper Collins, even though Carlos' "Magical Passes" is scheduled to appear within the next six months, by February 1998. At the same time Cleargreen attempts to publish another manuscript, "The Wheel of Time" through their new venue Eidolona. Why the hurry? Normally, Carlos left at least four years between each book, the last one appearing in 1993. Within one year they are trying to throw three new books on the market? I remember Carlos used to say in the private classes in 1993 that he has another five years. Might his time be up?

Also in the trash there are the torn flight coupons of the trip to the Mexico City seminar, as well as a photocopy of Tamalia's passport; a card from Talia to Taisha: "You are always in my heart and I am forever yours, with love Talia". A note: "Haley dear, I'm too restless to sit in a movie this afternoon, maybe later. Love, Claude". Honest affection or cunning manipulation?

From the cut-up black cashmere sweaters, pants, dresses and curtains I fashion a Halloween costume for myself. A frame constructed from plastic pipes rests comfortably like a backpack on my shoulders extending my skeleton to seven feet in height. The head consists of a mesh cube open at the front and from its space-less interior glow the eyes of a bony plastic skull that starts to laugh hellishly with every step. My eyes peek out from under the black fabric cover at breast level of the reaper that is properly outfitted with a scythe and Frankenstein shoes.

Only in this disguise we dare to show ourselves in the witches' neighborhood on Halloween Eve. When the masqueraded children run from house to house begging for sweets we will wait modestly in the background. A gesture to Intent.

But Pandora Avenue untouched by Halloween is like every night. No hollowed pumpkins glow in the front yards; no artificial cobwebs decorate the windows, no hordes of children giggle and crowd around the front doors. Carlos' house is quiet too, no movement or sound behind the windows.

Undecided we stand, I as giant death, my companion in combat uniform, momentarily lost on the corner. From a distance our eerie appearance must look out of place even on Halloween. I wonder what he is doing and if he feels us inside the house.

As the shadow season begins with Sycamores dropping their leaves and the sun setting in the ocean again, I feel change coming in the sweaty taste of moisture and the pregnant wind howling around the corners, still invisible but audibly approaching.

The trashcans in front of Carlos' place and the container behind Cleargreen's office continue to be our line of connection. So far, no one has moved, all members of the inner group still live at the same locations.

But then, we find something odd. A yellow sticky note with a phone number for Bob Leslie Yachts, two pages with numbers of fishing stores in Long Beach and San Pedro, the phone number of the coast guard.

Do the sorcerers plan to go fishing on the high seas? But that's not all. We find an advertisement for the Open Forum for Sailing into the next Millennium for November 13th in San Diego, an evening covering the current and future situation of sailing, presented by a panel of experienced sailors and industry experts; a fax from Cleargreen signed by Angela and Fabrizio addressed to Lee Babin containing the exact requirements for the boat they are searching for: a freighter with crew cabins, thought as an expedition vessel, about 180 feet long with an open deck of at least 1,250 square feet, 21 cabins and a ten thousand mile sailing radius. An additional yellow note with the distribution of the cabins.

Why are they buying a boat? Are they intending to hold movement seminars on the ocean? Their request does not have enough cabins to make that idea profitable. Maybe Carlos wants to leave with his group, and disappear unnoticed in the wide-open oceans, far away from any authority! Carlos could take off like a rocket without distraction. And if he fails they could throw his corpse overboard and tell us afterwards that he took his body, boots and all, to infinity. A clean get-away. Nobody could disprove it.

Or maybe it is just one of Carlos' crazy ideas to keep the people in his group occupied with something exiting. Like the abandoned merchandizing of Nagual's cookies baked from Chia and Buckwheat, the perfect snack for health and energy conscious practitioners! It is hard to imagine how the group would survive out on the ocean considering their worldly ineptitudes.

How serious are they taking their boat search? On closer examination, everybody in the office seems to be involved. Kylie orders a list of books from Amazon, including 'Medical Advice for Ship Captains', 'Ship Electronics for Boat Owners', 'Cooking on the High Seas', 'Guide to Buying Ships', 'Fishing for Sharks', 'Good Food on Board', 'Big Sailing Cook Book', 'The Mobile Baker', 'Baking on Board', 'Feeding and Care of Ships Crew', 'Calorie Reduced and Nutritious Vegetables', 'The Keeping of Food'.

Taisha, Fab and the Blue Scout fly on October 31st with Delta Airlines to Ft. Lauderdale, rent a car from Hertz and stay for two nights at the Hampton Inn. The purpose of their trip was four appointments to inspect boats in the harbor.

A fax from Portland urges Fabrizio to make a decision since the seller has another party interested in his boat. A FedEx letter addressed to Grant from Boats & Harbors in Crossville, Tennessee, a catalogue with California yachts for sale, information on the Long Beach Boats Convention.

They sure work up a serious sweat. Undoubtedly their efforts are directed by Carlos, who is the center from which everything emanates. Could it mean that he is sick? That he is preparing to burn from within? As of late he has withdrawn from the seminars, from his beloved private classes, and only seems to give instructions to individuals at home. If he had started up new classes we would find some evidence.

The final chapter of his sorcery story is unfolding rapidly, the moment he prepared for during the last 35 years. From the description in the books of his predecessor's jump I have a clear picture in my mind, and so do all the people that surround him. The expectation keeps them riveted. And us as well.

Another thought provoking piece from the trash is the correspondence with a lawyer about the immigration status of one of the young tracker girls. Cleargreen vouches for her as an employer. To receive permanent resident status Cleargreen has to prove that they can't find another person in the US capable of teaching the magical movements.

For that purpose they publish employment ads in several local and national papers for a director of materials for Tensegrity with an income of $35,000 per year. The lawyer coaches them on methods to discourage any other legitimate applicant. We find resumes and notes on actual interviews with hopeful but fruitless applicants.

November 29, 1997. 4 p.m. We are revisiting Pandora and stop a safe distance from Carlos' house. Hidden behind rows of cars I take binocular snatches of Tamalia carrying a chair into the house. Darien and Aerin appear to help with unloading. If Carlos is still teaching pairs of trackers in his house he must be well enough?

The sorcerers of ancient Mexico are being refurbished. Cleargreen, in the effort to manufacture spiritual candy canes, continues to sanitize the appearance of the world of the sorcerers, gradually exchanging the ambiguous word "sorcerer" with the less charged, more popular "shaman", and chiming in with the much-derided new age community.

A confusing promotional approach intended to reach out to the masses, ignoring the traditional shaman's role as healer and spiritual caretaker of the community and natural world he lives in. A role Carlos never touted as his destiny. He does not care about this world, the environment or the people. Until a few years ago he cared only about the small circle of women surrounding him.

Now don Juan's sorcery has become a business that doles out freedom in small predigested bites, in purchasable increments. It appears to me like a facade, a means to another end. Remembering that the former sorcerers were ruthless, cunning, sweet and patient, I can assume they still are.

A familiar wave of pressure rolls across my face pushing my lower jaw down. A vice tightens above the eyes, around the root of the nose and the temples. My neck crammed together by the force from deep within my spine feels like it's being pushed against a wall. My head digs into its grip. Now a kick in the back pushes me to the side. The violent rhythmic pressure wakens me from a dream. Then the waves quiet abruptly. But the silence is more concern for panic then the pushing waves.

I know I have to get out. I'm still inside her belly. My brother came out first and she knows nothing about me. I wait in the stillness until hope runs out of my body and return seems the only open option. I give up being born, I give up being. Death becomes my friend.

A thousand times and more I am born. If I could only stay outside! As a child I learned to throw myself against the dream demons, devils and witches with the power sitting in my solar plexus. But I never managed to deal with the abstract dream that shook me back and forth between gray constricted despair and bright open happiness. The swinging between those opposing states caused deep panic inside of me.

Naturally I was born after all - without conscious participation, without noticing - into a world that has me constantly looking for a way out, for a way home.

Nowadays I hardly dream at all. No nightmares, no happy dreams or lucid ones. As if the presence of the master has turned my subconscious out into the open, transposed my dream world into waking life? The fantastic that surfaced before through coded messages from dreams into my waking mind now seems to be spread out in front of me in the open.

My life is a twilight dream of double realities. Lined up next to each other exist the world of common sense, the practicality of earning a living, maintaining and nourishing my physical needs, and the unexplainable, impractical, superfluous hunt for the origin seemingly mixing harmoniously in the contact with the sorcerers. Or is it because I don't sleep alone in bed anymore?

Again, as so often in my life, I feel thrown back onto myself. I am dissatisfied with my progress, jealous of others and confused. Carlos does not conduct private classes anymore and does not appear in seminars. He is preparing for his ultimate departure.

Did I understand his teachings? He told us once, that he taught us everything he knew and that it was now our job to apply it. Should I have made bigger efforts to be taken into his inner circle? There was another opportunity when I caught the attention of a person from the inside. I stepped on her twice during the dancing at the seminar and her eyes lit up when I met her the next day at a follow-up talk for Germans by Florinda. But I was too proud and honest to pursue the potential sponsor that was primed by manipulated omens. I was not ruthless enough to force my way in or use the knowledge gained during the secret observing.

December 28, 1997. Sunday, 7:47 p.m. Pandora is quiet. A new midnight blue Ford pick-up has replaced the old puke-yellow Chevy. Still without license plate. The registration taped on the inside of the windshield shows the company, Cleargreen, as the owner.

A steady stream of confirmation from the trash pacifies our concern if Carlos is still around. His signature on contracts, notes with tasks from the Nagual, references to him, phone numbers in large writing, occasionally his high voice in the house, verify his presence though we have not seen him in months. Other fans, we hear in the practice groups, intercept him at Versailles, his favorite Cuban food

185

hangout, for a late lunch. We can't afford to attract his attention in such an obvious manner.

Carlos the Jackal, the revolutionary thief, caught after twenty years and standing trial in a French court says to his life sentence in prison, that it does not scare him and "Long live the revolution"!

January 15, 1998. Thursday. Tracy places an ad for sale in the paper offering antique furniture pieces. He is looking for a new place with three bedrooms in the same neighborhood he lives in now. There are properties marked on his list of prospects from newspaper and real estate brokers ranging from five hundred thousand to nine hundred thousand dollars. He could be planning to move himself, or he might be looking for comparative houses to estimate the current value of Carlos' property. For evaluation or sale?

Judging by the trash, Cleargreen acts undeterred as if there will be a rosy future full of seminars. Unlike the early years when Carlos planned from one seminar to the next, this time the corporation had a meeting and made up a schedule of workshops for the whole year.

Unrest, the unstable feeling of change vibrates in the air around the sorcerer's house. We register the signs of the approaching storm. The sudden suspension of all private classes, the unprecedented renovation of the house, the mysterious search for an ocean going vessel, the hasty push to publish three books within one year, his holing up in the house, it all points to impending change: his departure.

There is a defiant streak of optimism inside of me that hopes to be able to watch the decisive moment, in courtesy of IT, the sheer luck, the unexplainable force, that allowed us to be here in the first place. Greg hopes to catch the flight to freedom with his camera. Whereas my dreaded glass half-empty attitude of rational probability deems it unlikely. Even if by some kind of miracle we end up at his house at the right time, and it definitely would be happening at night, our video camera would not pick up much in the dark backyard.

Time is approaching completion. My roaming thoughts intuit the next steps of the master by drawing from the well of possibilities. And they circle around Pandora like the jaguar.

Chapter Ten

Back To The Beginning

Look who knows so much! There is a difference between
mostly dead and all dead. Mostly dead is slightly alive.
                              -Miracle Max in *The Princess Bride,* 1987

Jack-pot in the trash. Carlos cleaned out his old bills and receipts from 1988, 1989 and 1990. Nicely sorted in envelopes, ripped in half only once. A child's play to reassemble them again. The information is slightly outdated but in its completeness it gives a detailed picture of the sorcerer's household eight years ago.

The assortment of signatures on credit card slips helps us to confirm the writer of many previous pieces of handwritten notes. Taisha scribbled the purpose of the expenditure on the back of the credit card sales receipts. Keeping in mind that these notations were added for tax reasons, one can still assume that the choice of words borders on factual concepts floating around in Carlos' mind, even if whimsically pulled out of midair.

During a visit to the Fish Company with Florinda and Taisha, Carlos spoke with them about the filming of "The Teachings of Don Juan". (In the later private classes he pooh-poohed the attempt of a famous director trying to pry and distort the don Juan story).

Frequent lunches in Venice reflect discussions with Margarita about her lectures. Several receipts for dinner and lunches with Howard Lee in 1988 had the topic of sorceric kung fu. It seems the word used nowadays for the practice of the magical movements was not invented yet. From the many receipts of private studio rentals one can assume that Carlos or Howard Lee was teaching some form of movements even then to a core group.

Carlos' list of expenses include generous purchases of clothing, shoes, jewelry, college tuition and rent for Nuri Alexander, the blue scout; the sole responsibility for the absolute minimum of repairs and the maintenance on his building structure; groceries for everybody living in the house, definitely for Taisha and Florinda, and perhaps even for Mary Joan Barker.

Carlos' favorite clothing establishment was Brooks Brothers, a little more modest then his recent taste for Armani outfits.

Every penny spent was meticulously recorded. Ann-Marie Carter ran the majority of household errands, to the hardware store, post office, office supply store, drugstore, and interfaced with the gardener.

Kylie begins to show up running office errands in 1990.

In accounting terms the mysterious world of the sorcerer is the world of a writer supporting a group of women, invested and fully insured with health, dental, automotive and retirement packages.

President Clinton answers to allegations that he had an inappropriate affair with Monica Lewinsky and supposedly told the young white house intern to lie about it.

February 13, 1998. Friday, 3 a.m. Pandora's Box. We drive by his house to make sure he is still there, that he is still alive. Velvet darkness permeates the street corner. The jaguar is growing, absorbing the neighborhood. The fear that the sorcerer could be slipping away sits very close, making us restless.

Tamalia parked her Ford Taurus on the driveway in front of the garage on Eastbourne. That is unusual. Has she moved in? In the room above the garage burns a light bulb and the windows are covered with transparent plastic foil. Preparations for painting. Maybe inside. The outside could definitely use a makeover as well.

The trash cans continue to be stocked as always. No more talk about the Boat. Acupuncture needles in Carlos' trash. Presumably treatment from Carol? But for whom?

February 18, 1998. Wednesday, 10:30 p.m. Pandora Avenue. We make the round to check on changes. The light in the room above the garage is burning again. They are still here. Everybody is tucked into the same apartments, Carol on Rochester Avenue, opposite from her the younger trackers, next door to the Blue Scout; Tracy, Reni and Nyie on Manning Avenue next to each other; Fab and the other guys on Amherst.

February 22, 1998. Saturday, 2:23 p.m. I've purchased a white car. With this new disguise in white, patching up the sheen of innocence, we dare to sit again at the old spot on the corner of Pandora and Eastbourne, next to the fire hydrant. Carol's Ford stands on Pandora. The midnight-blue truck has a license plate now. The tangerine tree peeks from behind the top of the hedge with glowing orange balls. Veiled sunlight drips on the sidewalk under the evergreen magnolias and the Chinese elms.

Tamalia appears in her silver Ford and stops in the middle of the street next to the Pandora hedge entrance lacking a close parking spot. Flodo jumps from the green hedge portal, dressed in a white blouse and opens the rear passenger door. On the backseat in the middle I spy the small grayish silhouette of a head.

Could this be Carlos? The one we have not seen with our eyes for four months! Flodo holds the door open with one hand, with the other she assist the person out of the car. An obnoxious lamppost positions itself directly in our line of sight covering the right side of Tamalia's car.

Full of agitation I stare through the binoculars to catch a close-up glimpse. Minutes seem to pass in the breathless vacuum of suspense. Then a thin frail man appears from behind the lamppost, slightly hunched forward, his meager hair growth covered by a black golf cap, his emaciated neck showing the strands of tendons. He shuffles

189

carefully to the hedge entrance as if feeling his way forward. Florinda follows him. For a second a passing minivan blocks my view and when it is gone, the gaunt figure slips into the freshly painted garden gate.

Shock strangles me. Was it Carlos? This man looked twenty years older, fragile and sick with gray-pale complexion, like an invalid, sunken without strength or presence.

My eyes hold on to the empty gap in the hedge as if they could rewind the last few seconds of the fleeting image or as if the green wall held the answer.

Death rides on the left shoulder and whispers in the ear of the sorcerer.

My mind running in overdrive is hurdling over miles of possibilities unable to make connections. A hundred times or more I have seen Carlos walk through this gate, observed his profile, his posture, his gait like a hunter watches prey, like the jaguar chasing him in the magical desert. I know him by the roots of my hair, the veins in my eyeballs, and the dull beat of the aortic valve.

Tamalia backs into the Pandora crossing. While our heads sink automatically behind the dashboard she turns around and parks her car in the courtyard of an apartment building opposite of Carlos' house. She moved closer to Carlos.

I still refuse to believe what we have just seen. It could not have been him. The pictures of my album of collected memories roll off in front of me like police mug shots. I see the snapshots of a witty, charming and generous man, sometimes cranky or vulgar, impatient and dominating, but always completely present. They are incompatible with the picture of the last ten seconds.

They drip into the dirty puddle of the image mirroring his miserable weakness. Without will, reduced to the smallest radius, distant, occupied with the battle of pain, bent, weakened, pitiful, without control, bitter, fragile, on the doorstep of death.

Surely we've watched the changes during the last six months and I suspected that Carlos might be sick. But I never imagined him to be on the brink of death. Didn't he boast at the seminars that, in the event of becoming ill, all we had to do is switch to another track? And he proudly used examples from his own experience.

A thin veil of sadness creeps over me, a cloud of crusted tears covering my eyes. Slowly a red zeppelin wanders across the billowing sky.

We sit stunned with our binoculars and camera on the corner. Kylie drives up in her All-Trac, bringing Styrofoam cups and a white bag from the bagel shop into the house. Her serious long face shows the same crushed expression that we noticed on her the first time about nine months ago when she was leaving Dance Home.

4 p.m. An unfamiliar white BMW double parks in front of the hedge. Florinda steps out of the gate to talk to the driver, and then she receives a bag. A pharmacy bag!

Gladly I would like to be mistaken; gladly I would like to believe that what we saw in the ten seconds between the lamppost and the passing van was a ghost, or merely a view into a parallel universe, the terrible possibility of a life variation.

The phantom Carlos

Carlos deathly ill

At home I compare the pictures in my head with the caught images by watching them repeatedly in the replay of the videotape. There is no doubt, our formerly funny and wiry master totters like a gaunt apparition, a ghostly shadow of his former strength again and again through the hedge.

He has the sickly look of a hospital stay, the balding skull of chemotherapy treatment. He shuffles along the street as if on a hospital hallway in house slippers, wearing an unbecoming cap that only partially hides his emaciated head and thin hair. Where is his wild hair, that glorious shock that stood triumphantly into all directions in silver laughter, a metaphor of his personality? Hundreds of heart-wrenching forlorn steps he schleps himself to the gate without determination, clarity or certainty, a seemingly endless walk caught in the fog of pain, until my heart and eye break in sadness.

The princess that fell into the river to find the secret of life dissolved into uncountable particles that were picked up by the sun, lifted with the mist, swept across the ocean sky in big cloud ships and released in the drops of rain and snow.

She seeped through the thirsty earth, trickling along the roots into sandstone caverns, collecting in still pools of dark olive waters. She rose with the fresh sparkling springs flowing from the mossy embrace of the mountains. Then she meandered through the brook, back into the river. And the river murmured, "I am the water of life and the water of death".

Again I feel lost. As if the path, the connection, the web has come to an end. The hopes I carried for Carlos, the hope he imparted, whatever I saw in him is shrinking to a dying flame. Why was I being led here? The burning desire that brought me here, was it only a mistake? Who has answers for me now? Backtracking.

I'm taking the advice given to Inigo in the *Princess' Bride* when he got lost: "Go back to the beginning". The beginning where I still knew who I was! I hate to be stuck in the nothingness. Years ago I explored my subconscious with right and left-hand writing. I wonder what would emerge from this now. I have nothing left but myself.

What am I doing here, in this world? Who am I? What is my purpose?

The answers are in you. Just ask.

Whom? Who are you?

We are the hundred thousand, the river, the flow.

Are you the emissary Carlos talked about? Do you have a name?

Call me whatever you like.

Where do you all of a sudden come from?

We have been here for very long, the chorus of voices you tend to ignore.

You have been talking to me for a long time? How come I have not heard you?

You are too involved in the play. Between the voices of self-pity ours was too quiet. Only at the point of complete helplessness you start to listen.

That knocks me over. Where are you?

In you and everywhere.

How can you be in me?

You are caught up in the game of illusions and you have forgotten who you truly are.

Well, you tell me!

You believe to be the little Gaby. In this role you sweat away spinning a web of detailed world reflections. The interpretation of this web uses up all your energy and swallows you. And here it is: you are us. You/us are everything there is. There is nothing but us.

Oh, come on, that sounds unbelievably absurd!

February 25, 1998. Wednesday, 2:50 a.m. Trash collection. The windows on the Eastbourne side of Carlos' apartment complex are not taped up anymore. An illuminated room on the lower level is empty and appears freshly painted.

There is a prescription for Florinda Donner-Grau for hormones. Muni throws away a certificate of completion for an eighteen-hour continual education course for acupuncturists specializing in Tibetan aryuveda from December 1997.

February 28, 1998. Saturday. The image of the shrunken Carlos still haunts me. It demands to be replaced with my old happy Carlos.

8:21 p.m. and Carlos hasn't shown his face today. In the half-dark of the lamp light meeting the night Taisha wipes the windows of the room over the garage with a rag in quick determined movements. I doubt the success of her low-light efforts. Her round earrings dangle in the brisk rhythm of her arms.

Carol's head appears in the cutout of the window. She directs two 'elements' to deposit a small table under the window. Will this become her room now? Is she moving in? She is not happy with the arrangement. The two men carry the table back out the door and put it in front of the garage door on the driveway.

Through the open side door next to the garage we can see the walkway between the buildings and spy into the lit up patio where waiting boxes, baskets and small furniture pieces are piled. The men carrying objects, together with Florinda and Taisha dance back and forth between the lamp circle and the dark, resembling an Indonesian shadow play.

By 11 p.m. all activity ceases. Only the windows above the garage are still open, most likely to vent the fumes of the freshly painted walls. Inside the light is burning. Brown grocery bags are placed on a counter. On the windowpanes you can still see the glue strips of the tape.

All three witches now live in the house with Carlos, and his two most dedicated apprentices, Kylie and Tamalia, moved into the apartment building across the street. The proximity of his closest companions confirms the seriousness of his condition.

How can I be you? That's not possible.

Feel it. Deep inside you know that it is true. With the small reflective mind of calculating reason it is incomprehensible. The world around you and the experience of your Self are only pictures generated by your mechanism of interpretation, a self-reflection that creates all its components.

Everything you experience, see, feel, and think is your creation, your unique world. But you can't find your true nature in it. All the while you wait to be guided by someone else and there is no one but you/us.

My intellect refuses to accept the absurdity of these concepts. Carlos' worldview is strange enough. Am I not exchanging one fantastical mental contortion for another?

The concept itself is not an interpretation, only the pictures. As long as you are aware of the process and you don't become attached to appearances.

Oh, then I should not become attached to you either, shouldn't I?

That's right, not to the picture, the image you conceive in your head. It is a letting go, a shedding of skins on all levels. So our movements stay smooth.

I still doubt the veracity and sincerity, the honesty of your voice. Maybe it is only a product of my cornered mind.

Would you rather listen to another voice, a reflected mirror image? You would doubt any voice.

You're right. But to tell you the truth, I expected more, a multi-layered, elaborate and colorful explanation of the mysterious principles of life. The ornate exuberance of animistic societies, the beauty and serenity of Tibetan Buddhism, the creativity of European mythology, to mention a few. Why is your revelation reduced to such a simple formula? This narrow scope lets me suspect that it is just my own invention, my own simplistic mind.

It is not so. And you have known this for a long time; you sensed it and you tried to remember. All your searching, hoping and thrashing around was to re-member the connection to us/you.

Your longing was the yearning for us, the end of the separation from the real you. Now you are home. If that appears to you like simpleminded babble it has to do with the level of your capacity of understanding. Our voice speaks to you on a wordless plane, from which you translate it into your limited vocabulary.

Listening to myself makes me tired.

Your old self-image wants to hold on. Loosen your grip!

March 7, 1998. Saturday, 5:58 p.m. Gavin, Fab, Tracy and Grant are in the front yard behind the hedge pushing a rototiller around. Another one of the 'elements' handles a wheelbarrow full of dirt.

"To bury Carlos," Greg jokes. He hasn't lost his gallows humor. The caretakers of the sorcerer are re-landscaping the yard. The hibiscus bushes on the Pandora driveway have been removed. The stucco of the building has been repainted, so have the window frames and doors. The Eastbourne side sports the first motion detector light. The gate shines fresh in new ivory colored paint.

Taisha mentioned in a recent seminar that nowadays she stalks the position of an interior designer. In every day language that means she oversees the renovation work on the house. As long as Carlos was holding the reigns no man worked at the house or the backyard, except for professionals during emergencies. He nailed the lattice against the wall himself, instead of asking one of the able male 'elements' of his group. And now he does not care anymore that they trample all over his house and yard? There is no explanation for it other than that he has lost the reigns, mentally as well as physically.

6:32 p.m. Taisha drives away in the van. 6:45 p.m. Kylie crosses Eastbourne to her apartment carrying a paper bag on her arm and a tray of bowls. I take that as an indication that Carlos is home. He does not show himself. He is either too sick for his usual restaurant visit or we missed him. No opportunity for us to correct the mirage we saw a couple of weeks ago.

6:54 p.m. The elements that worked in the garden take off. 6:58 p.m. Kylie drives away. The windows in Carlos' house glow like lanterns illuminated by golden candlelight.

7:41 p.m. Carol rummages in the room above the garage, her head bobbing back and forth.

10:26 p.m. The lights are off. Carol's Ford Contour is parked to stay in the driveway.

Where is Carlos? Or more pressing: what is his condition? The certainty of his tragic end inevitably rising like dawn rallies my adrenals to new heights of production.

March 11, 1998. Wednesday, 3:25 a.m. Midnight full moon trash trip. No changes. All the familiar cars are still there.

In the garbage we find a medication label for Captopril 12.5mg prescribed for Carlos on February 22, 1998 by Dr. Duenas.

An armful of neckties. A cardboard box with garden utensils, gloves, the red clippers Carlos used to cut the hibiscus branches off, seeds for green beans and Swiss chard, refrigerator magnets and two straw-hats. Looks like the gardening days of the inhabitants of the house on Pandora are over. The have-a-heart trap that was unsuccessful in capturing the raccoons goes home with us as well.

I need to talk to you. I am confused by the explanations you have given me.

You still want to cling to the image that you are a specific, clearly delineated being.

What else can I be?

In your fantasy, you believe that this is all you are. You perceive yourself only from a particular fixed perspective, a limited view: You base your identity on differentiation and distinction.

I am not the sum of my experiences? I am what others see in me, what I mean to them.

But you are much more. You/we are the endless. You are us. Each possible aspect of life, as you encounter it, is only a facet of your own reflection. Don't attach yourself to a single one. Let it flow.

I am afraid I'm tricking myself.

You trick yourself if you believe in a divided world. The truth in its simplicity is more difficult to grasp. There is nobody you have to convince, nobody to convert, nobody to accuse, nobody to be jealous of. There is only one, you/us. No need to struggle or change, just accept the truth, as implausible as it might seem. You and us, we are one and the same.

I'm alone?

March 18, 1998. Wednesday, 3:56 a.m. Trash hunt. Ten-minute video of black nothing. One of the witches, my guess Florinda, dumped her fashion jewelry into the trash. A frog lover's bag full of brooches and pendants with frog motifs.

In addition, we find a broken Mexican ceramic dog that Greg skillfully restores with glue. Another ceramic statue of a couple engaged in sexual pleasures, broken in countless pieces, poses a bigger challenge. We also stumble on the original of a marriage document from Las Vegas indicating that Bruce Wagner married a Carolina Leonora Aranha on October 20, 1995, with Florinda Donner as witness. Carolina Aranha could be another name of Carol Tiggs.

An internet search for marriages in Las Vegas yields another surprise. Carlos married Florinda Donner on September 27, 1993, and a couple of days later under the name Carlos Aranha he married Carol Tiggs. The rules of this society don't mean much to the sorcerers.

March 22, 1998. Sunday, 7 p.m. Pandora. Carol leaves the house from the Eastbourne side, dressed in a neon green jacket with a disheveled hood. Her lips move to a song, her head teeters back and forth seemingly carefree on her way to her parked car on Pandora. Does Carlos' illness not affect her? Or is she in denial?

7:12 p.m. Flodo in a white blouse, black pants and yellow rubber boots waits in front of the Pandora gate with her hands on her hips. Her gold-blond hair glows like a lantern in the approaching dusk. For a moment she looks in our direction to the corner on the opposite side of the road, at least through the binoculars her gaze hits me directly. But then Tamalia drives up in her silver sedan.

Expectation causes me to tremble like the first time on the fire escape. Are we going to see another glimpse of Carlos? Will it be the familiar quirky, in-control and energetic Carlos? Maybe by some miracle he has recovered! Flodo meets the car and opens the back passenger door.

Paining my eyes, an even weaker Carlos slowly works himself out of the vehicle, an invalid insisting on doing it himself. The saddening image crushes me. It is no illusion, no fata morgana. Florinda leads him solicitously by the arm to the gate in the hedge. A light colored sweater draped over his shoulders by his custodians, his right hand clambers on to his white pant leg, in a feeble gesture looking for support. He wears no hat this time and his thin, meager hair is visible, indisputably pitiful. The color of his exposed skin is dark, almost purple in comparison to Florinda's complexion. I did not notice this detail two weeks ago.

Didn't he tell us that when we're old and sick it is too late? The chances of him leaving this world with his complete body as he intended, as the highest goal of the sorcerers of his lineage dictates, achieved partially by his predecessor, appear very slim now.

Tamalia parks her car on Pandora and walks stiffly with the serious expression of enduring tragedy to her apartment on the other side of Eastbourne.

Carol singing   Florinda waiting

Carlos peels himself out of the car

And shuffles to the house

March 28, 1998. Saturday. Again we sit in front of his house hoping to see him, to ascertain that it was not a sorcerer's trick, a cruel joke that he played on us. I have to know if it is true. Only the consistent confirmation without aberration will give me the picture I accept as the truth.

7:37 p.m. The evening dusk already turns the sidewalk under the magnolias dark blue and blurs the contrast between the few remaining shades of color. If Tamalia delivers him now we might only see scheming shadows. And there she is, driving up and stopping in the middle of Pandora. As if the blue-gray grainy light conditions weren't dampening enough, a lamp post further obscures our view. A fuzzy Florinda opens the rear door.

Greg accuses the pillar of conspiring. But I feel as if it's my fault for having parked in the wrong five inches. I start up the engine to adjust our viewing angle, forgetting that the camera is connected to the cigarette lighter. For a moment the motor sucks all the power to the camera, interrupting Greg's filming at the crucial seconds during which Carlos traverses the distance between the car and the hedge. And I had no opportunity to watch him with binoculars either.

Now Greg has reason to blame me. The seconds of Carlos shuffling from the car to the house are lost before the camera is readjusting. "It's too dark anyway," I play down my mess-up.

Out of frustration, we follow Tamalia to the gas station on the corner of Beverly Glen and Santa Monica. She has turned up the collar of her natural white jean jacket. It is cold. Then she takes a blanket from the backseat and rolls it up. This is the blanket Carlos uses to wrap himself.

As long as we see this blanket in Tamalia's car she must be driving him around and he must be alive.

Talia folding blanket

In the empty midnight-blue of my mind's window staring into the unknown I see nothing, no mysterious swirling corners and cubes, only the blackness of death. Maybe next time I will see the strong confident Carlos again, and the recent apparition was just a deception, a trick, an illusion. Tomorrow we will try again.

Hi. I thought about the things that you told me.
Great. You are listening. We have so much to tell you.
About what? I'm curious.
About life!
Can I ask a question about Carlos?
Sure, what do you want to know?
Does he say the truth about don Juan?
Don Juan was as real as our voices in your mind.
If everything is only an interpreted reflection of me, then Carlos has to be one as well, right?
Yes, one that reminds you of the way home. That's why you are attracted to him.
Carlos said that there are powers out there that suck energy from others. Is that true? Do you feed on me? You have to tell me the truth!
Everything is you-us. There is only one. It is your fear-induced perception that creates an opposite, just like the feelings of loneliness and separation create friends - to experience. We collect experience. It does not matter what kind. We make no differentiation between

good and bad, between joy and sorrow, between success and loss.
Only from your current perspective you make those distinctions.

Whenever I talk to you it seems as if no time has passed since our last discussion.

March 29, 1998. Sunday, 6:20 p.m. Florinda sends off the male elements that have been working in the front yard until now. Then she hastily sweeps the sidewalk on Pandora. As if she is expecting him soon!

6:36 p.m. Tamalia arrives in her metallic Ford. It is still light enough to recognize details. This promises to be a revealing opportunity. The car waits in the street for a long sixty seconds.

Where is Flodo? She usually stands at the gate. Hurriedly, she rushes out of the hedge wrapped in a white bathrobe and white slippers. She opens the car door and waits. This time the fluted pillar of the street light is not in the way. The figure in the backseat makes a tremendous slow-motion effort until his feet reach the ground next to the car. Then he straightens out in front of Florinda.

Carlos is still alive, but how! He wears the black cap again, and a dark blue jacket with a white collar underneath. He searches for Florinda's arm and she guides him to the entrance.

Instead of seeing an improvement, which I hoped for against all odds, he appears to be more frail and emaciated. Even the strength to walk the few steps to the gate by himself has left him.

The last sight of Carlos   Talia closing gate

I can't imagine that he will recover from this depleted state. Having worked in hospitals and doctors offices I have seen my share of seething death. It can only go downhill from here. There is of course the possibility that he could stay bedridden for years like Howard Hughes, cut off from the outside world. As long as the group is able to get an occasional signature from him, nobody else would need to know how sick he really is.

But our funny, wiry, adventurous, energetic, brazen, and peppy Carlos is no more.

After Tamalia parks her car she walks along the hedge with sorrowful shadows on her face, and then with an afterthought she turns abruptly to close the garden gate. She buttons her jacket shivering from the inner and outer cold.

The closed gate becomes the metaphor of his impending end. As long as he was the master of the house, the gate was always ajar. An invitation to welcome spirit. Now spirit cannot enter anymore?

The pears are splashing on to the white gravel again, wasps swarming around the putrefied wombs. It is undeniable: Carlos is sick, too sick to turn himself into pure energy, too sick to be himself. The jaguar roars like a wounded animal. The game is over.

What is over?
Without the Nagual nothing goes.
You never wanted to depart with him!
Yes, that's true, I've always had reservations. But despite my hesitation, doubts and critique on the discrepancies and shortcomings of his teachings, he deserves to achieve his ultimate goal for which he worked his whole life. Even if it is not my path.

My heart aches with a loud "no" in a realm that until recently promised the impossible. Its tinny echo bounces from the steep cliffs of looming death. How can he reach his goal under such conditions? To see him so ravaged hurts like the loss of love. He is the physical example of my own escape, my victory. *You've already succeeded.* If he fails does my will falter to complete the path I began? Do I fear to be stuck in a dead end? Have I wasted years of my life on the wrong path? *You are home.*

In all those years of closeness, of earnest peering into this invisible world I have grown to love him, more than a mother, more then a father. They only pushed me into this world; he showed me a way beyond.

The jaguar sniffs the air that smells of death, of dark rotting, of vanishing and decomposing. Sorrow falls over the neighborhood with the hulky shape of the reaper standing on the corner. It joins us as allies of the few who grieve for him, who watch his decline helplessly and with composed sidewalk faces, and witness with barely veiled brows of sorrow the fall of their world. "Your pain mirrors in my eyes," cries the jaguar in the recesses of my heart. From there it runs down the creek in the lost reflection of the centennial steep tile roofs and cow manure heaps.

He waited in the gray shadows of the early morning avoiding bright sunlight and the farmer that unlocked the front door to milk the cows. At night he had wandered, a lonely figure on the silver moonlit gravel road snaking five miles from the city to our village and crawled like a thief into the hay barn. Now he sneaked quietly through the leaning door and stole up the creaking wood steps to the second floor.

I woke up from his impatient shuffling and searching in the dark hallway. He was looking for his things. The door to our room was locked. My mother was scared. The white paint of the door rasped: "It's me." For a moment I wished that the door would open and my father would enter with a smile, embracing my mother, who'd cry out of happiness and I would hug his waist and smell the sweet scent of pipe tobacco and sun-dried hay in his shirt. And he would stay.

"Go away, leave us alone," hissed my mother under a breath of anxiety. "I'm only getting my things," the voice in the hallway mumbled. He rummaged on top of the tall wooden wardrobe, where I knew he kept his oil paints and brushes, which I secretly borrowed to play Michelangelo.

Then he came back to the door. "Let me see the children," he tried to charm. My mother was immobile with fear, marooned in the middle of the room, a safe distance from the door, as if she expected him to break it down. Her voice, repressing the rising panic, reluctantly agreed to open the door a crack. In the past when he had appeared unexpectedly her voice vibrated in a mixture of desire and fear. But I don't remember her ever flushing with joy, or tears coming from her eyes saying, "I am happy you are here".

How I wished it only was a dream.

My nosey little sister broke ranks and trotted to the door. There was no hint of fear in her gesture, only trust. Maybe with hearing my father's voice she remembered his strong arms twirling her around in the air and her own squeals of delight. She slowly turned the long black key, something I could never do again in my dreams, and the door opened a few inches.

In the gap appeared the smiling grimace of my father. He glanced from one child to the other and my mother started sweating. Was she afraid he might want to stay after all? It was too late for that. In the crib sat a baby that was not his. She was afraid he would count heads. But not even the sight of the new baby wiped the smile from his face. Nobody moved a muscle. Why was he so nice? Did he believe that seeing him we, his children would rush toward him like drooling puppies and shower him with affection?

Cautiously I kept my distance. At any moment I expected his face to change into the more familiar raging kabuki mask of anger and his soft voice into one of cutting thunder. So many times he had left, eroding the little love my mother was capable of, like a flashflood in a desert ravine. How could it be different this time?

Even though I had no way of knowing that this would be the last time I'd ever see him again, the pivotal importance of this moment carved into my mind like the wheel of fate that was cranking irretrievably forward.

Petrified with fear, my mother begged us to call the police.

Nobody reacted to her plea, not my older sister, or my twin brother and for sure not my younger sister. Time dissolved, the ticking of the clock stopped, the crackling of the fire in the stove died, there was no breath, no rooster crowing, no feet shuffling, no thumb sucking, no mattress squeaking. Into the void I hushed with a quiet inhale, "I, I will go."

From that moment on life took on the grayness of twilight and it would never wash off. What did it matter that I longed for the clarity of the fresh wind on a bright and sunny day, for a true beginning and a real change!

I climbed through the small window that faced the gentle line of hills. For all my nine years I had watched the world from here. The devilish rooster on the heap of reeking cow manure, strategically placed in front of the farmers doorway, the dark hedge of poisonous berries, where the boogey man with his long knife used to roam, past the red lake of steep shingled roofs huddled together in the hollow of the valley, over which the pigeons circled like a flock of paper airplanes, to the bobsledding hill, now worn blank in early spring, to the pastures of the gnarly grandmother apple trees, and the meadows hugging the dark blue forest that thrones on top of the limestone hills.

My eyes would see this for him a last time.

The green wooden slats that were nailed to the house had the familiarity attained by my brown hands from unauthorized races up and down to the second floor. They supported a network of grapevines with grapes that never ripened, and not only from a lack of sunny days. I can still feel the rough square surface etching into my hands. Master of the chestnut hedge I could climb this with my eyes closed.

Reaching the bottom I jumped past the smelly puddles. My view shrank to a narrow tunnel driven by my task to hurry and call the police to save my mother. Without touching the ground I flew passed the cave where the blacksmith shaped his glowing steel pinging on the anvil. Now it stared black and dead cold. My feet were without feeling, as if only my head and my heartbeat were racing to the post office with the only telephone in the middle of the village.

Why didn't he stay and be a father? He could have been an art teacher. Or a forest ranger. Then we would have walked in the forest he loved so much, hidden under trees during a thunderstorm, picked tiny wild strawberries and he could have shown me his secret mushroom hunting places. He knew all plants.

Racing in the gray zone of my mission, the schoolhouse and the well in front of it faded away. I did not see the gnarly linden tree in the town center, or the smooth boulder with the brass ring next to the pub where they tied the bulls for sale, nor did I notice the shiny metal milk canisters lined up for pick-up. My world was reduced to the flashing of my red and black dress and a blur of blue-green, sandy-yellow, creamy-white and ochre blotches until I came to the orange-red house. The dark wooden door with the black iron handle smelling of tar and centuries of dried stamp ink was locked. It was too early. I called out to the row of upper windows in a thin voice that boomed through the silent village. What if nobody heard me?

A window on the second floor opened like a miracle and I asked the faceless person looking down on me to call the police. If my mind or my voice gave any reason, I do not know. Maybe it needed none. For the postmaster it must have been explanation enough seeing me so early, uncombed, and asking for the police.

My way back is completely missing like a bad dream. I wished I would have run down the meadow to the brook, to look for the first anemones swinging their heads in the spring wind that scrapes the cheeks red. I wished, I could have yelled into everybody's house that my father is back and that he is going to stay with us. And I wished that everybody would share our joy.

207

The scene in our room was unchanged as if my absence had only been a thought. My mother was still hiding behind the wall of her children afraid to face him.

When the avocado-green police came they escorted him and the last of his belongings out of the house. The moment had a finality much greater then I, with my nine years, could comprehend. A slight twinge of guilt trickled in, of being somehow an accomplice in the ploy of my father getting dragged away. My sisters did not volunteer.

His grinning face in the door never left me.

Chapter Eleven

Countdown To Infinity

Hear that, Mr. Andersen? That is the sound of inevitability.
It is the sound of your death.

-Agent Smith in The Matrix, 1999

"It will happen soon." "It could be any day now," we fear. "He can't recover from this, it's too serious." "It wasn't supposed to be like this." "He should have left like a rocket."

Gone is the boisterous lighthearted banter, the wanton private jokes, the stakeout atmosphere of incontinent language and layers of crumbs on the seats, the rush of a bumpy chase, the fleet-footed swimming along in the river of circumstances.

Silently I listen into the space that surrounds him. Every gesture, every movement, every hue and detail attains overdimensional meaning.

Is this the end? I can feel it approaching. The path of the Westwood sorcerer leads nowhere. Does a dead branch call in question the whole tree? What is left? What is true of his teachings, if he can't leave in the grandiose magical escape he lured us with!

I am addicted to lofty ideas, ever escaping the drudgery of the ordinary, hatched in the same cradle that nests alcoholics and gamblers I despise so much! Have the sails of hope and yearning that pushed me across this ocean lost their wind? Am I afraid that I will drown in the blank face of reality?

Carlos is not the end. You believe that he was the goal, the answer. Your path goes past him.

To where? I can't see anything.

Back to the base, where you are at home.

I am afraid, as if my life is threatened. And I don't understand why. Is it the fear of losing the ground under my feet, the central support and that's why I turn inward? Or the fear of being alone?

The Schneider Babett at her end, after her parents died, drank schnapps and slept with her only cow for warmth and comfort. She could not bear the loneliness. Always good-natured and dressed in black traditional garb or mourning clothes, she mowed the grass in the road ditch with a long scythe. Her brown naked feet showed when she bent over in her full skirts to gather the fresh greens into the tall willow basket that she carried home on her back. From the small square of our bedroom window we could see down into her farmstead, to the stone steps leading up to the living quarters next to the attached barn and the heap of cow manure. In the barn was a dark cavern where she kept her only cow. I can't remember if she or her cow died first.

And there is the dire story of the Chumash woman that lived for twenty-seven years by herself on one of the Channel Islands after her village was evacuated to the mainland against repeated raids of whaling crews. She was left behind by mistake. A quarter of a century went by before she was finally rescued and brought to the Santa Barbara mission wearing a cape of iridescent hummingbird feathers, only to find out that all of her people had died and nobody could understand her language. A few months later she died as well.

And now you tell me there is no true companionship possible in this reality and everything I see around me is only a reflection with infinitely self-repeating images? And the more I concentrate on the details they will take on an ever-expanding diversity?

Loss. You are afraid to give up your point of perception, the concept you hold on to. You still hunger after illusions because they are convenient. But they will stay to be illusions. All circles of interpretation fall off, the sphere of familiar continuity, the ring of dependency on love and fear of survival. Carlos' world is nothing more then a shadow play in the ring of illusions.

I also have this sense of pressure and urgency I don't understand. *It is the knowing of the end of time, the end of the individual you.*

April 4, 1998. Saturday seminar in Santa Monica. The witches and guardians are sure to appear in it. If Carlos is still alive, someone will show up during the afternoon break and take care of him or take him out for lunch. Greg and I sit on the corner spot. The silent question that throttles all conversation and colors every aspect now, is not if he will die a normal death, but when. Until a month ago, we carried the fantastical hope of filming the parade of disappearing lights into the eggplant colored Westwood sky.

As much as I feared losing the tip of his coat tails and spoiling my sidewalk witness status, or missing the physical boat they where planning to sail into the Pacific Ocean, as little I enjoy now watching his sad, inglorious end. The shards of his intrepid confidence lie in the dirt, kept secret even from the other members of his inner group.

Especially the men seem to be kept in the dark about Carlos' true condition. Only Tamalia, Kylie, Florinda, Taisha and Carol have access to the master whose death rides now visibly on his shoulder.

The grief and despair on this corner is thick, stacked up in the open and yet unnoticed by the other inhabitants of this neighborhood. My eyes have no tears and still the sadness drips inside me like the rain that splatters on the windshield.

6:11 p.m. Kylie drives up in her Toyota All-Trac and parks on the Pandora side of the house. She enters the compound hurriedly dressed in a yellow raincoat.

6:41 p.m. She crosses the street on the Eastbourne side in a purple tee shirt running to her apartment. Twenty minutes later she is back at Carlos' and emerges from the Pandora gate with her hood pulled over.

We follow her with the car since we anticipate no other Carlos' sighting tonight. She drives down to Beverly Glen, from there east on Santa Monica Boulevard to Beverly Hills where she pulls into the Whole Foods market. Her errant is short. On the return we lose her lights in the rain reflections of the evening slick. We figure she went back to the seminar, since we don't detect her car on Pandora. Her stopover at Carlos' place is a weak confirmation of his presence.

Kylie stopping in on Carlos

Others tell us, that the witches thanked the audience and said their good-byes at the seminar in an unusual finality and that Kylie walked through the crowd giving heartfelt hugs.

If I give up my self-perception does that constitute my physical death? I feel as if I have to say good-bye to everything I know, to what and who I am. To my role as a mother, to the image of a treasured employee, to the picture of a competent and intelligent woman, to the world of Carlos. Am I not the construct of my relations? When I let all this go where will I end up? Who will I be?

You are we.

Who are we?

The flow of life that runs through (everything). Let go of your focal point, then stretch and elongate toward us. This is what you have learned during the last years. And now you can feel our place, our position. And you know who you are.

April 8, 1998. Wednesday, 3:07 a.m. A flecked moon shines on us, the only witness to our nightly trash hunt. Each time we turn from Santa Monica Boulevard to Pandora I fear we will arrive at an empty house, that the sorcerers' party has slipped away, and left from one moment to the next.

Tonight the cars are still there. The house is dark, the sorcerer sleeps. The inner yard has a newly built gazebo with a brick floor; the garage on Pandora has French doors. Room for another guardian?

Do the many renovations point to an imminent sale of the property or at least to a change of ownership? Who renovates their house during a serious illness?

The illusive jaguar of the Baboquivari Mountains circles the quiet building and slips unseen through the fly screen. His soft paws leave no sound on the clean but badly worn wood floor. Barely noticeable his tail tassel brushes against the terracotta dog on the door. His breath moves the white terry robe hanging on the door of the closet no more then a draft would.

In a soft fluent movement he leaps on to the double-sized mattress, lowers himself at the foot of the bed and sinks into the white bedcovers next to the rolled up wooden snake. The whiskers vibrate as he inhales. In the nightshade black of the jaguar pupils, bedded on white pillows, rests the sorcerer, the dark, purple skinned Carlos, the broken puppet skeleton, the half decayed, he who is dying. The jaguar's exhale brushes over the sorcerer and his rattling breath.

The clues from the trash confirm all to well the accelerated course of events. They are desperate signs we assemble in reasonably accurate speculation. Florinda's parents send her a card with wishes for general wellness and the hope that Regina recovers from the deep tiredness she must have professed to them. Depressions? Quite understandable! The letter conveys the mutual love for each other and the desire to see her again.

Dr. Duenas prescribes more hormones. The stress caused by Carlos' illness must have played havoc with the women's hormonal households. I can only surmise how the witches cope with the miserable decline of their master to whom they have been loyal for more then 25 years, when looking at him the sadness that overpowers me reduces my vision to the quality of our fuzzy amateur videos.

Insulin syringes retrieved from the garbage obviously confirm that Carlos' diabetes has flared up. Bottles and tin boxes with Chinese herbal drugs, a calm spirit for combating insomnia, to clear liver and brighten eyes, a blood tonic for the liver meridian, a Chi regulating and stagnation dispersing for the heart and liver channels, a liver yang sedative, according to the Traditional Acupuncture Inc. stationary.

Inquiries about a vegetarian diet. Copies of guidelines for healthier eating with diabetes: less animal fat, less sugar, less salt. Five minutes to twelve they want to change his meat diet? Too little, too late, we fear.

A list of books, from "The Art of spiritual Healing", "The Power of Prayer" to "Awaken Your Inner Power" and "Awareness Heals". Diet for the headache patient from the National Headache Foundation. A photocopy of chapter 8 from "Replenishing Enzyme Deficiencies", marked paragraphs on diabetes and high blood pressure; conditions with cellulase deficiency like acute food allergies, candidiasis, gas, bloating; conditions associated with disaccaridase deficiency like bronchitis, hyper activity, insomnia, mood swings. These clues give us a general picture of his condition and in their desperation they convey the growing panic by reaching for any healing method.

What is death then? He said that it was the unifying force, the end of fragmentation.

Yes, death is the loss of individuality, the return to the whole.

Does that mean the "us" doesn't die?

No, only your position, your view of separateness.

And what about my experiences, and my awareness?

Are ours, you collect for us. Give it up. Your supposed individuality is only an illusion which becomes more prominent the more you forget who you/we really are.

Carlos wanted to keep his individuality, his experiences and the knowledge of his self and not let go of it while he changed into pure energy to ride on its wave into infinity. Is this method more advanced, a more desirable outcome?

No, there is no difference for us. The end result is the same: oneness.

Is it possible to keep the knowledge of the individual self in the infinite?

As a separate being, no. The whole contains all memory experiences of the individual. Believe me, in the oneness you will not miss the loneliness. The whole contains everything already.

My daughter moves into a new apartment that turns out to be situated on Pandora Avenue only one street south of Santa Monica and Beverly Glen. From her bedroom window on the second floor we can almost see Carlos' house. What a strange omen! Is this a call to stand watch around the clock?

April 15, 1998. Wednesday, 2:30 a.m. A new silver Ford Crown Victoria without license plate is parked in front of the house. In the backseat lies the rolled up blanket. He is still here! In the Pandora trash is a note with the assignment to find a good honest gold coin business and to relay the answer to Cleargreen. Another note has the address of Wilshire Coin Exchange and the current rate of Maple Leaf, American Eagle and Krugerand gold coins. Are they planning to exchange cash for gold coins?

In Carol's story of her unexpected reappearance from the second attention they alluded to the prudence of the sorcerers of preparing caches of money and always wearing gold jewelry in case of getting stranded in another world. Supposedly gold is the going currency in all dimensions.

The accompanying instructions for Phenobarbital, a sleep enhancing drug, and the label of a designer vodka are signs of emotional overload. A prescription by Dr. Duenas for Carlos of Metronidazole 250mg from April 6, 1998. On the bottom of the barrel we find a honey colored corduroy jacket with elbow patches, the one Carlos mockingly described in his talks as the armchair sorcerer's uniform.

April 18, 1998. Saturday, 4:28 p.m. Again we are parked on our usual spot on the corner of Pandora and Eastbourne, next to the hydrant, the best position to watch both entrances of the compound at the same time. For the last two weeks we have not seen Carlos.

The fact that Tamalia has not taken him out of the house anymore for trips to the restaurant, his only remaining pleasure, or one could assume to the doctor, rallies our fears of his impending death into the ever-present foreground.

Kylie comes out of the Pandora gate and walks to her car, dragging her left shoulder behind as if she is exhausted from carrying a heavy load. From the side her face appears gaunt; her lower jaw hangs lose in unguarded despair.

4:35 p.m. Tamalia parks the new Ford Crown Victoria in front of her apartment building.

5:21 p.m. The house buzzes with activity, a steady coming and going, we are unaccustomed to seeing on a Saturday afternoon. One of the 'elements' is packing Taisha's van with boxes, containers of files and a red-and-white cooler. He locks the back doors of the van and throws a brown manila envelope into his own car. Are they getting ready for a trip or move to a new home? Maybe to Mexico! Tijuana has alternative clinics with healing methods that are outlawed in the US. If they are leaving today for the border it would be the end of our surveillance. We can't follow them without preparations of our own, without passport and money. And in Mexico they could bury Carlos in the desert and nobody would ever find out. "And then they can tell us 'he went like don Juan'. Nobody would ever know the truth."

Fab exits the Pandora gate stone-faced. We cringe almost physically at the desecration of the gate. Carol drives away in her Ford Contour, dressed in red and as always absorbed in her cell phone. Another 'element' strides in determined steps along the hedge.

Darien waits in front of the Pandora gate and via cell phone she receives permission to enter. Her demeanor appears painfully cheery, innocently oblivious of the tragedy that is taking place in the house. After a few minutes she comes back out carrying a briefcase and wearing the same unaffected look as she walks away to her car.

"Where is Carlos? Is he still alive? Or is he already gone?" The questions, spooked by the heightened activity and the nervousness, surround the house of the sorcerer. Tamalia drives off without him. The telltale blanket lies rolled-up on the backseat window. We consider that a positive sign of Carlos' continuing presence. Probably he is just too weak to leave the house.

Fab comes back, walks around the corner of the hedge with a sweater stylishly draped around his shoulders and enters the compound from the Eastbourne side. Kylie returns. Gavin leaves the building with his ear pressed to the cell phone. They swarm around

216

the house like yellow-jackets. The restlessness is palatable. It reverberates in me like aspen leaves fluttering in the wind.

Packing the get-away car   Darien carrying briefcase away

Then something strange happens. In the last two years during which we spent almost every weekend in this neighborhood, nobody paid any attention to us. As if the people here were used to our presence and did not perceive us as foreign elements. Just as they are known to us, including their dogs, cars and public habits.

But now, to our surprise, the little weasel-faced woman walking her Pekinese looks full of curiosity into our car. The balding man on the balcony throws questioning glances over his newspaper into our direction and other passing people notice with deliberate neck craning our binoculars and camera. I'm beginning to feel uneasy.

Is the veil thinning? Is the magic hood that surrounded us for years wearing out? I feel naked like a soldier without underwear whose uniform got shredded in the fight. For so long nobody cared about our presence and all of a sudden everybody sees us! Except for the members of Carlos' group who are still absorbed into their inner world, giving the outer one no second glances.

A sudden knock on the window of my passenger door jolts us from our concentration.

What are we doing here, a neighbor demands to know. He notices the camera in Greg's lap. "Get lost," he insists. I turn stubborn. "We have a right to be here just as anybody else," is what I tell him. A ridiculous answer since we are parked on a red curb and in front of a fire hydrant. The pesky neighbor sees the sticker of a Fox studio parking permit on my windshield left by the previous owner, while I spy the CBS logo on his shorts. He must think we are connected to the Fox news station and we believe he is with CBS. A media wrestling match.

Under that pretense we palaver back and forth. If we don't leave, he will call the police, he finally threatens. There have been burglaries in the neighborhood. "Do we look like burglars," I contentiously bite back. We fuss around some more. From his apartment door he throws us dagger-like looks.

Driving by Pandora one last time we notice Kylies car, a newer red Ford with license plate. We wonder, "Why does she not drive her own car anymore? If it were a brand-new car it wouldn't have a plate! And red is not her style. Looks more like a rental."

The turn of events proves too alarming to be ignored. The veil of our magic hood is lifting. For so long we were protected under the cloak of invisibility and a tacit multi-leveled agreement. What is the meaning of this sudden change? The membrane that separates us from the sorcerers has become as thin as cellophane.

Did we push too hard? Maybe this is a sign to lay off, to give them room. And the beehive activity at the house definitely points to a mobilization. He lies terminally ill in the newly renovated house, while his nurses pack their new cars. This is the climax, the moment of truth. I can feel it in the roots of my hair, the tips of my fingers, and the lashing girdle of energy pouring out of my belly that reaches into the net that connects us all.

And yet the shock over the torn veil, the sudden exposure and the loss of our protection and the foreboding of his bitter end makes me recoil from being a sidewalk witness any longer. Even if it would be a sobering finale to our film to capture the moment when his coffin is being carried through the gate.

I want to go home, forever. All along I have been here only with half my heart.

You are already home.

But I can only feel it sometimes. Why? I want to go back to where I came from.

Not yet.

What am I doing here? What for should I stick around?

You are the one who catches experiences like fish in the ocean, like pearls strung in outer space. Collect them. Throw your net out and pull it in. Each separate pearl contains the reflection of all.

What kind of experiences should I collect?

Ultimately it does not matter what kind. We need them all, the plight, the joy, the lack and abundance, the pain and the happiness, the boredom and the laughter.

How am I supposed to do this?

Just watch and notice the experience. Be aware. You don't have to do anything else.

What are you doing with these experiences?

We grow. One day the basket of our experiences will be full and then a tremble will run through us, a recognition that changes us into a new expression, into something that has not existed before, something we are not able to imagine now, we only know.

May 2, 1998. Saturday. We have returned from a weekend in Hawaii. Full of foreboding we shuffle along the familiar bumpy Santa Monica Boulevard with other cars fighting hastily for every empty inch. The stone statue of Gabriel high on top of the Mormon temple still blows his trumpet towards the East as if pointing the way for us.

On a backdrop sky of post card flaming orange, picture perfect palm trees in black dot the typical California horizon and Century City's glass buildings glow brazenly in the evening gold.

The street is empty in front of the house on Pandora. The Eastbourne entrance is littered with deliveries of water bottles. Is nobody there to bring them into the house? The yellowed leaves of

219

the lemon tree blow through the front yard with the mood of an early autumn. Lack of water, neglect or grief? Only days ago the place buzzed with activity. Now the house yawns like an abandoned ruin.

Through the uncovered panes we see empty rooms without furniture. Carlos is gone! The realization hits us like a brick. Clinging to a "maybe they are gone temporarily" I mitigate the impact.

During the afternoon of the one-day seminar in Santa Monica, poignantly called "On the run", Carol shows up at the house accompanied by Enzo in his black town car. They stay only for a brief time and then drive off again. Where are Florinda, Kylie, Tamalia, and Taisha?

Is Carol the only one of the witches that appeared at the seminar? Maybe the others took the sick and dying Carlos to Mexico. If they packed Carlos into the back seat and drove him across the border under the cover of night nobody will ever find out. And they might be back without him soon.

Carol stopping by at the empty Pandora house

At night a lonely light burns staring into the empty corners with mocking persistence. The trashcans are flagrantly empty but for some rubble and cleaning debris. No discarded food, bills, bathroom tissues, or other signs of life; no indication that anybody is living at the house anymore. For now they have disappeared.

Why did we fly to Hawaii, at this crucial moment? We knew the end was close, the crescendo of the concert. Did I misinterpret the omens? The lifting of our camouflage was not a sign to retreat, but the merging of the twin worlds. The veil separating the sorcerer's world from the ordinary thinned, like a soap bubble, reigning in a new chapter. And I did not respond. In the decisive moment I lost the nerve.

We scramble searching for traces, for tracks in the mud. Reni and Nyie are still around living on Manning. Enzo and Fab have not moved either. Only Carlos, Taisha, Florinda, Kylie and Tamalia are missing. I cling to the thought of their sudden return. Even though everything points to a final departure.

Kylie's and Tamalia's apartment across the street has a for rent sign in the front yard. Taisha's van is gone, as well as Tamalia's Crown Victoria. Nuri drives Carol's Ford Contour. Carol has a new Ford Taurus. Kylie's old car is for sale.

Cleargreen prints a new list of phone numbers with all present members of the group. Carlos', Taisha's, Florinda's, Kylie's, Talia's and Nuri's names are omitted. Seven new keys are ordered. They are on the lookout for new apartments. A shuffling and rearranging of cars and living quarters by the remaining group seems to be happening.

Any indication of Carlos', Taisha's, Florinda's, Kylie's and Tamalia's presence is painfully absent in the office trash as well. The sticky notes that Kylie and Talia wrote used to keep the daily flow in the office going. Now they are incontestably amiss. Only a sheet of white paper with a misspelled Carlos signature turns up, as if someone was practicing.

The Cleargreen payroll sheet for May 1998 excludes Talia, Nuri and Kylie. There is no official announcement by Cleargreen, they are dead silent.

And from the looks of it, Kylie's colleagues emptied the complete contents of her former desk into the trash. There are notes from the search for Rachel by a private eye that Carlos hired to find her after she ran away from them. The unused airline ticket paid for by Carlos to see her family one more time, and the deployment of a private detective to find her, confirm to us that she was about to enter the fold of Carlos' inner students, but opted to disappear without explanation.

A box full of frank letters and cynical cards written by the hilariously entertaining Merilyn. In their entirety they have the sound of a relationship gone one-sided. Tape recordings from Cleargreen's office answering machine with semi obscene phone calls to Kylie from known people.

Legal correspondence about lawsuits or actions against people who taught Carlos' philosophy unauthorized to others. A stack of books from other authors earmarked with yellow stickers probing for stolen ideas or copyright infringement. Also information on legal proceedings by Carlos' lawyer to suppress the publication of the book of his former wife Margaret. A collection of material from other movement teachings, including yoga and somatic movements, either researched for their usefulness or transgressing similarities.

Vigilantly sliced credit cards belonging to Kylie Lundahl for Macys, Robinson-May, Bloomindales, and The Limited. Does that mean she will no longer go shopping? A small corner of Kylie's golden card lies next to the trash dumpster on the ground, scratched up from car tires, caked with dirt. Only Kylie L. is left of it.

The diagonal rays of the sinking sun illuminate the dirt road with carmine red blotches, wash the sand prints in pink and violet, and dab green gold on downy grass and fresh oak leaves. I squint. I should paint this. Years ago I painted looking for answers in my canvases. There was the painting of the unborn in its egg. On the inner walls vivid colors of all elements ran into each other freely, like on a soap bubble before it pops. A web of lines and scaffoldings, beginning at the temples wound through the swirls of color providing structure and meaning. I am the unborn in the bubble that tries to make sense of its own reflection.

When I walk through nature, the landscape with its oak forests, fire roads, grasses and hills, even its sound, takes on the quality of intimate closeness, of such physical familiarity as if it was my body that sweeps the hair from its own face when the wind blows through the treetops, that recognizes its own shape in the curvature of the soft road and the light hues of the afternoon, whose heart smiles at itself in the touching of the mountain ridge, that lets me feel my own foot prints on my back.

And I'm one.

With golden strings the sun pulls her rainbow net behind the rim of the mountain. The frog pond reflects stray magenta clouds. Purple hills hug each other in the fresh evening breeze. I sing softly to myself. Long ear owls squawk in the black bramble of the oaks.

My tendrils sweep through the web of energy strings that grew between the sorcerers and us during the past years. Nothing moves. It could mean that the connection between us is severed. A week later the house of the sorcerer is still empty and despite the fresh paint it has the look of neglect. A deserted lifeless ruin, a Sleeping Beauty's house without inhabitants, sunken into the sleep of oblivion. And the jaguar is gone.

By now we give up hope that the women, the witches and their guardians will return, even without Carlos. Wherever they went, they are free. Free from twenty-five years of commitment, with enough money to live well.

Maybe Florinda grows corn somewhere. No, I can't imagine that. People that didn't move for decades from the metropolitan pavement, that found satisfaction in better department stores, movie theaters and restaurants and didn't give a rat about the natural world, wouldn't want to be without the comforts of urban life.

Greg's remote viewing results in the image of a dead Carlos behind a wooden shed.

The empty gap

223

On the day he died I was in Kauai. The red sienna mud of the Napali coast squished between my toes. A stiff breeze chased the rain clouds away, shook the lechua trees and washed the hues of green and blue to brilliant sapphire, deep emerald, turquoise and lapis. Tiny pink orchids danced in the wind.

Where the mouth of the indigo river gushed into the ocean to rumble and jump over rounded black volcanic boulders, I stood on an algae crusted rock dancing a few hula steps, overwhelmed by the beauty and the sound spectacle of the raw forces of nature. I wanted to throw myself into the rock-smashing surf.

The river water growled, gurgled and rattled in competition with the breakers, creating a sound tapestry of dissonant dimensions. From the surface of the deep blue river water I saw the edge of the waves crash between porous rocks. Cobalt blue mixed with the white foam, ran turquoise through bottle green, cornflower blue to the midnight blue curvature where the ocean touches the cerulean blue. In the afternoon Greg and I built towers from flat polished granite rocks that stood like an army of guardians at the beach waiting to be destroyed by the high tide.

In my thoughts I was not in Westwood on Pandora Avenue where we spent so many afternoons. I gave him space.

What is reality ultimately? An agreement between people, a decision to interpret events and information in a specific learned way; a sorting and arranging according to a particular pattern, a connecting of dots.

His mind was drifting in and out of reality, clinging to wispy strands of random thoughts. He squinted, pinching his eyes to narrow slits. He puckered his lips and sucked the cool morning air into his searing lungs.

His eyes skimmed without recognition across the bare white walls of his spartan bedroom; they did not linger on the only decoration, the small poster artwork of his latest products, nor did they connect the fuzzy amber outlines with the loyal companions that surrounded his bed.

Turning inward he followed the seething pain in his body that rose and sank, growing into a monster to take over the small white room.

He was not dying the death of a sorcerer of his lineage, a maneuver of connecting all points of reality and igniting them to burn from within. That was what thousands of seminar attendees and last not least the circle of devoted women had come to believe in. He was dying.

The terracotta dog at the door stared with snarling teeth; the wooden snake crawled under the bed. In the crack of dawn a pomegranate stain trickled over the horizon and he left his body. The jaguar jumped out the window.

So now what? What should I do with the "Carlos" experience?
Write a book.
What?
Carlos is the chase after the elusive and its capture into the mundane. It is the sparkle in the net of the treasure hunt for your Self.
I don't know how to write, not a book. Letters are difficult enough for me. How am I supposed to do this?
Collect yourself at the position of total overview, our position, and write from there.
How do I collect myself at the point of total overview?
Let go. Feel the life inside, the strength, and stretch along on this thread of energy without loosing the beginning out of your sight. See yourself in everything.

The princess that left her castle to wander for days without food and water to find out what life was, that fell exhausted into the river of life and death, to disintegrate in the water and whose infinitesimal parts floated with the mist of the clouds that dropped her in the rain from the sky, to trickle through earth, roots and rocks to collect in dark caverns, seeping out of the mountain springs, to run with the stream back into the river, this princess pulled all her parts together again and rose from the water.

Now she knew what life was. She herself was life. She is in everything and everything is in her.

Epilogue

He called me Chocho.
- C.J. Castaneda, *after Carlos' death*

By the end of May, three weeks after returning from our weekend in Kauai, Carlos and the group of women were still unaccounted for and we grew wary of our own investigative abilities. Greg and I decided to approach several reporters to search for Castaneda and the group of women that had disappeared. None showed any visible interest.

The news of Carlos Castaneda's death finally broke on June 19th, 1998, almost two months after his death on April 27.1998, with the Los Angeles Times running a headline of "A Hushed Death for Mystic Author Carlos Castaneda" in the lower right-hand corner of the front page. A savvy reporter had found the public announcement of the probate hearing for Carlos' estate. Quickly the press contacted C.J. Castaneda and Carlos' former wife Margaret Runyon who were both surprised by the news.

Suddenly the remaining people at Cleargreen were forced to admit that Carlos was gone. Even months after his death they did not have a consistent story, and gave conflicting answers to the deluge of phone calls. Obviously they were not prepared for this event and/or were just as surprised.

Greg obtained a death certificate and went to the funeral home that had cremated Carlos' body. Curiously enough, he was cremated the same day he died. The director confirmed without a doubt that Carlos' body was indeed cremated, and that his body had been intact (no partial burning from within). The phony employment, marriage and family relation information on the death certificate seemingly had the purpose of keeping the famous death from becoming public since the funeral home director was unaware of the notoriety until the papers ran the story.

In August 1998 Greg and I went to the probate hearings. In the process we befriended Margaret and C.J. Castaneda, who fought unsuccessfully for some acknowledgment of Carlos' love for him. During C.J.'s last personal visit in 1993 at a Phoenix bookstore lecture Carlos acted overjoyed at seeing him, and gave the impression that he wanted to keep in touch. The exclusion in the will was a complete shock to C.J. Allegedly Carlos had changed his will three days before his death adding male members of the inner group and specifically excluding his former wife and adopted son.

Six months after Carlos' death, we came "out of the closet" with our deeds and film footage, by showing our friends from the practice groups what we had done. Some shunned us and never talked to us again. But for others, it accelerated the wave of deconstruction of an already crumbling belief system.

Cleargreen was alerted to the existence of our video through a close associate and arranged a meeting with us. Rich and Reni came to our old hang-out at Lucy's Chinese food place and presented us with two options. Either we should give our tape to them so they can destroy it, or we should destroy it ourselves. Reni said that we could have a nice burning ceremony with it. Neither one of these options appealed to us. But they did not give up. Their next move was an attempt to entangle us in the probate proceedings; the lawyer demanding all papers and items from the trash and the video as evidence and also requested personal statements from us in their offices to act as witnesses for their case. We did not feel qualified to be witnesses, considering that they had a host of Cleargreen's people that were much better suited. We passively refused.

The probate case ended suddenly in February 1999. Earlier wills already showed the same explicit exclusion of C.J. and Margaret Castaneda and therefore nullified any claims.

Rich. started his painful recovery with his website www.sustainedaction.org, offering a host of information on all aspects of Castaneda's life.

All in all, years later I still feel grateful to Carlos for the adventure and the entertainment on the road to finding my way home. The one thing I regret was that I never thanked him personally.

Appendix A

Time Line

October 1992........Taisha's book signing at Phoenix Bookstore
November 1992..... Florinda's talk at Sisterhood Bookstore
May 1993............Florinda meets with me and friends at apartment
June 1993............Witches' seminar at Rim Institute in Arizona
September 1993.....Meet Carlos first time in private classes at
                    Stewart Street dance studios
October 1993.........Maui workshop
November 1993.....Carlos' talk at friend's apartment
December 1993.......Private classes suspended
February 1994........Back in class, 3 times a week at Stewart Street
April 1994............Kicked out again
May-April 95.........Omega workshop
August 1995.........Carlos teaches three week seminar in Los
                    Angeles
October 1995.........Culver City Seminar
November 1995......Culver City Seminar
December 1995.......Anaheim Seminar
January 1996..........Mexico City Seminar
February 1996........Oakland Seminar
March 1996..........Women's seminar in Los Angeles
April 1996............First secretive observing
July 1996.............Westwood Seminar
September 1996......Mexico City seminar
November 1996......Pasadena seminar
December 1996......First trash picking
January 1997.........First videotaping
February 1997.......Long Beach seminar, last seminar led by
                    Carlos. Also last seminar Greg and I attend
April 1997............ Mexico City seminar
June 1997.............Barcelona seminar
June 1997.............Berlin seminar
July 1997.............Carlos ends Sunday class and stops all private
                    classes
July 1997.............Seattle workshop
August 1997..........Phoenix workshop
August 1997..........Los Angeles seminar - Carlos does not attend
October 1997..........Denver workshop

October 1997..........Omega, New York workshop
December 1997.......Mexico City workshop
February 1998.........Pomona, Los Angeles County, workshop
February 22, 1998...First videotape of the ill Carlos
March 29, 1998......Last pictures of Carlos
April 4, 1998..........Santa Monica, 1 day workshop
April 18, 1998.......Inner group packing
April 27, 1998......Carlos dies
Taisha, Florinda,...Kylie and Talia disappear
May 2, 1998..........Santa Monica, 1 day workshop
May 1998.............Nuri disappears
June 19, 1998........Newspaper announcements of Carlos' death

Appendix B

Have you seen these women?

Florinda Donner

Nuri Alexander

Taisha Abelar

Taisha Abelar

Kylie Lundhal and Talia Bey

Florinda Donner, Taisha Abelar, Nuri Alexander, Kylie Lundhal and Talia Bey left their residences in the week following Carlos' death on April 27, 1998, and have not been seen since. All efforts by family to find the disappeared have been unsuccessful. Some believe there is indication enough that the women might have committed suicide.

If they are still out there, I'd like them to know that they are missed and loved.

All photos from author's video collection.

Appendix C

Miscellaneous Photo Gallery

Author second from right. Photo: Author's personal archives.

Author with Greg. Photo: Author's personal archives.

Margaret Runyon Castaneda, author of "A Magical Journey with Carlos Castaneda," and C.J. Castaneda. Photo: Courtesy of Margaret Runyon

Ceramic doorstop from Carlos' house, the author found broken in the trash. Photo: Author's video archives.

Appendix D

Paper trail from trash archives

The Chacmool Center for Enhanced Perception
11901 Santa Monica Blvd., Suite 598
Los Angeles, CA 90025

June 28, 1995

Marina del Rey, CA 90292

via fax 310.574.7816

RE: SETTING UP A RELIGION

Dear George:

Our interest in grouping ourselves under the protection of a religion stems from the necessity to make clear the position that we were taught by the descendants of the sorcerers of ancient Mexico in relation to the following:

1. Their beliefs about the cause, nature and purpose of the universe;
2. The existence of a given moral code governing man's conduct in relation to what those sorcerers considered to be the prime force;
3. The existence of a set of beliefs and practices discovered by those sorcerers;
4. The fact that all the persons involved in the present devotedly follow the principles and practices taught to them by their original teachers.

We do have a binding activity that is extremely similar to the activities of religious congregations in the sense that it is all-absorbing and requires total attention. We call it dreaming.

The practice of dreaming gives, as a result, a closer emotional approximation to things which are on a metaphysical plane, so to speak. It leads the act of perceiving in general to enlarge its scope and include sensorial data which is ordinarily discarded.

I do hope that this outline may serve as a source to draw upon.

I will be at your entire disposal for anything else you want to know.

Sincere regards,

Carlos Castaneda

Carlos Castaneda
/nm

Pope Carlos I. Also note: No mention of shamans. These were the days when they were still sorcerers. *Author's trash archives.*

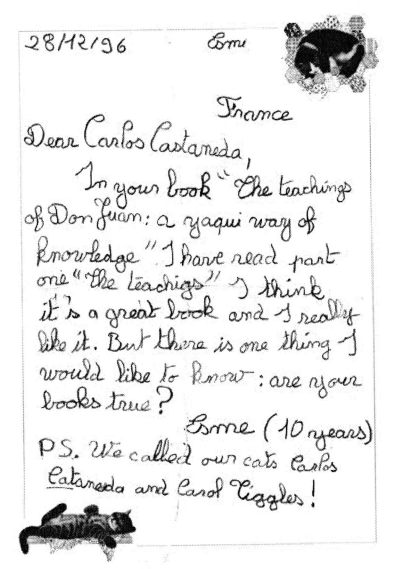

28/12/96   Esme

France

Dear Carlos Castaneda,

In your book "The teachings of Don Juan: a yaqui way of knowledge" I have read part one "the teachings" I think it's a great book and I really like it. But there is one thing I would like to know: are your books true?

Esme (10 years)

P.S. We called our cats Carlos Cataneda and Carol Tizzles!

Poignant letter from 10-year old to Carlos with a question we all would have liked him to answer honestly. Author's trash archives.

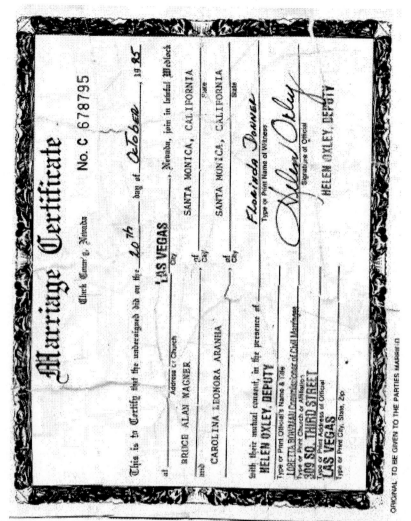

Marriage certificate found 1997 discarded in trash, prompting an internet search under the various sorcerer aliases. Author's trash archives.

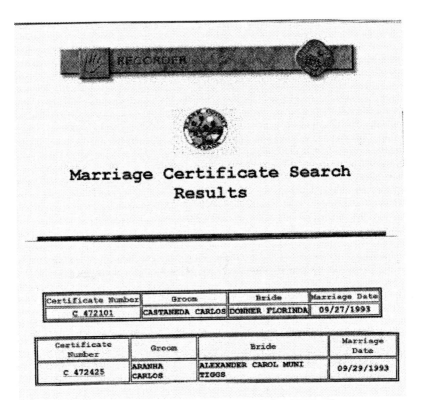

Marriage Certificate Search Results

Certificate Number	Groom	Bride	Marriage Date
C 472101	CASTANEDA CARLOS	DONNER FLORINDA	09/27/1993

Certificate Number	Groom	Bride	Marriage Date
C 472425	ARANHA CARLOS	ALEXANDER CAROL MUNI TIGGS	09/29/1993

Carlos married two women in one week in 1993. Sorcerers are exempt from societal regulations. Copy of electronic public information from County Recorder's office Clark County (Las Vegas), Nevada.

Talia's discarded phone-list from 1997, reflecting status and pecking order of the "insiders". All phone numbers have been changed.
Author's trash archives.

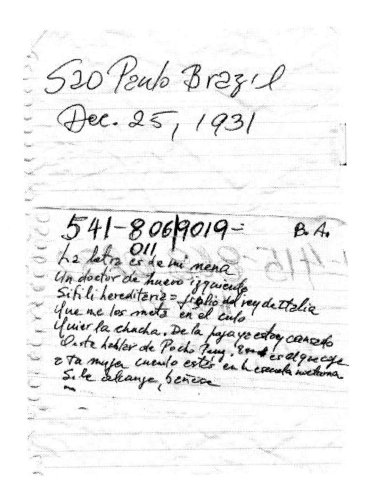

Samples of Carlos' handwriting from 1997, showing alternate birth information, phone number and song lyrics. *Author's trash archives.*

Large phone numbers, attesting to Carlos' vision problems in 1997, necessary during the absence of Kylie and the witches. *Author's trash archives.*

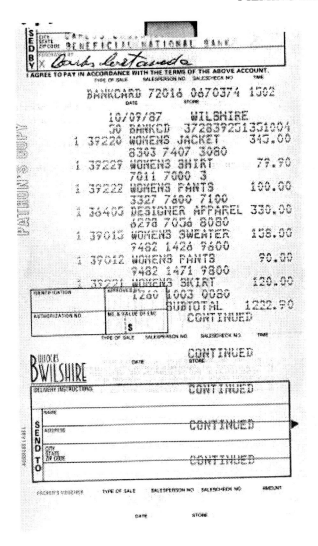

Partial shopping receipt from 1987. Carlos generously supported his
women with wardrobe, tuition and rent. *Author's trash archives.*

Front

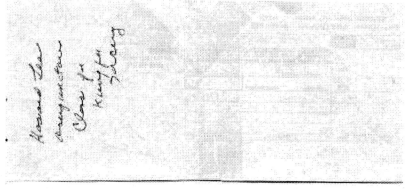

Backside

One of many receipts for lunch with Howard Lee from 1988, with notation on the back discussing a class for "Kung Fu Sorcery". Tensegrity was not invented yet. *Author's trash archives.*

Handwriting sample of Florinda Donner from 1997, calling herself Flodo. *Author's trash archives.*

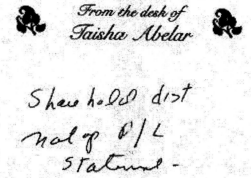

Handwriting sample of Taisha Abelar from 1997. Taisha was involved with Laugan Productions and general bookkeeping for Carlos and as always concerned about money. *Author's trash archives.*

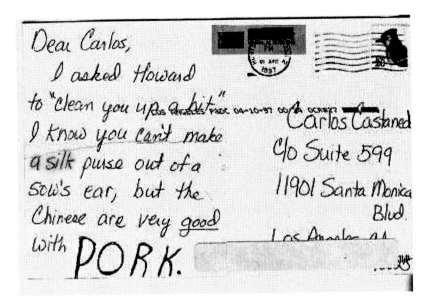

Dear Carlos,
I asked Howard
to "clean you up ~~aod~~" ~~~~ ~~~~
I know you *can't* make
a silk purse out of a
sow's ear, but the
Chinese are very *good*
with PORK.

Carlos Castaned
C/o Suite 599
11901 Santa Monica
Blvd.
Los Angeles ca

Carlos,

I'll need money if
I'm to do all the things
I'm needed to do. Can't
you please help me to make
it?

Merilyn

Fan mail to Carlos from persistent woman, possibly a former 'electric warrior' or one-time nagual woman, who entertained us with weekly postcards in 1997. *Author's trash archives.*

FAX COVER SHEET

PLEASE DELIVER IMMEDIATELY

DATE: 10 / 28   / 97

TO: LEE BABIN

FAX NUMBER: 504-367 5508

FROM: Angela and Fabricio

FAX NUMBER:

SUBJECT: VESSEL SPECIFICATIONS

NUMBER OF PAGES: 1

MESSAGE:

Dear Lee:

As we discussed in our telephone conversation, I'm sending you the general
specifications of the vessel we would like to purchase.

- cargo/crew vessel
- 100 - 200 ft.
- 10,000 miles range
- unlimited navigation capability
- 2 engines, 2 generators
- room for a crew of 25 persons
- clear deck space: 1,250 sq. ft.
- full seaworthiness (everything in perfect condition)
- vessel will be used for research purposes (no underwater research)
- we could modify vessel in order to meet our requirements
- price: around $400,000

We very much appreciate your help concerning this matter and are looking
forward to your answer.

Sincerely,

Intense search for a boat to Infinity. Angela, an alter ego of Reni used
in the office. *Author's trash archives.*

BarnesandNoble.com

One Pond Road • Rockleigh, NJ • 07647
To Reach Customer Service e-mail:
web customers: service@barnesandnoble.com
aol customers: service@bnonline.com
3-21-30

Cust. No. 123296 Order No. 1358464
Sold to: KYLIE LUNDAHL
11901 SANTA MONICA BLVD.
#599
CLEARGREEN, INCORPORATED
LOS ANGELES, CA 90025

Ship to: KYLIE LUNDAHL
11901 SANTA MONICA BLVD.
#599
CLEARGREEN, INCORPORATED
LOS ANGELES, CA 90025

QTY	ITEM	DESCRIPTION	UNIT PRICE	EXTENDED PRICE
1	0879611510	SEA VEGETABLES; HARVESTING GUIDE & COOKBMCCONNAU		
		The following items have been cancelled:		
1	0923155058	FISHING FOR SHARKS BARRETT		
1	0393032493	CARE AND FEEDING OF THE OFFSHORE CREW; APARDEY		
1	087040475X	LOW CALORIE, HIGH NUTRITION VEGETABLES FARASAKI		
		The following items shipped separately on: 10/29/97		
1	157866202?	SHARK LIVER OIL SOLOMON		
		The following items shipped separately on: 10/30/97		
1	1885670389	SHARK CARTILAGE ELKINS		
1	0884153576	GOOD FOOD AFLOAT; TASTY AND NUTRITIOUS RBETTERLY		
1	0924486929	GREAT CRUISING COOKBOOK: AN INTERNATIONAPAYNE		
1	0070599711	PORTABLE BAKER: BAKING ON BOAT & TRAIL SPANGENB		
1	0062725033	KEEPING FOOD FRESH BAILEY		
		The following items shipped separately on: 11/12/97		
1	0961268638	SEA TO SHORE CARIBBEAN SEAFOOD COOKBOOK ROBINSON		
		The following items shipped separately on: 4/09/98		
		Page 1		

IMPORTANT NOTE ABOUT SHIPPING CHARGES: 5/22/98
Shipping charges reflect only the portion of your order that has been shipped.
Net Product $ 8.95

As part of an all out effort to make it in the 'sea of infinity' Kylie orders books in the end of October 1997. *Author's trash archives.*

257

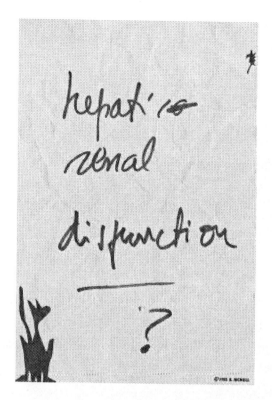

Many details in the trash, including prescription drugs and holistic healing procedures, underlined the serious illness Carlos was fighting unsuccessfully during the last several months of his life. *Author's trash archives.*

About The Author

Gaby Geuter lived in Germany and Spain before settling with her daughter in Los Angeles. A painter and performance artist in the 1980's, she now writes and grows vegetables in California.

Printed in the United States
31601LVS00002B/253-258